New Perspectives on
Creating Web Pages
with **HTML**

INTRODUCTORY

The New Perspectives Series

The New Perspectives Series consists of texts and technology that teach computer concepts and microcomputer applications (listed below). You can order these New Perspectives texts in many different lengths, software releases, custom-bound combinations, CourseKits™ and Custom Editions®. Contact your Course Technology sales representative or customer service representative for the most up-to-date details.

The New Perspectives Series

Computer Concepts

Borland® dBASE®

Borland® Paradox®

Corel® Presentations™

Corel® Quattro Pro®

Corel® WordPerfect®

DOS

HTML

Lotus® 1-2-3®

Microsoft® Access

Microsoft® Excel

Microsoft® Internet Explorer

Microsoft® Office Professional

Microsoft® PowerPoint®

Microsoft® Windows® 3.1

Microsoft® Windows® 95

Microsoft® Windows NT® Server 4.0

Microsoft® Windows NT® Workstation 4.0

Microsoft® Word

Microsoft® Works

Microsoft® Visual Basic® 4 and 5

Netscape Navigator™

Netscape Navigator™ Gold

New Perspectives on
Creating Web Pages
with **HTML**

INTRODUCTORY

Patrick Carey
Carey Associates, Inc.

COURSE
TECHNOLOGY

ONE MAIN STREET, CAMBRIDGE, MA 02142

an International Thomson Publishing company I(T)P®

Cambridge • Albany • Bonn • Boston • Cincinnati • London • Madrid • Melbourne • Mexico City
New York • Paris • San Francisco • Singapore • Tokyo • Toronto • Washington

New Perspectives on Creating Web Pages with HTML — Introductory
is published by Course Technology.

Associate Publisher	Mac Mendelsohn
Series Consulting Editor	Susan Solomon
Product Manager	Donna Gridley
Developmental Editor	Kathleen Finnegan
Production Editor	Nancy Shea
Text and Cover Designer	Ella Hanna
Cover Illustrator	Douglas Goodman

© 1998 by Course Technology— I(T)P®

For more information contact:

Course Technology
One Main Street
Cambridge, MA 02142

International Thomson Editores
Seneca, 53
Colonia Polanco
11560 Mexico D.F. Mexico

ITP Europe
Berkshire House 168-173
High Holborn
London WCIV 7AA
England

ITP GmbH
Königswinterer Strasse 418
53227 Bonn
Germany

Nelson ITP, Australia
102 Dodds Street
South Melbourne, 3205
Victoria, Australia

ITP Asia
60 Albert Street, #15-01
Albert Complex
Singapore 189969

ITP Nelson Canada
1120 Birchmount Road
Scarborough, Ontario
Canada M1K 5G4

ITP Japan
Hirakawacho Kyowa Building, 3F
2-2-1 Hirakawacho
Chiyoda-ku, Tokyo 102
Japan

ISBN 0-7600-5532-7

Printed in the United States of America

3 4 5 6 7 8 9 B 01 00 99

At Course Technology we have one foot in education and the other in technology. We believe that technology is transforming the way people teach and learn, and we are excited about providing instructors and students with materials that use technology to teach about technology.

Our development process is unparalleled in the higher education publishing industry. Every product we create goes through an exacting process of design, development, review, and testing.

Reviewers give us direction and insight that shape our manuscripts and bring them up to the latest standards. Every manuscript is quality tested. Students whose backgrounds match the intended audience work through every keystroke, carefully checking for clarity and pointing out errors in logic and sequence. Together with our own technical reviewers, these testers help us ensure that everything that carries our name is error-free and easy to use.

We show both how and why technology is critical to solving problems in college and in whatever field you choose to teach or pursue. Our time-tested, step-by-step instructions provide unparalleled clarity. Examples and applications are chosen and crafted to motivate students.

As the New Perspectives Series team at Course Technology, our goal is to produce the most timely, accurate, creative, and technologically sound product in the entire college publishing industry. We strive for consistent high quality. This takes a lot of communication, coordination, and hard work. But we love what we do. We are determined to be the best. Write to us and let us know what you think. You can also e-mail us at NewPerspectives@course.com.

The New Perspectives Series Team

Joseph J. Adamski	Michael Ekedahl	John Leschke
Judy Adamski	Jessica Evans	Mac Mendelsohn
Roy Ageloff	Marilyn Freedman	William Newman
Tim Ashe	Kathy Finnegan	Dan Oja
David Auer	Robin Geller	David Paradice
Daphne Barbas	Kate Habib	June Parsons
Dirk Baldwin	Donna Gridley	Harry Phillips
Rachel Bunin	Roger Hayen	Sandra Poindexter
Joan Carey	Cindy Johnson	Mark Reimold
Patrick Carey	Charles Hommel	Ann Shaffer
Sharon Caswell	Janice Jutras	Karen Shortill
Barbara Clemens	Chris Kelly	Susan Solomon
Rachel Crapser	Mary Kemper	Susanne Walker
Kim Crowley	Stacy Klein	John Zeanchock
Melissa Dezotell	Terry Ann Kremer	Beverly Zimmerman
		Scott Zimmerman

Preface The New Perspectives Series

What is the New Perspectives Series?

Course Technology's **New Perspectives Series** is an integrated system of instruction that combines text and technology products to teach computer concepts and microcomputer applications. Users consistently praise this series for innovative pedagogy, creativity, supportive and engaging style, accuracy, and use of interactive technology. The first New Perspectives text was published in January of 1993. Since then, the series has grown to more than 100 titles and has become the best-selling series on computer concepts and microcomputer applications. Others have imitated the New Perspectives features, design, and technologies, but none have replicated its quality and its ability to consistently anticipate and meet the needs of instructors and students.

What is the Integrated System of Instruction?

New Perspectives textbooks are part of a truly Integrated System of Instruction: text, graphics, video, sound, animation, and simulations that are linked and that provide a flexible, unified, and interactive system to help you teach and help your students learn. Specifically, the *New Perspectives Integrated System of Instruction* includes a Course Technology textbook in addition to some or all of the following items: Course Labs, Course Test Manager, Online Companions, and Course Presenter. These components—shown in the graphic on the back cover of this book—have been developed to work together to provide a complete, integrative teaching and learning experience.

How is the New Perspectives Series different from other microcomputer concepts and applications series?

The **New Perspectives Series** distinguishes itself from other series in at least four substantial ways: sound instructional design, consistent quality, innovative technology, and proven pedagogy. The applications texts in this series consist of two or more tutorials, which are based on sound instructional design. Each tutorial is motivated by a realistic case that is meaningful to students. Rather than learn a laundry list of features, students learn the features in the context of solving a problem. This process motivates all concepts and skills by demonstrating to students why they would want to know them.

Instructors and students have come to rely on the high quality of the **New Perspectives Series** and to consistently praise its accuracy. This accuracy is a result of Course Technology's unique multi-step quality assurance process that incorporates student testing at at least two stages of development, using hardware and software configurations appropriate to the product. All solutions, test questions, and other supplements are tested using similar procedures. Instructors who adopt this series report that students can work through the tutorials independently with minimum intervention or "damage control" by instructors or staff. This consistent quality has meant that if instructors are pleased with one product from the series, they can rely on the same quality with any other New Perspectives product.

The **New Perspectives Series** also distinguishes itself by its innovative technology. This series innovated Course Labs, truly *interactive* learning applications. These have set the standard for interactive learning.

How do I know that the New Perspectives Series will work?

Some instructors who use this series report a significant difference between how much their students learn and retain with this series as compared to other series. With other series, instructors often find that students can work through the book and do well on homework and tests, but still not demonstrate competency when asked to perform particular tasks outside the context of the text's sample case or project. With the **New Perspectives Series**, however, instructors report that students have a complete, integrative learning experience that stays with them. They credit this high retention and competency to the fact that this series incorporates critical thinking and problem-solving with computer skills mastery.

How does this book I'm holding fit into the New Perspectives Series?

New Perspectives applications books are available in the following categories:

Brief books are typically about 150 pages long, contain two to four tutorials, and are intended to teach the basics of an application.

Introductory books are typically about 300 pages long and consist of four to seven tutorials that go beyond the basics. These books often build out of the Brief editions by providing two or three additional tutorials. The book you are holding is an Introductory book.

Comprehensive books are typically about 600 pages long and consist of all of the tutorials in the Introductory books, plus a few more tutorials covering higher-level topics. Comprehensive books typically also include two Windows tutorials and three or four Additional Cases.

Advanced books cover topics similar to those in the Comprehensive books, but go into more depth. Advanced books present the most high-level coverage in the series.

Custom Books The **New Perspectives Series** offers you two ways to customize a New Perspectives text to fit your course exactly: *CourseKits*™, two or more texts packaged together in a box, and *Custom Editions*®, your choice of books bound together. Custom Editions offer you unparalleled flexibility in designing your concepts and applications courses. You can build your own book by ordering a combination of titles bound together to cover only the topics you want. Your students save because they buy only the materials they need. There is no minimum order, and books are spiral bound. Both CourseKits and Custom Editions offer significant price discounts. Contact your Course Technology sales representative for more information.

New Perspectives Series Microcomputer Applications

■ Brief Titles or Modules	■ Introductory Titles or Modules	■ Intermediate Tutorials	■ Advanced Titles or Modules	□ Other Modules

Brief	**Introductory**	**Comprehensive**	**Advanced**	**Custom Editions**
2 to 4 tutorials	6 or 7 tutorials, or Brief + 2 or 3 more tutorials	Introductory + 4 or 5 more tutorials. Includes Brief Windows tutorials and Additional Cases	Quick Review of basics + in-depth, high-level coverage	Choose from any of the above to build your own Custom Editions® or CourseKits™

In what kind of course could I use this book?

This book can be used in any course in which you want students to learn all the most important topics of HTML, including creating an HTML document; viewing an HTML file in a Web browser; working with tag text elements, including headings, paragraphs, and lists; inserting special characters, lines, and graphics; creating hypertext links; working with color and images; creating text and graphical tables; using tables to enhance page design; creating and working with frames; and controlling the behavior of hyperlinks on a page with frames. It is particularly recommended for a short course on HTML or as part of a full-semester course on the Internet. This book assumes that students have learned basic Windows 95 or Windows NT navigation and file management skills from *Course Technology's New Perspectives on Microsoft Windows 95—Brief, New Perspectives on Microsoft Windows NT Workstation 4.0—Introductory*, or an *equivalent* book.

How do the Windows 95 editions differ from the Windows 3.1 editions?

SESSION 1.1

Sessions We've divided the tutorials into sessions. Each session is designed to be completed in about 45 minutes to an hour (depending, of course, upon student needs and the speed of your lab equipment). With sessions, learning is broken up into more easily assimilated portions. You can more accurately allocate time in your syllabus, and students can better manage the available lab time. Each session begins with a "session box," which quickly describes the skills students will learn in the session. Furthermore, each session is numbered, which makes it easier for you and your students to navigate and communicate about the tutorial. Look on page HTML 1.4 for the session box that opens Session 1.1.

Quick Check

Quick Checks Each session concludes with meaningful, conceptual Quick Check questions that test students' understanding of what they learned in the session. Answers to the Quick Check questions in this book are provided on pages HTML 2.35 through HTML 2.37 and pages HTML 5.40 through HTML 5.42.

New Design We have retained the best of the old design to help students differentiate between what they are to *do* and what they are to *read*. The steps are clearly identified by their shaded background and numbered steps. Furthermore, this new design presents steps and screen shots in a larger, easier to read format. Some good examples of our new design are pages HTML 1.16 and HTML 1.17.

What features are retained in the Windows 95 editions of the New Perspectives Series?

"Read This Before You Begin" Page This page is consistent with Course Technology's unequaled commitment to helping instructors introduce technology into the classroom. Technical considerations and assumptions about software are listed to help instructors save time and eliminate unnecessary aggravation. See pages HTML 1.2 and HTML 3.2 for the "Read This Before You Begin" pages in this book.

Tutorial Case Each tutorial begins with a problem presented in a case that is meaningful to students. The problem turns the task of learning how to use an application into a problem-solving process. The problems increase in complexity with each tutorial. These cases touch on multicultural, international, and ethical issues—so important to today's business curriculum. See page HTML 1.3 for the case that begins Tutorial 1.

1.
2.
3.

Step-by-Step Methodology This unique Course Technology methodology keeps students on track. They enter data, click buttons, or press keys always within the context of solving the problem posed in the tutorial case. The text constantly guides students, letting them know where they are in the course of solving the problem. In addition, the numerous screen shots include labels that direct students' attention to what they should look at on the screen. On almost every page in this book, you can find an example of how steps, screen shots, and labels work together.

TROUBLE?

TROUBLE? Paragraphs These paragraphs anticipate the mistakes or problems that students are likely to have and help them recover and continue with the tutorial. By putting these paragraphs in the book, rather than in the Instructor's Manual, we facilitate independent learning and free the instructor to focus on substantive conceptual issues rather than on common procedural errors. Some representative examples of Trouble? paragraphs appear on page HTML 1.14.

REFERENCE
window

Reference Windows Reference Windows appear throughout the text. They are succinct summaries of the most important tasks covered in the tutorials. Reference Windows are specially designed and written so students can refer to them when doing the Tutorial Assignments and Case Problems, and after completing the course. Page HTML 1.24 contains the Reference Window for Creating Lists.

Tutorial Assignments, Case Problems, and Lab Assignments Each tutorial concludes with Tutorial Assignments, which provide students with additional hands-on practice of the skills they learned in the tutorial. See page HTML 3.43 for examples of Tutorial Assignments. The Tutorial Assignments are followed by four Case Problems that have approximately the same scope as the tutorial case. In the Windows 95 applications texts, the last Case Problem of each tutorial typically requires students to solve the problem independently, either "from scratch" or with minimum guidance. See page HTML 3.49 for examples of Case Problems. Finally, if a Course Lab accompanies a tutorial, Lab Assignments are included after the Case Problems. See page HTML 1.41 for examples of Lab Assignments.

EXPLORE

Exploration Exercises The Windows environment allows students to learn by exploring and discovering what they can do. Exploration Exercises can be Tutorial Assignments or Case Problems that challenge students, encourage them to explore the capabilities of the program they are using, and extend their knowledge using the Help facility and other reference materials. Page HTML 3.49 contains Exploration Exercises for Tutorial 3.

What supplements are available with this textbook?

Course Labs: Now, Concepts Come to Life Computer skills and concepts come to life with the New Perspectives Course Labs—highly-interactive tutorials that combine illustrations, animations, digital images, and simulations. The Labs guide students step-by-step, present them with Quick Check questions, let them explore on their own, test their comprehension, and provide printed feedback. Lab icons at the beginning of the tutorial and in the tutorial margins indicate when a topic has a corresponding Lab. Lab Assignments are included at the end of each relevant tutorial. The Lab available with this book and the tutorial in which it appears is:

TUTORIAL 1

The Internet
World Wide Web

Course Test Manager: Testing and Practice at the Computer or on Paper
Course Test Manager is cutting-edge, Windows-based testing software that helps instructors design and administer practice tests and actual examinations. This full-featured program allows students to randomly generate practice tests that provide immediate on-screen feedback and detailed study guides. Instructors can also use Course Test Manager to produce printed tests. Course Test Manager can automatically grade the tests students take at the computer and can generate statistical information on individual as well as group performance.

Course Presenter: This lecture presentation tool allows instructors to create electronic slide shows or traditional overhead transparencies using the figure files from the book. Instructors can customize, edit, save, and display figures from the text in order to illustrate key topics or concepts in class.

Online Companions: Dedicated to Keeping You and Your Students Up-To-Date When you use a New Perspectives product, you can access Course Technology's faculty sites and student sites on the World Wide Web. You can browse this text's password-protected Faculty Online Companion to obtain an online Instructor's Manual, Solution Files, Student Files, and more by visiting Course Technology's Online Resource Center at **http://www.course.com.** Please see your Instructor's Manual or call your Course Technology customer service representative for more information. Students can access this text's Student Online Companion, which contains student files and additional coverage of selected topics in the text.

Instructor's Manual **New Perspectives Series** Instructor's Manuals contain instructor's notes and printed solutions for each tutorial. Instructor's notes provide tutorial overviews and outlines, technical notes, lecture notes, and extra Case Problems. Printed solutions include solutions to Tutorial Assignments, Case Problems, and Lab Assignments.

Student Files Student Files contain all of the data that students will use to complete the tutorials, Tutorial Assignments, and Case Problems. A Readme file includes technical tips for lab management. See the inside covers of this book and the "Read This Before You Begin" pages for more information on Student Files.

Solution Files Solution Files contain every file students are asked to create or modify in the tutorials, Tutorial Assignments, and Case Problems.

The following supplements are included in the Instructor's Resource Kit that accompanies this textbook:

- Instructor's Manual
- Solution Files
- Student Files
- Internet /World Wide Web Course Lab
- Course Test Manager Test Bank
- Course Test Manager Engine
- Course Presenter
- HTML files of the Faculty Online Companion

Some of the supplements listed above are also available over the World Wide Web through Course Technology's password-protected Faculty Online Companion for this text. Please see your Instructor's Manual or call your Course Technology customer service representative for more information.

Acknowledgments

This book would not have been started without the support and enthusiasm of Mac Mendelsohn, Associate Publisher, and Mark Reimold, Acquisitions Editor, who initially proposed the project. Special thanks to Kathy Finnegan who improved the book with her editorial skill and valuable ideas, and to Donna Gridley who kept the project on track and on time and provided useful input. Other people at Course Technology who deserve credit are Karen Shortill, Editorial Assistant; Nancy Shea, Production Editor; Devra Kunin, Jeri Friedman, copyeditors; and John McCarthy, QA tester. Feedback is an important part of writing any book, and thanks go to the following reviewers for their ideas and comments: John Chenoweth, East Tennessee State University; Ramona Coveny, Patrick Henry Community College; Joseph Farrelly, Palomer College; Ralph Hooper, University of Alabama; Stuart Varden, Pace University; and Dr. Ahmed Zaki, College of William & Mary. Finally, I want to thank my wife Joan for her encouragement, suggestions and photographs (which I liberally used in creating my sample Web pages!) and my four sons: John Paul, Thomas, Peter, and Michael, to whom this book is dedicated.

Patrick Carey

Table of **Contents**

N E W
PERSPECTIVES
S E R I E S

Creating Web Pages with **HTML**

LEVEL I

TUTORIALS

Read This **Before You Begin**

STUDENT DISK

To complete HTML Tutorials 1–2 and end-of-tutorial assignments in this book, you need a Student Disk. Your instructor will either provide you with a Student Disk or ask you to make your own.

If you are supposed to make your own Student Disk, you will need one blank, formatted high-density disk. You will need to copy a set of folders from a file server or standalone computer onto your disk. Your instructor will tell you which computer, drive letter, and folders contain the files you need. See the inside front or inside back cover of this book for more information on Student Disk files, or ask your instructor or technical support person for assistance.

COURSE LAB

Tutorial 1 features an Interactive Course Lab to help you understand Internet World Wide Web concepts. There are Lab Assignments at the end of the tutorial that relate to this Lab. To start the Lab, click the Start button on the Windows 95 Taskbar, point to Programs, point to Course Labs, point to New Perspectives Applications, and click the Internet World Wide Web.

USING YOUR OWN COMPUTER

If you are going to work through this book using your own computer, you need:

■ **Computer System** A text editor and a Web browser (preferably Netscape Navigator or Internet Explorer, versions 3.0 or above) must be installed on your computer. If you are using a non-standard browser, it must support frames and HTML 3.2 or above. Most of the tutorials can be completed with just a text editor and a Web browser. However, to complete the last sections of Tutorial 2, you will need software that connects you to the Internet and an Internet connection.

■ **Student Disk** Ask your instructor or lab manager for details on how to get the Student Disk. You will not be able to complete the tutorials or end-of-tutorial assignments in this book using your own computer until you have a Student Disk. The Student Files may also be obtained electronically over the Internet. See the inside front or inside back cover of this book for more details.

VISIT OUR WORLD WIDE WEB SITE

Additional materials designed especially for you are available on the World Wide Web. Go to **http://www.course.com**. For example, see our Student Online Companion that contains additional coverage of selected topics in the text. These topics are indicated in the text by an online companion icon located in the left margin.

To complete HTML Tutorials 1–2 and end-of-tutorial assignments in this book, your students must use a set of files on one Student Disk. These files are included in the Instructor's Resource Kit, and they may also be obtained electronically over the Internet. See the inside front or inside back cover of this book for more details. Follow the instructions in the Readme file to copy the files to your server or standalone computer. You can view the Readme file using WordPad.

Once the files are copied, you can make a Student Disk for the students yourself, or you can tell students where to find the files so they can make their own Student Disks. Make sure the files get correctly copied onto the Student Disk by following the instructions in the Student Disk section above, which will ensure that students have enough disk space to complete all the tutorials and end-of-tutorial assignments.

COURSE LAB SOFTWARE

The Course Lab software is distributed on a CD-ROM included in the Instructor's Resource Kit. To install the Course Lab software, follow the setup instructions in the Readme file on the CD-ROM. Refer also to the Readme file for essential technical notes related to running the Lab in a multi-user environment. Once you have installed the Course Lab software, your students can start the Lab from the Windows 95 desktop by following the instructions in the Course Lab section above.

COURSE TECHNOLOGY STUDENT FILES

You are granted a license to copy the Student Files to any computer or computer network used by students who have purchased this book.

Creating a Web Page

Web Fundamentals and HTML

HTML

OBJECTIVES

In this tutorial you will:

- Explore the structure of the World Wide Web

- Learn the basic principles of Web documents

- Get to know the HTML language

- Create an HTML document

- View an HTML file in a Web browser

- Tag text elements, including headings, paragraphs, and lists

- Insert character tags

- Add special characters

- Insert horizontal lines

- Insert an inline graphic image

LAB

The Internet
World Wide Web

CASE

Creating an Online Resume

Mary Taylor just graduated from Colorado State with a master's degree in telecommunications. Now she has to find a job. Mary wants to explore as many employment avenues as possible, so she decides to post a copy of her resume on the World Wide Web. Creating an online resume offers Mary several advantages. The Web's skyrocketing popularity gives Mary the potential of reaching a large and varied audience. She can continually update an online resume, offering details on her latest projects and jobs. An online resume also gives a prospective employer the opportunity to look at her work history in more detail than is normal with a paper resume, because she can include links to other relevant documents. Mary asks you to help her create an online resume. You're happy to agree because it's something you wanted to learn anyway. After all, you'll be creating your own resume soon enough.

In this session you will learn the basics of how the World Wide Web operates. Then you will begin to explore the code used to create Web documents.

Introducing the World Wide Web

The **Internet** is a structure made up of millions of interconnected computers whose users can communicate with each other and share information. The physical structure of the Internet uses fiber-optic cables, satellites, phone lines, and other telecommunications media that send data back and forth, as Figure 1-1 shows. Computers that are linked together form a **network**. Any user whose computer can be linked to a network that has Internet access can join the worldwide Internet community.

Figure 1-1 ◄
Structure of the
Internet

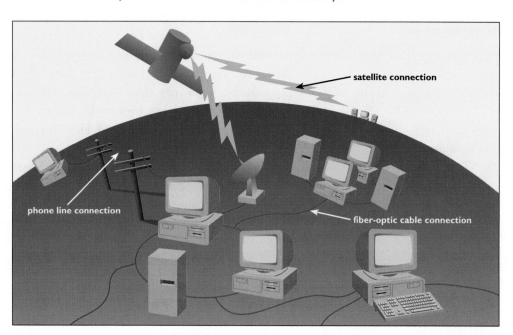

For years, anyone with Internet access could take advantage of the opportunities the Internet offered but not without some problems. New users often found their introduction to the Internet an unpleasant one. Many Internet tools required you to master a bewildering array of terms, acronyms, and commands before you could begin navigating the Internet. Navigation itself was a hit-and-miss proposition. A computer in Bethesda might have information on breast cancer, but if you didn't know that computer existed and how to reach it, the Internet offered few tools to help you get there. What Internet users needed was a tool that would be easy to use and would allow quick access to any computer on the Internet, regardless of its location. This tool would prove to be the World Wide Web.

The Development of the World Wide Web

The Internet World Wide Web

The **World Wide Web** organizes the Internet's vast resources to give you easy access to information. In 1989, Timothy Berners-Lee and other researchers at the CERN nuclear research facility near Geneva, Switzerland, laid the foundation of the World Wide Web, or the Web. They wanted to create an information system that made it easy for researchers to share data and that required minimal training and support. They developed a system of hypertext documents that made it very easy to move from one source of information to another. A **hypertext document** is an electronic file that contains elements that you can select, usually by clicking a mouse, to open another document.

Hypertext offers a new way of progressing through a series of documents. When you read a book you follow a linear progression, reading one page after another. With hypertext, you progress through pages in whatever way is best suited to your goals. Hypertext lets you skip from one topic to another, following a path of information that interests you. Figure 1-2 shows how topics could be related in a hypertext fashion as opposed to a linear fashion.

Figure 1-2 ◀
Linear vs. hypertext documents

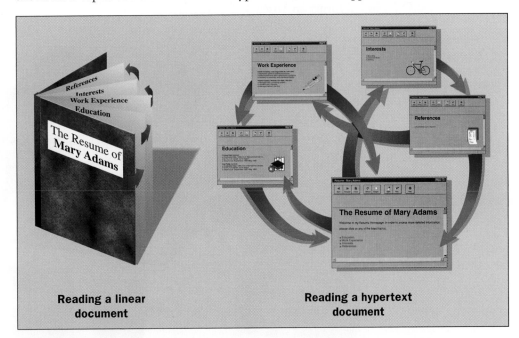

You might already be familiar with two common sources of hypertext: Windows Help files and Macintosh HyperCard stacks. In these applications, you move from one topic to another by clicking or highlighting a phrase or keyword known as a **link**. Clicking a link takes you to another section of the document or it might take you to another document entirely. Figure 1-3 shows how you might navigate a link in a Help file.

Figure 1-3 ◀
Clicking a link in a Help file

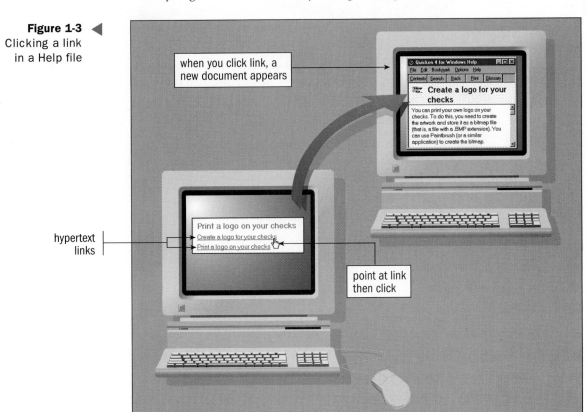

Hypertext as implemented by the CERN group involves jumping from one document to another on computers scattered all over the world. In Figure 1-4, you are working at a computer in Canada that shows a hypertext document on traveling in the United States. This document contains a link to another document located on a computer in Washington D.C. on the National Park Service. That document in turn contains a link to a document located in California on Yosemite National Park.

Figure 1-4 ◀
Navigating
hypertext
documents on
the Web

You move from document to document (and computer to computer) by simply clicking links. This approach makes navigating the Internet easy. It frees you from knowing anything about the document's location. The link could open a document on your computer or a document on a computer in South Africa. You might never notice the difference.

Your experience with the Web is not limited to reading text. Web documents, also known as **pages**, can contain graphics, video clips, sound clips, and, more recently, programs that you can run directly from the page. Moreover, as Figure 1-5 shows, Web pages can display text in a wide variety of fonts and formats. A Web document is not only a source of information, it can also be a work of art.

Figure 1-5 ◄
Web page
featuring
interesting
fonts, graphics
and layout

A final feature that contributes to the Web's popularity is that it gives users the ability to easily create their own Web documents. This is in marked contrast to other Internet tools, which often required the expertise of a computer systems manager. Figure 1-6 illustrates the Web's explosive growth: in 1993 there were only a couple hundred Web sites worldwide; by the beginning of 1997 there were almost 650,000. Even more impressively, the number of sites doubled in less than six months, according to estimates from Matthew Gray of the Massachusetts Institute of Technology. The Web has grown so fast, that it is almost impossible to estimate its current size. Is there any doubt why Mary sees the Web as a dynamic place to post a resume?

Figure 1-6 ◄
Growth of the
World Wide
Web

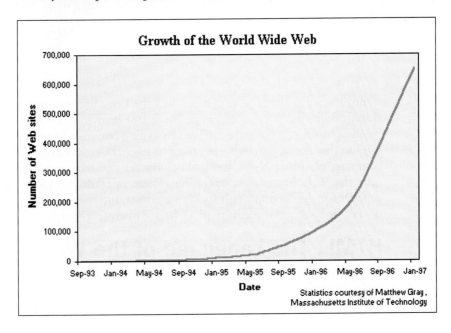

Web Servers and Web Browsers

The World Wide Web has the two components shown in Figure 1-7. The **Web server** is the computer that stores the Web document that users access. The **Web browser** is the software program that accesses the Web document and displays its contents on the user's computer. The browser can locate a document on a server anywhere in the world and display it for you to see.

Figure 1-7 ◀
Using a browser to view a Web document on a server

Netscape Navigator browser

browser in California locates and displays document stored on server in Florida

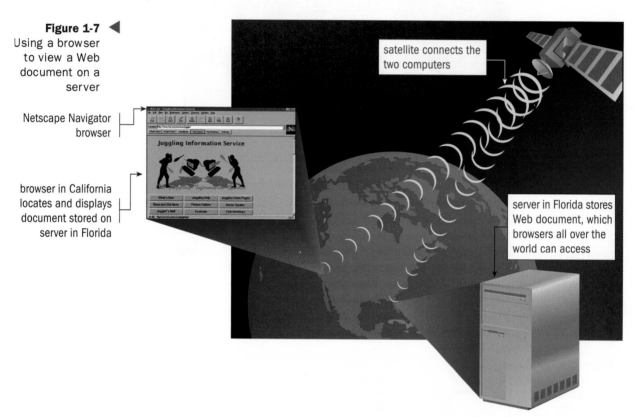

satellite connects the two computers

Juggling Information Service

server in Florida stores Web document, which browsers all over the world can access

Browsers can either be text-based like the Lynx browser found on UNIX machines or graphical like the popular Netscape Navigator browser shown in Figure 1-7. With a text-based browser you navigate the Web by typing commands; with a graphical browser you can use the mouse to move from page to page. Browsers are available for virtually every computer platform. No matter what computer you have, you can probably use it to navigate the Web. In its latest operating system upgrade, Windows 95, Microsoft includes support for the Web through its Web browser, Internet Explorer. Web access will probably become a standard feature of all future operating systems.

HTML: The Language of the Web

When a browser locates a Web document on a server, it needs a way to interpret what it finds. To create a Web document, you use a special language that browsers can read called a **markup language**. The most common markup language is the **Hypertext Markup Language** or **HTML**. HTML is one example of a more general markup language called **Standard Generalized Markup Language (SGML)**. SGML encompasses several types of markup languages called **Document Type Definitions (DTD)**. So if you want to engage in a little acronym overload, you can tell your friends that HTML is an SGML DTD used on the WWW.

HTML

HTML was designed to describe the contents of a Web page in a very general way. As you've seen in previous figures, a browser can display a Web page with a variety of fonts and styles. If you've used a word processor you know that you can specify the appearance of text in terms of a font type such as Arial or Times Roman, or an attribute such as bold or italic. HTML doesn't describe how text looks. Instead it uses a **code** that describes the function the text has in the document. Text appearing in the document heading is marked with a heading code. Text appearing in a bulleted list is marked with a list code. A Web browser interprets these codes to determine the text's appearance. Different browsers might make different choices. One browser might apply a Times Roman font to text in the document heading, while another browser might use an Arial font. Figure 1-8 shows how the same HTML file might appear on two different browsers.

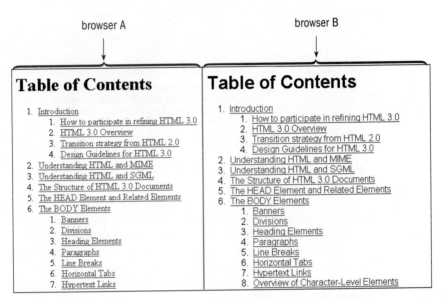

Figure 1-8 ◀
Two different browsers displaying the same HTML file

There are a couple reasons for this. The Web must work across computer platforms, a feature known as **portability**. Because each computer differs in terms of what, if any, fonts it can display, the browser determines how text is to be displayed. Portability frees Web page authors from worrying about making their pages compatible with the large variety of computers and operating systems on the Internet. HTML works with a wide range of devices, from clunky teletypes to high-end workstations. It also works with nonvisual media such as speech and Braille.

Another advantage of HTML is speed. While it might be possible to include exact specifications on how to display each character within the Web document, doing so would dramatically increase both file size and the time required to retrieve it. It is much quicker to render the document on the local computer using local specifications. The downside of this approach is that you cannot be sure exactly how every browser will display the text on your page. Some Web authors therefore test their code on several different browsers before posting their pages on the Internet.

Versions of HTML

The language HTML uses to mark text has a grammar or set of rules under which it operates, called its **syntax**. There must be a consensus on the syntax used in HTML files. If there were not, you would have no guarantee that other browsers on the Internet will recognize the code in your Web document. It wouldn't do Mary much good to create a stunning online resume that her potential employers cannot read. This consensus is referred to as the **specifications** or **standards** that have been developed by a consortium of Web authors, software companies, and interested users.

Figure 1-9 lists four versions of HTML; each follows a defined set of standards.

Figure 1-9 ◄
Versions of
HTML

Version	Description
HTML 1.0	The first public version of HTML, which included browser support for inline images and text controls.
HTML 2.0	The version supported by all graphical browsers, including Netscape Communicator, Internet Explorer and Mosaic. It supported interactive form elements such as option buttons and text boxes. A document written to follow 2.0 specifications would be readable by most browsers on the Internet.
HTML 3.2	This version included more support for creating and formatting tables and expanded the options for interactive form elements. It also allows for the creation of complex mathematical equations.
HTML 4.0	This version adds support for style sheets to give Web authors greater control over page layout. It adds new features to tables and forms and provides support for international features. This version also expands HTML's scripting ability and support for multimedia elements.

For detailed information on HTML standards and any updates, see the Web page at http://www.w3.org/MarkUp/.

Some browsers also support **extensions**, features that add new possibilities to HTML. The most well-known extensions were created for the Netscape Navigator browser. Because only Netscape Navigator browsers can interpret these extensions, many people argue that Netscape Navigator has undermined a fundamental advantage of the World Wide Web: the ability of a Web document to work on different platforms and browsers. On the other hand, Web authors clearly want the additional functions the Netscape Navigator extensions offer. These extensions foreshadowed many of the enhancements added in HTML 3.2. Moreover, the Netscape Navigator extensions didn't alter existing features. If you plan to use extensions in your Web documents, you should indicate this on your page and identify the browsers that support those extensions.

Tools for Creating HTML Documents

HTML documents are simple text files. The only software package you need to create them is a basic text editor like the Windows Notepad application. If you want a software package to do some of the work of creating an HTML document, you can use an HTML converter or an HTML editor.

An **HTML converter** takes text in one format and converts it to HTML code. For example, you can create the source document with a word processor like Microsoft Word and then have the converter save the document as an HTML file. Converters have several advantages. They free you from the occasionally laborious task of writing HTML code, and, because the conversion is automated, you do not have to worry about typographical errors ruining your code. Finally, you can create the source document using a software package that you might be more familiar with. Be aware that a converter has some limitations. As HTML specifications are updated and new extensions created, you will have to wait for the next version of the converter to take advantage of these features. Moreover, no converter can support all HTML features, so for anything but the simplest Web page, you still have to work with HTML.

An **HTML editor** helps you create an HTML file by inserting HTML codes for you as you work. HTML editors can save you a lot of work, but they have many of the same advantages and limitations as converters. They do let you set up your Web page quickly, but to create the finished document, you probably still have to work directly with the HTML code. You can read reviews of popular HTML editors on the Web page located at http://www.webcommando.com/editrev/index.html.

Quick Check

1. What is hypertext?

2. What are a Web server and a Web browser? Describe how they work together.

3. What is HTML?

4. How do HTML documents differ from documents created with a word processor like Word or WordPerfect?

5. What are the advantages of letting Web browsers determine the appearance of Web pages?

6. What are HTML extensions? What are some advantages and disadvantages of using extensions?

7. What software program do you need to create an HTML document?

SESSION

1.2

In this session you begin entering the text that will form the basis of your Web page. You will insert the appropriate HTML codes and create a simple Web page detailing Mary's work experience and qualifications.

Creating an HTML Document

It's always a good idea to plan the appearance of your Web page before you start writing code. In her final semester Mary developed a paper resume that she distributed at campus job fairs. Half her work is already done, because she can use the paper resume as her model.

Figure 1-10 shows Mary's hardcopy resume.

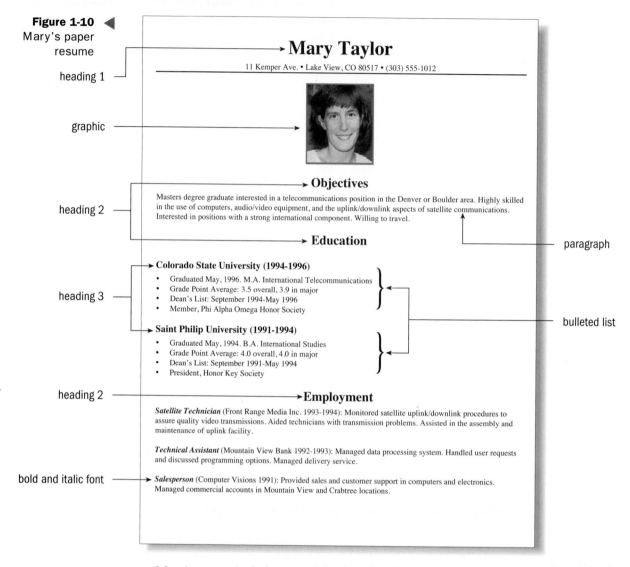

Figure 1-10
Mary's paper
resume

heading 1

graphic

heading 2

paragraph

heading 3

bulleted list

heading 2

bold and italic font

Mary's resume includes several features that she would like you to implement in the online version. A heading at the top prominently displays her name in a large font. Beneath the heading is her photo. Mary's resume is divided into three sections: Objectives, Education, and Employment. Within the Objectives section, a paragraph describes Mary's interests and future goals. Within the Education section, two smaller headings name the two universities she attended. Under each of these headings, a bulleted list details her accomplishments. The Employment section describes each position she's held, with the official title bolded and italicized. Mary's paper resume has three heading levels, bulleted lists, formatted characters, and graphics. When she creates her online resume with HTML, she wants to include these features. As you help Mary create this document for the World Wide Web, you will probably want to refer to Figure 1-10 periodically as the page develops.

HTML Syntax

The HTML syntax for creating the kinds of features that Mary wants in her page follow a very basic structure. An HTML document has two elements: document content and tags. **Document content** are those parts of the document that you want the user to see, such as text and graphics. **Tags** are the HTML codes that indicate the document content. You apply a tag to document content using the syntax:

```
<Tag Name Properties> Document Content </Tag Name>
```

You can always identify a tag by the brackets (<>) that enclose the tag name. Some tags can include **properties**, or additional information placed within the brackets that defines the tag's appearance. Tags usually come in pairs: the **opening tag** is the first tag, which tells the browser to turn on the feature and apply it to the document content that follows. The browser applies the feature until it encounters the **closing tag**, which turns off the feature. Note that closing tags are identified by the slash (/) that precedes the tag name. Not every tag has an opening and closing tag. Some tags are known as **one-sided tags** because they require only the opening tag. **Two-sided tags** require both opening and closing tags.

Look at the first line of Mary's resume, the name "Mary Taylor," in Figure 1-10. HTML uses the tag name <H1> for a heading 1. The HTML command that describes this line reads:

```
<H1 ALIGN=CENTER>Mary Taylor</H1>
```

Here the <H1 ALIGN=CENTER > opening tag tells the browser that the text that follows, "Mary Taylor," should appear as a heading 1. This tag also includes a property, the **alignment property** (ALIGN), which tells the browser how to align the text: in this case, centered. After the opening tag comes the content, Mary Taylor. The </H1> tag signals the browser to turn off the H1 heading. Remember that each browser determines the exact look of the H1 heading. One browser might apply a 14-point Times Roman bold font to Mary's text, whereas another browser might use 18-point italic Arial. Figure 1-11 shows how three different browsers might interpret this line of HTML code.

Figure 1-11
Examples of how different browsers might interpret the HTML<H1> tag

Browser interpreting the <H1> tag	Appearance of the document content
Browser A	**Mary Taylor**
Browser B	Mary Taylor
Browser C	*Mary Taylor*

Tags are not case sensitive. That means typing "<H1>" has the same effect as typing "<h1>." Many Web authors like to use only uppercase for tags to distinguish tags from document content. We'll follow that convention in the examples that follow.

Creating Basic Tags

When you start entering HTML code, it's best to identify the document's main components. First you enter tags that indicate the language in which Mary's document is written, identify the document's key sections, and give it a title. For now, type the text exactly as you see it. The text after the steps explains each line. To start entering code you need a text editor.

To start creating an HTML file:

1. Place your Student Disk in drive A.

   TROUBLE? If you don't have a Student Disk, you need to get one. Your instructor will either give you one or ask you to make your own. See the "Read This Before You Begin" page at the beginning of the tutorials for instructions.

   TROUBLE? If your Student Disk won't fit in drive A, try drive B. If it fits in drive B, substitute "drive B" for "drive A" in every tutorial.

2. Open a text editor on your system, and start a new document.

   TROUBLE? If you don't know how to locate, start, or use the text editor on your system, ask your instructor for help.

3. Type the following lines of code into your document. Press **Enter** after each line (twice for a blank line).

```
<HTML>
<HEAD>
<TITLE>The Resume of Mary Taylor</TITLE>
</HEAD>

<BODY>
</BODY>

</HTML>
```

4. Save the file as **Resume.htm** in the Tutorial.01 folder on your Student Disk, but do not exit your text editor. If you are working with Windows 95, UNIX, or a Macintosh, you can save it with the more conventional **html** file extension. The text you typed should look something like Figure 1-12.

   TROUBLE? If you don't know how to save a file on your Student Disk, ask your instructor for assistance.

   TROUBLE? Don't worry if your screen doesn't look exactly like Figure 1-12. The text editor shown in the figures is the Windows 95 Notepad editor. Your text editor might look very different. Just make sure you entered the text correctly.

   TROUBLE? If you are using the Windows 95 Notepad text editor to create your HTML file, make sure you don't save the file as a text document type. Notepad automatically adds the .txt extension to the filename. This renders the file unreadable to the Netscape Navigator browser, which expects an htm or html file extension. Instead, save the file as type, All Files=(*.*), and add the htm or html extension to the filename yourself.

Figure 1-12 ◄
HTML codes
entered in text
editor

HTML tags
indicate code is
written in HTML

<HEAD> tags
surround information
about Web page

<BODY> tags
surround the portion
of the document
that appears
in the browser

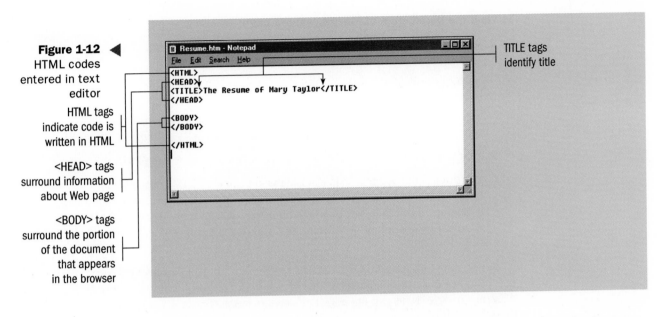

TITLE tags
identify title

The opening and closing HTML tags bracket all the remaining code in the document. This indicates to a browser that the page is written in HTML. While you don't have to include this tag, it is necessary if the file is to be read by another SGML application. Moreover, it is considered "good style" to include it.

The <HEAD> tag is where you enter information about the Web page. One such piece of information is the title of the page. The <TITLE> tag includes a title that names Mary's page "The Resume of Mary Taylor." This title will appear in the title bar of the Web browser window displaying Mary's page.

Finally, the portion of the document that Web users will see is contained within the <BODY> tags. At this point, the page is blank with no text or graphics. You'll add those later. The HEAD and BODY tags are also not strictly required, but you should include them to better organize your document and make its code more readable to others. The extra space before and after the BODY tags is also not required, but it will make your code easier to view as you add more features to it.

Displaying Your HTML Files

The file you are creating is the HTML file. A browser, of course, will not display the HTML file but will display the formatted page. As you continue adding to Mary's HTML file you should occasionally display the formatted page with your Web browser to verify that there are no syntax errors or other problems. You might even want to view the results on several browsers to check for differences between one browser and another. In the steps and figures that follow, the Netscape Navigator browser is used to display Mary's resume page as it gradually unfolds. If you are using a different browser, ask your instructor how to access local files.

To view the beginnings of Mary's resume page:

1. Start your browser. You do not need to be connected to the Internet to access a file loaded on your computer.

   TROUBLE? If you try to start your browser and are not connected to the Internet, you might get a warning message. Netscape Navigator, for example, gives a warning message telling you that it was unable to create a network socket connection. Click OK to ignore the message and continue.

2. After your browser loads its home page, click **File** then click **Open File**.

   TROUBLE? You use the Open File command to view an HTML document in Netscape Navigator 3.0. The Netscape Navigator 3.0 Gold command is Open File in Browser. If you are using a different browser, look for a similar command. In Internet Explorer, for example, you click Open on the File menu, and then click the Open File button.

3. Locate the **Resume.htm** file that you saved in the Tutorial.01 folder on your Student Disk, then click **Open**. Your browser displays Mary's file as shown in Figure 1-13. Note that the page title appears in the Netscape Navigator title bar.

   TROUBLE? If your browser displays something different, compare the code in your file to the code shown in Figure 1-12, and correct any errors.

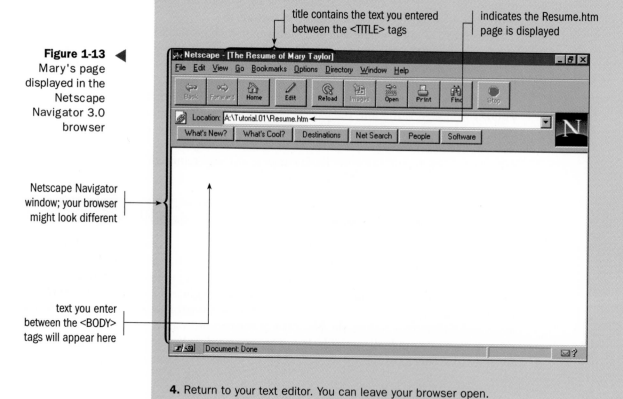

title contains the text you entered between the <TITLE> tags

indicates the Resume.htm page is displayed

Figure 1-13 ◄
Mary's page displayed in the Netscape Navigator 3.0 browser

Netscape Navigator window; your browser might look different

text you enter between the <BODY> tags will appear here

4. Return to your text editor. You can leave your browser open.

Creating Headings, Paragraphs, and Lists

Now that the basic structure of Mary's page is set, you turn to filling in the details. The best place to start is with the headings for the various sections of her document. Her document needs a heading for the entire page and headings for each of three sections: Objectives, Education, and Employment. The Education section has two additional headings that provide information about the two universities she attended. You can create all these headings using HTML heading tags.

Creating Heading Tags

HTML has six levels of headings, numbered 1 through 6, with 1 being the most prominent. Headings appear in a larger font than normal text. Some headings are also bolded. The general syntax for a heading tag is:

```
<Hy>Heading Text</Hy>
```

where *y* is a heading numbered 1 through 6.

Figure 1-14 illustrates the general appearance of the six heading styles. Your browser might use slightly different fonts and sizes.

Figure 1-14 ◀
Six heading
levels

This is an H1 Header

This is an H2 Header

This is an H3 Header

This is an H4 Header

This is an H5 Header

This is an H6 Header

REFERENCE window

CREATING A HEADING TAG

- Open the HTML file with your text editor.
- Type <H*n*> where *n* is the heading number you want to use.
- Specify the alignment property setting after *n* and before > if you want to use a special alignment.
- Type the text that you want to appear in the heading.
- Type </H*n*> to turn off the heading tag.

Starting with HTML 3.2, the heading tag can contain additional properties, one of which is the alignment property. Mary wants some headings centered on the page, so you take advantage of this property. Although Mary's address is not really heading text, you decide to format it with a heading 5 tag, because you want it to stand out a little from normal paragraphed text.

To add headings to the resume file:

1. Return to your text editor, and open the **Resume.htm** file, if it is not already open.

2. Type the following text between the <BODY> and </BODY> tags (type the address and phone number all on one line, as shown in Figure 1-15):

```
<H1 ALIGN=CENTER>Mary Taylor</H1>
<H5 ALIGN=CENTER>11 Kemper Ave. Lake View, CO 80517
   (303) 555-1012</H5>
<H2 ALIGN=CENTER>Objectives</H2>
<H2 ALIGN=CENTER>Education</H2>
<H3>Colorado State University (1994-1996)</H3>
<H3>Saint Philip University (1991-1994)</H3>
<H2 ALIGN=CENTER>Employment</H2>
```

The revised code is shown in Figure 1-15. In order to make it easier to follow the changes to the HTML file, new and altered text is highlighted in red.

3. Save the revised Resume.htm file into the Tutorial.01 folder on your Student Disk. You can leave the text editor open.

Figure 1-15 ◀
Entering HTML
code to mark
headings

enter the new code
between the
<BODY> tags

code you just
entered specifies
the headings
in Mary's resume

```
<BODY>
<H1 ALIGN=CENTER>Mary Taylor</H1>
<H5 ALIGN=CENTER>11 Kemper Ave. Lake View, CO 80517 (303) 555-1012</H5>
<H2 ALIGN=CENTER>Objectives</H2>
<H2 ALIGN=CENTER>Education</H2>
<H3>Colorado State University (1994-1996)</H3>
<H3>Saint Philip University (1991-1994)</H3>
<H2 ALIGN=CENTER>Employment</H2>
</BODY>
```

The section headings all use the ALIGN=CENTER property to center the text on the page. The tags for the two university headings, however, do not include that property and will be left-justified because that is the default alignment setting. If a browser that displays Mary's page does not support HTML 3.2 (or above) or does not support the alignment property through an extension, the headings will appear but all of them will be left-justified.

To display the revised Resume.htm file:

1. Return to your Web browser.

2. If the previous version of the file still appears in the browser window, click **View** then click **Reload** if you are using Netscape Navigator to reload the file. Otherwise open the file using the techniques you learned earlier.

The updated Resume.htm file looks like Figure 1-16.

Figure 1-16
Headings as
they appear
in the browser

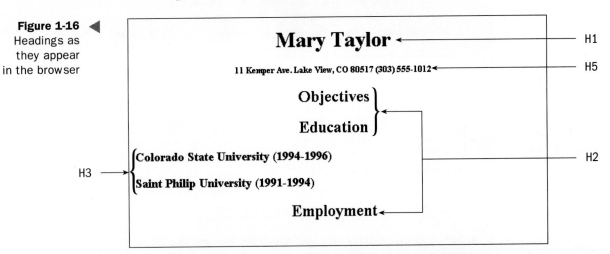

Mary Taylor ← H1

11 Kemper Ave. Lake View, CO 80517 (303) 555-1012 ← H5

Objectives
Education

H3 → Colorado State University (1994-1996)
Saint Philip University (1991-1994)   H2

Employment

Entering Paragraph Text

The next thing that you have to do is enter information for each section. If your paragraph does not require any formatting, you can enter the text without tags.

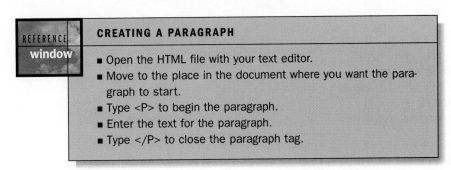

REFERENCE window

CREATING A PARAGRAPH

- Open the HTML file with your text editor.
- Move to the place in the document where you want the paragraph to start.
- Type <P> to begin the paragraph.
- Enter the text for the paragraph.
- Type </P> to close the paragraph tag.

Mary's career objective, which appears just below the Objectives heading, does not require formatting.

To enter paragraph text:

1. Return to your text editor, and reopen the **Resume.htm** file, if it is not already open.

2. Type the following text directly after the line of code that specifies the Objectives heading:

   Masters degree graduate interested in a telecommunications position in the Denver or Boulder area. Highly skilled in the use of computers, audio/video equipment and the uplink/downlink aspects of satellite communications. Interested in positions with a strong international component. Willing to travel.

   Your text should be placed between the Objectives head and the Education head as shown in Figure 1-17. Check your work for mistakes, and edit the file as necessary.

TROUBLE? If you are using a text editor like Notepad, the text might not wrap automatically. You might need to select the Word Wrap command on the Edit menu, or a similar command, to force the text to wrap so you can see it all on your screen.

Figure 1-17 ◀
Entering
paragraph text

enter Objectives
paragraph here

```
<BODY>
<H1 ALIGN=CENTER>Mary Taylor</H1>
<H5 ALIGN=CENTER>11 Kemper Ave. Lake View, CO 80517 (303) 555-1012</H5>
<H2 ALIGN=CENTER>Objectives</H2>
Masters degree graduate interested in a telecommunications position in the
Denver or Boulder area. Highly skilled in the use of computers, audio/video
equipment and the uplink/downlink aspects of satellite communications.
Interested in positions with a strong international component. Willing to
travel.
<H2 ALIGN=CENTER>Education</H2>
```

3. Save the changes you made to the Resume.htm file.

4. Return to your Web browser, and reload the **Resume.htm** file to view the text you've added. See Figure 1-18.

Figure 1-18 ◀
Paragraph text
as it appears
in the browser

Objectives text

Mary Taylor

11 Kemper Ave. Lake View, CO 80517 (303) 555-1012

Objectives

Masters degree graduate interested in a telecommunications position in the Denver or Boulder area. Highly skilled in the use of computers, audio/video equipment and the uplink/downlink aspects of satellite communications. Interested in positions with a strong international component. Willing to travel.

Education

5. Now enter the Employment paragraph text by returning to your text editor and reopening the **Resume.htm** file if needed.

6. Go to the end of the file, and, in the line before the final </BODY> tag, enter the following text:

Satellite Technician (Front Range Media Inc. 1993-1994): Monitored satellite uplink/downlink procedures to assure quality video transmissions. Aided technicians with transmission problems. Assisted in the assembly and maintenance of uplink facility.

Technical Assistant (Mountain View Bank 1992-1993): Managed data processing system. Handled user requests and discussed programming options. Managed delivery service.

Salesperson (Computer Visions 1991): Sales and customer support in computers and electronics. Managed commercial accounts in Mountain View and Crabtree locations.

Figure 1-19 shows the new code in Mary's resume file.

Figure 1-19 ◀
Entering
Employment
paragraph text

enter employment
descriptions here

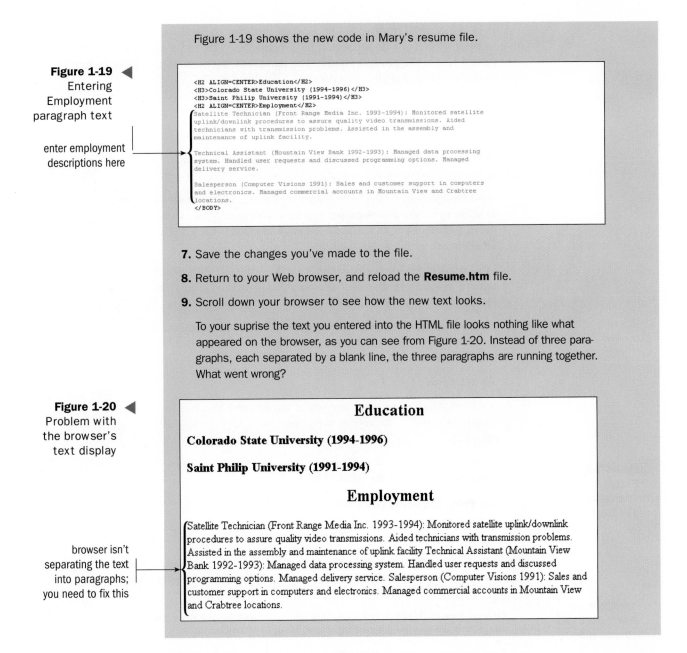

```
<H2 ALIGN=CENTER>Education</H2>
<H3>Colorado State University (1994-1996)</H3>
<H3>Saint Philip University (1991-1994)</H3>
<H2 ALIGN=CENTER>Employment</H2>
Satellite Technician (Front Range Media Inc. 1993-1994): Monitored satellite
uplink/downlink procedures to assure quality video transmissions. Aided
technicians with transmission problems. Assisted in the assembly and
maintenance of uplink facility.

Technical Assistant (Mountain View Bank 1992-1993): Managed data processing
system. Handled user requests and discussed programming options. Managed
delivery service.

Salesperson (Computer Visions 1991): Sales and customer support in computers
and electronics. Managed commercial accounts in Mountain View and Crabtree
locations.
</BODY>
```

7. Save the changes you've made to the file.

8. Return to your Web browser, and reload the **Resume.htm** file.

9. Scroll down your browser to see how the new text looks.

To your suprise the text you entered into the HTML file looks nothing like what appeared on the browser, as you can see from Figure 1-20. Instead of three paragraphs, each separated by a blank line, the three paragraphs are running together. What went wrong?

Figure 1-20 ◀
Problem with
the browser's
text display

Education

Colorado State University (1994-1996)

Saint Philip University (1991-1994)

Employment

browser isn't
separating the text
into paragraphs;
you need to fix this

Satellite Technician (Front Range Media Inc. 1993-1994): Monitored satellite uplink/downlink procedures to assure quality video transmissions. Aided technicians with transmission problems. Assisted in the assembly and maintenance of uplink facility Technical Assistant (Mountain View Bank 1992-1993): Managed data processing system. Handled user requests and discussed programming options. Managed delivery service. Salesperson (Computer Visions 1991): Sales and customer support in computers and electronics. Managed commercial accounts in Mountain View and Crabtree locations.

The problem here is that HTML formats text through the use of tags. HTML ignores such things as extra blank spaces, blank lines, or tabs. As far as HTML is concerned, the following three lines of code are identical, so a browser interprets and displays each line just like the others, ignoring the extra spaces and lines:

```
<H1>To be or not to be. That is the question.</H1>

<H1>To be or not to be.        That is the question.</H1>

<H1>To be or not to be.
        That is the question.</H1>
```

At first glance the Employment section seemed not to need formatting; however, each job description needs to be separated by a blank line. To add a blank line to an HTML document, you use the paragraph tag. The **paragraph tag** adds an extra line before text to separate it from any text that precedes it.

To incorporate paragraph tags into the resume file:

1. Return to your text editor.

2. Modify the Employment text, bracketing each paragraph between a **<P>** and **</P>** tag, so that the lines read:

   <P>Satellite Technician (Front Range Media Inc. 1993-1994): Monitored satellite uplink/downlink procedures to assure quality video transmissions. Aided technicians with transmission problems. Assisted in the assembly and maintenance of uplink facility.</P>

   <P>Technical Assistant (Mountain View Bank 1992-1993): Managed data processing system. Handled user requests and discussed programming options. Managed delivery service. </P>

   <P>Salesperson (Computer Visions 1991): Sales and customer support in computers and electronics. Managed commercial accounts in Mountain View and Crabtree locations.</P>

3. Save the revised text file.

4. Return to your Web browser, and reload the **Resume.htm** file. The text in the Employment section is properly separated into distinct paragraphs as shown in Figure 1-21.

Figure 1-21 ◀
Paragraphs
with paragraph
tags inserted

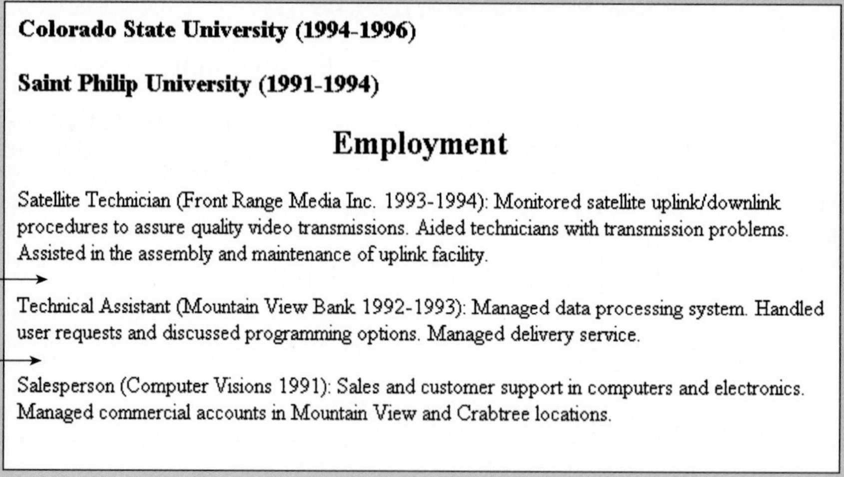

Colorado State University (1994-1996)

Saint Philip University (1991-1994)

Employment

Satellite Technician (Front Range Media Inc. 1993-1994): Monitored satellite uplink/downlink procedures to assure quality video transmissions. Aided technicians with transmission problems. Assisted in the assembly and maintenance of uplink facility.

paragraph tags
now in place so
spaces appear

Technical Assistant (Mountain View Bank 1992-1993): Managed data processing system. Handled user requests and discussed programming options. Managed delivery service.

Salesperson (Computer Visions 1991): Sales and customer support in computers and electronics. Managed commercial accounts in Mountain View and Crabtree locations.

If you start examining the HTML code for pages that you encounter on the Web, you might notice that the <P> tag is used in different ways on other pages. In the original version of HTML, the <P> tag inserted a blank line into the page. In HTML 1.0, <P> was placed at the end of each paragraph; no </P> tag was required. In versions 2.0 and 3.2, the paragraph tag is two-sided: both the <P> and </P> tags are used. Moreover, the <P> tag is placed at the beginning of the paragraph, not the end. Starting with HTML 3.2, you can specify the alignment property in a paragraph tag. In HTML 1.0 and 2.0, you cannot—paragraphs are always assumed to be left-justified. For the Web documents that you intend to create today, you should use the style convention shown in this example.

Creating Lists

You still need to enter the lists describing Mary's achievements at Colorado State and Saint Philip University. HTML provides tags for such lists. HTML supports three kinds of lists: ordered, unordered, and definition.

An **ordered list** is a list in numeric order. HTML adds the numbers. If you remove an item from the list, HTML automatically updates the numbers. For example, Mary might want to list her education awards in order from the most important to the least important. To do so, you could enter the following code into her HTML document:

```
<H3>Education Awards</H3>
<OL>
<LI>Enos Mills Scholarship
<LI>Physics Expo blue ribbon winner
<LI> Honor Key Award semi-finalist
</OL>
```

A Web browser might display this code as:

Education Awards

1. Enos Mills Scholarship

2. Physics Expo blue ribbon winner

3. Honor Key Award semi-finalist

This example shows the basic structure of an HTML list. The list text is bracketed between the <OL> and </OL> tags, where OL stands for ordered list. This tells the browser to present the text between the tags as an ordered list. Each list item is identified by a single <LI> tag, where LI stands for list item. There is no closing tag for list items.

An **unordered list** is one in which list items have no particular order. Browsers usually format unordered lists by inserting a bullet symbol before each list item. The entire list is bracketed between the <UL> and </UL> tags, where UL stands for unordered list. If Mary wants to display her awards without regard to their importance, you could enter the following code:

```
<H3>Education Awards</H3>
<UL>
<LI>Enos Mills Scholarship
<LI>Physics Expo blue ribbon winner
<LI>Honor Key Award semi-finalist
</UL>
```

A Web browser might display this code as:

Education Awards

■ Enos Mills Scholarship

■ Physics Expo blue ribbon winner

■ Honor Key Award semi-finalist

The third type of list that HTML can display is a definition list. A **definition list** is a list of terms, each followed by a definition line, usually indented slightly to the right. The <LI> tag used in ordered and unordered lists for individual items is replaced by two tags: the <DT> tag used for each term in the list and the <DD> tag used for each term's definition. As with the <LI> tag, both of these tags are one-sided. The entire list is bracketed by the <DL> and </DL> tags indicating to the browser that the list is a definition list. If Mary wants to create a list of her educational awards and briefly describe each, she could use a definition list. To create a definition list for her awards, you could enter this code into her HTML file:

```
<H3>Education Awards</H3>
<DL>
<DT>Enos Mills Scholarship<DD>Awarded to the outstanding
  student in the senior class
<DT>Physics Expo blue ribbon winner<DD>Awarded for a research
  project on fiberoptics
<DT>Honor Key Award semi-finalist<DD>Awarded for an essay on
  the information age
</DL>
```

A Web browser might display this code as:

Education Awards

Enos Mills Scholarship
  Awarded to the outstanding student in the senior class

Physics Expo blue ribbon winner
  Awarded for a research project on fiberoptics

Honor Key Award semi-finalist
  Awarded for an essay on the information age

REFERENCE window

CREATING LISTS

- Open the HTML file with your text editor.
- Move to the place in the document where you want the list to appear.
- Type <OL> to start an ordered list or <UL> to start an unordered list.
- For each item in the list, type <LI> followed by the text for the list item.
- To turn off the list, type </OL> for an ordered list or </UL> for an unordered list.
- To create a definition list, type <DL> and </DL> as brackets, then within each bracket type <DT> before the term and <DD> before the definition.

On her paper resume (Figure 1-10) Mary's educational accomplishments are in a bulleted list. You can include this feature in Mary's online resume by using an unordered list.

To add an unordered list to the resume file:

1. Return to your text editor, and reopen the **Resume.htm** file if it is not still open.

2. Type these lines of code between the headings "Colorado State University" and "Saint Philip University":

<UL>
<LI>Graduated May, 1996. M.A. International Telecommunications
<LI>Grade Point Average: 3.5 overall, 3.9 in major
<LI>Dean's List: September 1994-May 1996
<LI>Member, Phi Alpha Omega Honor Society
</UL>

3. Type these lines of code after the heading "Saint Philip University":

<UL>
<LI>Graduated May, 1994. B.A. International Studies
<LI>Grade Point Average: 4.0 overall, 4.0 in major
<LI>Dean's List: September 1991-May 1994
<LI>President, Honor Key Society
</UL>

The new lines in the resume file should look like Figure 1-22.

Figure 1-22 ◀
Entering
unordered lists

unordered lists ———

```
<H2 ALIGN=CENTER>Education</H2>
<H3>Colorado State University (1994-1996)</H3>
<UL>
<LI>Graduated May, 1996. M.A. International Telecommunications
<LI>Grade Point Average: 3.5 overall, 3.9 in major
<LI>Dean's List: September 1994-May 1996
<LI>Member, Phi Alpha Omega Honor Society
</UL>
<H3>Saint Philip University (1991-1994)</H3>
<UL>
<LI>Graduated May, 1994. B.A. International Studies
<LI>Grade Point Average: 4.0 overall, 4.0 in major
<LI>Dean's List: September 1991-May 1994
<LI>President, Honor Key Society
</UL>
<H2 ALIGN=CENTER>Employment</H2>
```

4. When you are sure that the revised resume matches the code in Figure 1-22, save the file as **Resume.htm**.

5. Switch to your Web browser and reload the **Resume.htm** file.

Mary's resume file now includes lists formatted much like those on her paper resume. If your browser does not create a page that looks like Figure 1-23, return to the HTML file, and check for inconsistencies.

Figure 1-23 ◀
Unordered lists
as they appear
in the browser

browser formats
unordered lists
with bullets

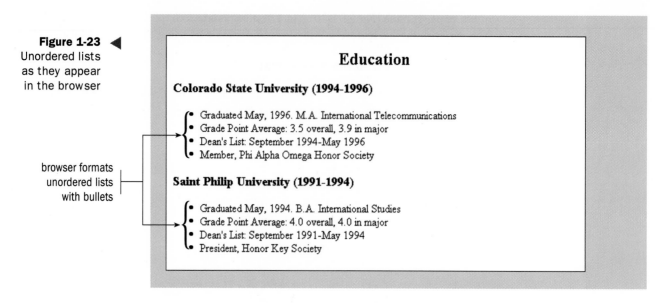

Education

Colorado State University (1994-1996)

- Graduated May, 1996. M.A. International Telecommunications
- Grade Point Average: 3.5 overall, 3.9 in major
- Dean's List: September 1994-May 1996
- Member, Phi Alpha Omega Honor Society

Saint Philip University (1991-1994)

- Graduated May, 1994. B.A. International Studies
- Grade Point Average: 4.0 overall, 4.0 in major
- Dean's List: September 1991-May 1994
- President, Honor Key Society

Creating Character Tags

Until now you've worked with tags that affect either the entire document or individual lines. HTML also lets you modify the characteristics of individual characters. A tag that you apply to an individual character is called a **character tag**. You can use two kinds of character tags: logical and physical. **Logical character tags** indicate how you want to use text, not necessarily how you want it displayed. Figure 1-24 lists some common logical character tags.

Figure 1-24 ◀
Common logical
character tags

Tag	Description
<EM>	Indicates that characters should be emphasized in some way. Usually displayed with italics.
<STRONG>	Emphasizes characters more strongly than <EM>. Usually displayed in a bold font.
<CODE>	Indicates a sample of code. Usually displayed in a Courier font or a similar font that allots the same width to each character.
<KBD>	Used to offset text that the user should enter. Often displayed in a Courier font or a similar font that allots the same width to each character.
<VAR>	Indicates a variable. Often displayed in italics or underlined.
<CITE>	Indicates short quotes or citations. Often italicized by browsers.

Figure 1-25 shows examples of how these tags might appear in a browser. Note that you can combine tags, allowing you to create bolded and italicized text by using both the <EM> and the <STRONG> tags.

Figure 1-25 ◄
Logical
character tags
as they appear
in the browser

examples of
individual logical
character tags

combined logical
character tags

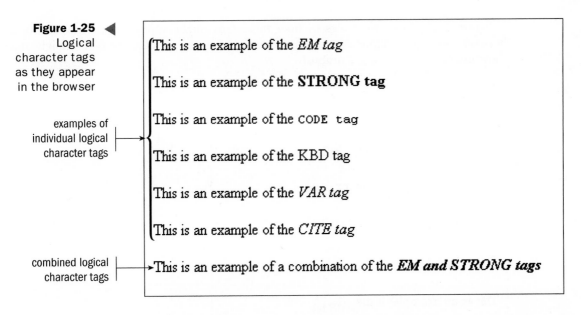

This is an example of the *EM tag*

This is an example of the **STRONG tag**

This is an example of the `CODE tag`

This is an example of the KBD tag

This is an example of the *VAR tag*

This is an example of the *CITE tag*

This is an example of a combination of the ***EM and STRONG tags***

HTML authors can also use **physical character tags** to indicate exactly how characters are to be formatted. Figure 1-26 shows common examples of physical character tags.

Figure 1-26 ◄
Common
physical
character tags

Tag	Description
<B>	Indicates that the text should be bold
<I>	Indicates that the text should be italic
<TT>	Indicates that the text should be used with a font like Courier that allots the same width to each character
<BIG>	Indicates that the text should be displayed in a big font. Available only in HTML 3.0 and above.
<SMALL>	Indicates that the text should be displayed in a small font. Available only in HTML 3.0 and above.
<SUB>	The text should be displayed as a subscript, in a smaller font if possible. Available only in HTML 3.0 and above.
<SUP>	The text should be displayed as a superscript, in a smaller font if possible. Available only in HTML 3.0 and above.

Figure 1-27 shows examples of how these tags might appear in a browser. Some browsers also support the <U> tag for underlining text, but other browsers might not show underlining, so use it cautiously.

Figure 1-27 ◀
Physical
character tags
as they appear
in the browser

This is an example of the **B tag**

This is an example of the *I tag*

This is an example of the ⊤⊤ tag

This is an example of the **BIG tag**

This is an example of the SMALL tag

This is an example of the ₛᵤᵦ tag

This is an example of the ˢᵁᴾ tag

Given the presence of both logical and physical character tags, which should you use to display some text in an italicized font: <EM> or <I>? The answer depends on who will view your Web page. Some browsers, like the UNIX browser Lynx, are text-based and cannot display italics. These browsers ignore the <I> tag, so emphasis you want to place on a certain piece of text is lost. In this case you would use a logical tag. On the other hand, if you decide that only graphical browsers such as Netscape Navigator or Internet Explorer will access your page, you might want to use a physical tag since it more explicitly defines what the resulting text looks like on the browser.

Because Mary is not certain who will access her online resume, you decide to use logical tags so the formatting appears on the widest range of browsers. Only one part of her resume requires character tags: the Employment section, where Mary wants to emphasize the title of each job she has held. You decide to use a combination of the <EM> and <STRONG> tags.

To add character tags to the resume file:

1. Return to your text editor, and reopen the **Resume.htm** file if necessary.

2. Type the **<EM>** and **<STRONG>** tags around the job titles in the Employment section of the resume (just after the <P> tags), so that they read:

<EM><STRONG>Satellite Technician</STRONG></EM>
<EM><STRONG>Technical Assistant</STRONG></EM>
<EM><STRONG>Salesperson</STRONG></EM>

Adjust any word wrapping in your editor to make the code easier to follow. See Figure 1-28.

Figure 1-28
Applying
character tags

character tags

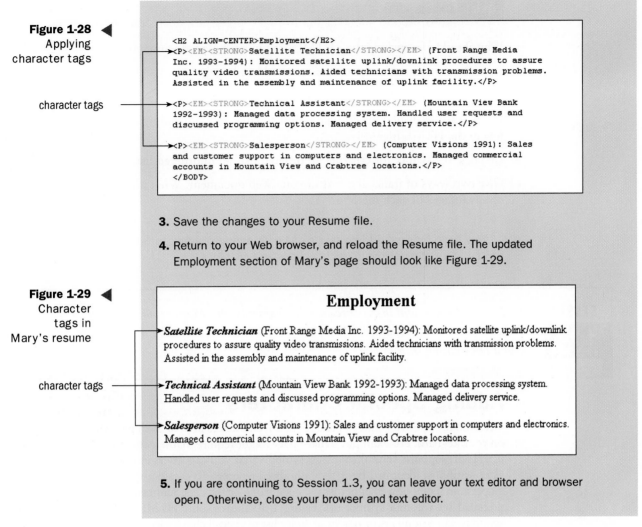

```
<H2 ALIGN=CENTER>Employment</H2>
<P><EM><STRONG>Satellite Technician</STRONG></EM> (Front Range Media
Inc. 1993-1994): Monitored satellite uplink/downlink procedures to assure
quality video transmissions. Aided technicians with transmission problems.
Assisted in the assembly and maintenance of uplink facility.</P>
<P><EM><STRONG>Technical Assistant</STRONG></EM> (Mountain View Bank
1992-1993): Managed data processing system. Handled user requests and
discussed programming options. Managed delivery service.</P>
<P><EM><STRONG>Salesperson</STRONG></EM> (Computer Visions 1991): Sales
and customer support in computers and electronics. Managed commercial
accounts in Mountain View and Crabtree locations.</P>
</BODY>
```

3. Save the changes to your Resume file.

4. Return to your Web browser, and reload the Resume file. The updated Employment section of Mary's page should look like Figure 1-29.

Figure 1-29
Character
tags in
Mary's resume

character tags

Employment

Satellite Technician (Front Range Media Inc. 1993-1994): Monitored satellite uplink/downlink procedures to assure quality video transmissions. Aided technicians with transmission problems. Assisted in the assembly and maintenance of uplink facility.

Technical Assistant (Mountain View Bank 1992-1993): Managed data processing system. Handled user requests and discussed programming options. Managed delivery service.

Salesperson (Computer Visions 1991): Sales and customer support in computers and electronics. Managed commercial accounts in Mountain View and Crabtree locations.

5. If you are continuing to Session 1.3, you can leave your text editor and browser open. Otherwise, close your browser and text editor.

When you apply two character tags to the same text you should place one set of tags completely within another. You combine the <EM> and <STRONG> tags like this:

<EM><STRONG>Satellite Technician</STRONG></EM>

not like this:

<EM><STRONG>Satellite Technician</EM></STRONG>

Although many browsers interpret both sets of code the same way, nesting tags within each other rather than overlapping them makes your code easier to read and interpret.

Quick Check

1. Why should you include the <HTML> tag in your Web document?

2. Describe the syntax for creating a centered heading 1.

3. Describe the syntax for creating a paragraph.

4. If you want to display several paragraphs, why can't you simply type an extra blank line in the HTML file?

5. Describe the syntax for creating an ordered list, an unordered list, and a definition list.

6. Give two ways of italicizing text in your Web document. What are the advantages and disadvantages of each method?

You have finished adding text to Mary's online resume. In Session 1.3, you will add special formatting elements such as lines and graphics.

SESSION

1.3

In this session you will insert three special elements into Mary's online resume: a special character, a line separating Mary's name and address from the rest of her resume, and a photograph of Mary.

Adding Special Characters

Occasionally you will want to include special characters in your Web page that do not appear on your keyboard. For example, a math page might require mathematical symbols such as ß or µ. HTML supports several character symbols that you can insert into your page. Each character symbol is identified by a code number or name. To create a special character, type an ampersand (&) followed either by the code name or the code number. Code numbers must be preceded by a pound symbol (#). Figure 1-30 shows some HTML symbols and the corresponding code numbers or names. A fuller list of special characters is included in Appendix B.

Figure 1-30 ◀
Common
special
characters

Symbol	Code	Description
©	&#169	Copyright symbol
®	&#174	Registered trademark
•	&#183	Middle dot
°	&#186	Masculine ordinal
TM	&#153	Trademark symbol
		Non-breaking space, useful when you want to insert several blank spaces one after another
<	&lt	Less than sign
>	&gt	Greater than sign
&	&amp	Ampersand

As Mary views her resume file, she notices a place where she could use a special symbol. In the address information under her name, she finds that the street address, city, and phone numbers all flow together. She cannot add extra spaces because HTML will ignore the blank spaces and run the text together anyway. She decides instead to insert a bullet (•) between the street address and the city and another bullet between the zip code and the phone number.

To add a character code to the resume file:

1. Make sure the **Resume.htm** file is open in your text editor.

2. Revise the address line at the beginning of the file, inserting the code for a middle dot, &#183, between the street address and the city, and between the zip code and the phone number so that the line reads:

<H5 ALIGN=CENTER>11 Kemper Ave. &#183 Lake View, CO 80517 &#183 (303) 555-1012</H5>

TROUBLE? In your text editor this line probably appears as a single line.

3. Save the changes to your Resume file.

4. Return to your Web browser, and reload the Resume file. Figure 1-31 shows Mary's resume with the bullets separating the address elements.

Figure 1-31 ◀
Special characters as they appear in the browser

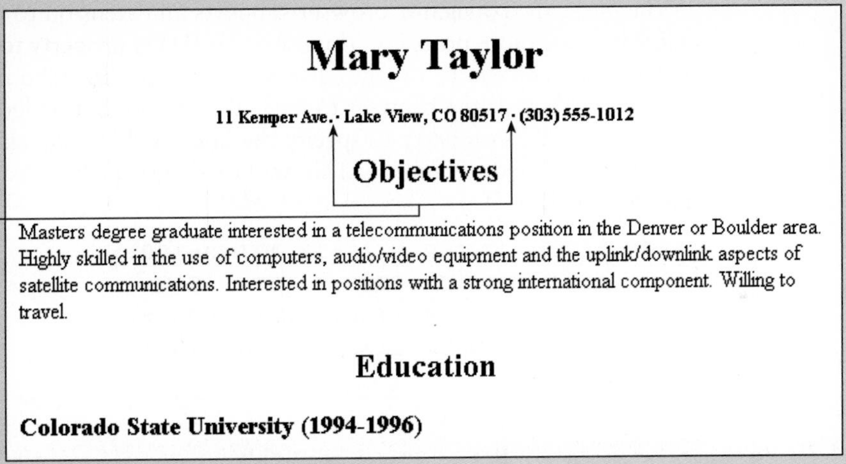

bullets now appear in the address line

Mary Taylor

11 Kemper Ave. · Lake View, CO 80517 · (303) 555-1012

Objectives

Masters degree graduate interested in a telecommunications position in the Denver or Boulder area. Highly skilled in the use of computers, audio/video equipment and the uplink/downlink aspects of satellite communications. Interested in positions with a strong international component. Willing to travel.

Education

Colorado State University (1994-1996)

Inserting Horizontal Lines

The horizontal line after Mary's name and address lends shape to the appearance of her paper resume. She'd like you to duplicate that in the online version. You use the <HR> tag to create a horizontal line, where HR stands for horizontal rule. The <HR> tag is one-sided. When a text-based browser encounters the <HR> tag, it inserts a line by repeating an underline symbol across the width of the page.

To add a horizontal line to the Resume file:

1. Return to your text editor, and reopen the **Resume.htm** file if necessary.

2. At the end of Mary's address line, press **Enter** to insert a new blank line.

3. In the new line, type **<HR>**.

4. Save the changes to your Resume file.

5. Return to your Web browser, and reload the Resume file. The Resume file with the new horizontal line appears in Figure 1-32.

Figure 1-32
Horizontal line
as it appears
in the browser

horizontal line ⟶

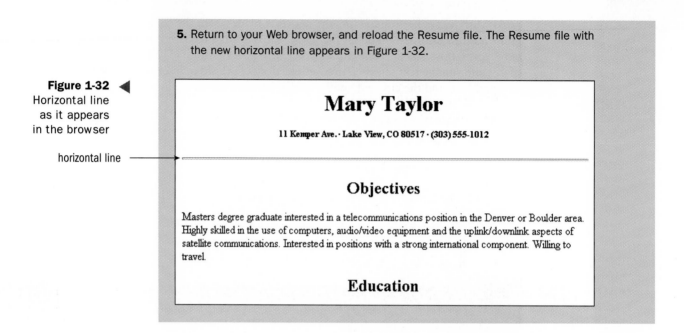

The Netscape Navigator browser supports an extension to the <HR> tag that lets you define line size more precisely. You use the WIDTH property to tell the browser what percentage of the width of the display area the line should occupy. For example, WIDTH=50% tells the browser to place the line so that its length covers half the screen. You use the SIZE property to specify the line's width in pixels. A **pixel**, short for picture element, is ½" wide. Figure 1-33 shows how Netscape Navigator interprets the following lines of HTML code:

```
<HR ALIGN=CENTER SIZE=12 WIDTH=100%>
<HR ALIGN=CENTER SIZE=6 WIDTH=50%>
<HR ALIGN=CENTER SIZE=3 WIDTH=25%>
<HR ALIGN=CENTER SIZE=1 WIDTH=10%>
```

Figure 1-33
Experimenting
with different
line styles

SIZE=12
WIDTH=100%

SIZE=6
WIDTH=50%

SIZE=3
WIDTH=25%

SIZE=1
WIDTH=10%

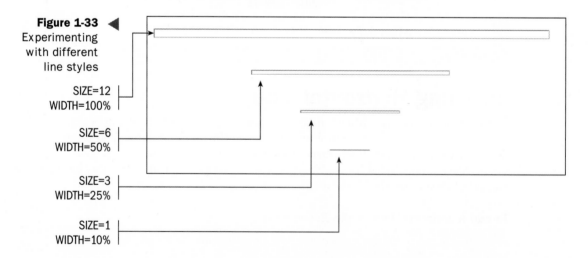

Other extensions allow you to use a graphic image for the line. As always, you should remember that using extensions might produce wildly different results on browsers that do not support the extension.

Inserting a Graphic

One feature of Web pages that has made the World Wide Web so popular is the ease of displaying a graphic image. The Web supports two methods for displaying a graphic: as an inline image and as an external image.

An **inline image** appears directly on the Web page and is loaded when the page is loaded. The Web only supports two graphic types for inline images: GIF (Graphics Interchange Format) and JPEG (Joint Photographic Experts Group). Of these, the GIF file format is the more common on the Web and not all browsers support JPEG files. Before you display a graphic image, your best bet is to convert it to a GIF file format. For example, if you create a graphic in an application like the Windows 95 Paint accessory, which supports only BMP files, you need to locate a graphics converter to convert your BMP file to a GIF file.

An **external image** is not displayed with the Web page. Instead the browser must have a **file viewer**, an application that the browser loads automatically whenever it encounters the image file and displays the image. You can find file viewers at several Internet Web sites. Most browsers make it easy to set up viewers for use with the Web. External images have one disadvantage: you can't actually display them on the Web page. Instead they are represented by an icon that a user clicks to view the image. However, external images are not limited to the GIF or JPEG formats. You can set up virtually any image format as an external image on a Web page, including video clips and sound files.

REFERENCE window	**INSERTING AN INLINE IMAGE**
	■ Open the HTML file with your text editor. ■ Move to the place in the document where you want the inline image to appear. ■ Type <IMG SRC="*filename*"> where *filename* is the name of the graphics file (in GIF or JPEG format).

Mary is more interested in using an inline image than an external image. <IMG> is the tag for an inline image. You can place inline images on a separate line in your document, or you can place the image within a line of text (hence the term "inline"). To access the image file you need to include the filename within the tag. You do this using the SRC property, short for "source." The general syntax for an inline image is:

```
<IMG SRC="filename">
```

If the image file is located in the same directory as the HTML file, you do not need to include any directory information. However, if the image file is located in another directory or on another computer, you need to include the full path with the SRC property. Tutorial 2 discusses directory paths and filenames in more detail. For now, assume that Mary's image file is placed in the same directory as the HTML file. The image file that Mary has created is a photograph of herself in GIF format named Taylor.gif.

You'd like to center the image on the page. You can nest the image tag <IMG SCR="Taylor.gif"> within a paragraph tag and then set the ALIGN property to CENTER in the opening paragraph tag <P ALIGN=CENTER>. Note that the ALIGN property was introduced in HTML 3.2; in browsers that do not support this convention, Mary's image may be left-justified. Verify that the image file is in the same directory as your Resume.htm file, and then add the necessary code to your HTML file.

To add Mary's photo to the online resume:

1. Look in the Tutorial.01 folder on your Student Disk, and verify that both the **Resume.htm** file and **Taylor.gif** file are there.

2. Return to your text editor with the **Resume.htm** file open.

3. At the end of the line with the <HR> tag that you just entered, press **Enter** to create a new line.

4. Type **<P ALIGN=CENTER><IMG SRC="Taylor.gif"></P>** then save the changes to the Resume file.

5. Print a copy of your completed Resume.htm file, and then close your text editor unless you are continuing to the Tutorial Assignments.

6. Return to your Web browser, and reload the Resume file. Mary's online resume now includes an inline image. See Figure 1-34.

Figure 1-34 ◄
The final version of Mary's resume page

inline graphic appears directly on the Web page →

Mary Taylor

11 Kemper Ave.· Lake View, CO 80517 · (303) 555-1012

Objectives

Masters degree graduate interested in a telecommunications position in the Denver or Boulder area. Highly skilled in the use of computers, audio/video equipment and the uplink/downlink aspects of satellite communications. Interested in positions with a strong international component. Willing to travel.

Education

Colorado State University (1994-1996)

- Graduated May, 1996. M.A. International Telecommunications
- Grade Point Average: 3.5 overall, 3.9 in major
- Dean's List: September 1994-May 1996
- Member, Phi Alpha Omega Honor Society

Saint Philip University (1991-1994)

- Graduated May, 1994. B.A. International Studies
- Grade Point Average: 4.0 overall, 4.0 in major
- Dean's List: September 1991-May 1994
- President, Honor Key Society

Employment

Satellite Technician (Front Range Media Inc. 1993-1994): Monitored satellite uplink/downlink procedures to assure quality video transmissions. Aided technicians with transmission problems. Assisted in the assembly and maintenance of uplink facility.

Technical Assistant (Mountain View Bank 1992-1993): Managed data processing system. Handled user requests and discussed programming options. Managed delivery service.

Salesperson (Computer Visions 1991): Sales and customer support in computers and electronics. Managed commercial accounts in Mountain View and Crabtree locations.

7. Use your browser to print a copy of Mary's online resume. In Netscape Navigator, use the Print command on the File menu.

Compare the printout of the code, shown on the following page, to the online resume on your browser. When you finish, you can exit your browser unless you're continuing to the Tutorial Assignments.

```
<HTML>
<HEAD>
<TITLE>The Resume of Mary Taylor</TITLE>
</HEAD>

<BODY>
<H1 ALIGN=CENTER>Mary Taylor</H1>
<H5 ALIGN=CENTER>11 Kemper Ave. &#183 Lake View, CO 80517
   &#183 (303) 555-1012</H5>
<HR>
<P ALIGN=CENTER><IMG SRC="Taylor.gif"></P>
<H2 ALIGN=CENTER>Objectives</H2>
Masters degree graduate interested in a telecommunications
   position in the Denver or Boulder area. Highly skilled in
   the use of computers, audio/video equipment and the
   uplink/downlink aspects of satellite communications.
   Interested in positions with a strong international
   component. Willing to travel.
<H2 ALIGN=CENTER>Education</H2>
<H3>Colorado State University (1994-1996)</H3>
<UL>
<LI>Graduated May, 1996. M.A. International
   Telecommunications
<LI>Grade Point Average: 3.5 overall, 3.9 in major
<LI>Dean's List: September 1994-May 1996
<LI>Member, Phi Alpha Omega Honor Society
</UL>
<H3>Saint Philip University (1991-1994)</H3>
<UL>
<LI>Graduated May, 1994. B.A. International Studies
<LI>Grade Point Average: 4.0 overall, 4.0 in major
<LI>Dean's List: September 1991-May 1994
<LI>President, Honor Key Society
</UL>
<H2 ALIGN=CENTER>Employment</H2>
<P><EM><STRONG>Satellite Technician</STRONG></EM>
   (Front Range Media Inc. 1993-1994): Monitored satellite
   uplink/downlink procedures to assure quality video
   transmissions. Aided technicians with transmission
   problems. Assisted in the assembly and maintenance of
   uplink facility.</P>

<P><EM><STRONG>Technical Assistant</STRONG></EM> (Mountain
   View Bank 1992-1993): Managed data processing system.
   Handled user requests and discussed programming options.
   Managed delivery service. </P>
<P><EM><STRONG>Salesperson</STRONG></EM> (Computer Visions
   1991): Sales and customer support in computers and
   electronics. Managed commercial accounts in Mountain
   View and Crabtree locations.</P>
</BODY>

</HTML>
```

You show the completed online resume file to Mary; she thinks it looks great. You tell her that the next step is adding hypertext links to other material about herself for interested employers. You take a break while she heads to her desk to start thinking about what material she'd like to add. You'll learn about hypertext links in Tutorial 2.

Quick Check

[1] How would you insert a copyright symbol, ©, into your Web page?

[2] What is the syntax for inserting a horizontal line into a page?

[3] Using the Netscape Navigator extension, what is the syntax for creating a horizontal line that is 70% of the display width of the screen and 4 pixels high?

[4] What is an inline image?

[5] What is an external image?

[6] What is the syntax for inserting a left-aligned graphic named "mouse.jpg" into a Web document as an inline image?

[7] What graphic file formats can you use with inline images?

Tutorial Assignments

After thinking some more about her online resume, Mary Taylor decides that she wants you to add a few more items. In the Education section, she wants you to add that she won the Enos Mill Scholarship contest as a senior at St. Philip University. She also wants to add that she worked as a climbing guide for The Colorado Experience touring company from 1989 to 1991. She would like to add her e-mail address, mtaylor@tt.gr.csu.edu, in italics at the bottom of the page. You tell her that adding a horizonal line to separate it from the rest of the resume might look nice. She agrees, so you get to work.

1. Open the Resume.htm file located in the Tutorial.01 folder on your Student Disk. This is the file you created over the course of this tutorial.

2. Save the file on your Student Disk with a new name: Resume2.htm.

3. After the HTML line reading "President, Honor Key Society," enter a new line, "Winner of the Enos Mills Scholarship."
Use the <LI> tag to format this line as an addition to the existing list.

4. Move to the Employment section of the Resume2 file.

5. After the paragraph describing Mary's experience as a salesperson, insert the text, "Guide (The Colorado Experience 1989-1991): Climbing guide for private groups and schools."

   Make sure you mark the text with the correct code for a two-sided paragraph tag.

6. Using the <EM> and <STRONG> tags, bracket the word "Guide" in the line you just entered to make it both bold and italic.

7. After the paragraph on Mary's climbing guide experience, insert a horizontal line using the <HR> tag.

8. After the horizontal line, insert a new line with her e-mail address.

 9. Use the <CITE> tag to format her e-mail address as a citation:

   `<CITE>mtaylor@tt.gr.csu.edu</CITE>`

10. Save the changes to your Resume2.htm file and print it.

11. View the file with your Web browser.

12. Print a copy of the page as viewed by your browser.

13. Hand in both printouts to your instructor.

Case Problems

1. Creating a Web Page at the University Music Department You are an assistant to a professor in the Music Department who is trying to create Web pages for topics in classical music. He wants to create a page showing the different sections of the fourth movement of Beethoven's Ninth symphony. The page should appear as shown in Figure 1-35.

Figure 1-35 ◀

Beethoven's Ninth Symphony

The Fourth Movement

Sonata-Concerto Form

1. Open Ritornello
2. Exposition
    1. Horror/Recitative
    2. Joy Theme
    3. Turkish Music
3. Development
4. Recapitulation
    1. Joy Theme
    2. Awe Theme
5. Codas Nos. 1 2 3

The page needs three headings and a list of the fourth movement's different sections. Several of the sections also have sublists. For example, the Recapitulation section contains both the Joy and Awe themes. You can create lists of this type with HTML by inserting one list tag within another. The HTML code for this is simply:

```
<OL>
<LI>Recapitulation
    <OL>
    <LI>Joy Theme
    <LI>Awe Theme
    </OL>
</OL>
```

1. Open a text editor on your computer.

2. Enter the <HTML>, <HEAD>, and <BODY> tags to identify different sections of the page.

3. Within the HEAD section, insert a <TITLE> tag with the text: "Beethoven's Ninth Symphony, 4th Movement."

4. Within the BODY section, create an H1 heading with the text "Beethoven's Ninth Symphony," center the heading on the page with the ALIGN property.

5. Below the H1 heading, create an H2 heading with the text "The Fourth Movement," and then center the heading on the page.

6. Below the H2 heading, create an H3 heading with the text "Sonata-Concerto Form," but this time do not center the heading.

7. Create an ordered list using the <OL> tag with the list items "Open Ritornello," "Exposition," "Development," "Recapitulation," and "Codas Nos. 1 2 3."

 8. Within the Exposition list, create an ordered list with the items "Horror/Recitative," "Joy Theme," and "Turkish Music."

 9. Within the Recapitulation list, create an ordered list with the items "Joy Theme" and "Awe Theme."

10. Save the code in a file named Ludwig.htm in the Cases folder of the Tutorial.01 folder on your Student Disk, print it, then close your text editor.

11. View the file with your Web browser, print it, then close your browser.

12. Hand in the printouts to your instructor.

2. Sports Page Info, Inc. You work for a sports information company, Sports Page Info, Inc., that publishes sports information on the Internet. You have been asked to create a Web page that describes the final standings for the NFL season. The standings follow.

Team	Wins	Losses	%
Packers	11	5	0.6875
Lions	10	6	0.6250
Bears	9	7	0.5625
Vikings	8	8	0.5000
Buccaneers	7	9	0.4375

Unfortunately if you type the text "as is" into your HTML file, browsers remove all blank spaces when displaying the document. You can overcome the inability of HTML to display extra blank spaces or extra blank lines by using the <PRE> tag, where PRE stands for preformatted. Browsers format text entered with <PRE> tags exactly as it appears within the HTML file, including extra spaces and blank lines. The <PRE> tag's limitation is that it forces all text to display in a monospace font like Courier. Still, the <PRE> tag is often used as a quick way to present table text.

1. Open a text editor on your computer.

2. Enter the <HTML>, <HEAD>, and <BODY> tags to identify different sections of the page.

3. Within the HEAD section, insert a <TITLE> tag with the text "NFL Info Page."

4. Within the BODY section, create an H1 heading with the text "Central Division Final Standings" and center the heading on the page with the ALIGN property.

5. Below the H1 heading, enter a new line and type <PRE> to turn on the pre-formatted feature, then press the Enter key.

6. Enter the NFL statistics. Press the Spacebar as necessary to align the columns properly. Don't use the Tab key because browers interpret tabs differently. Press the Enter key after the last line of the table.

7. Type </PRE> to turn off the preformatted feature.

8. Save the code in a file named NFL.htm in the Cases folder of the Tutorial.01 folder on your Student Disk, then print your file and close your text editor.

9. Using your Web browser, view the NFL.htm file.

10. View the file with your Web browser, print it, then close your browser.

11. Hand in the printouts to your instructor.

3. Chester the Jester A friend of yours who performs as a clown named "Chester the Jester" wants to advertise his services on the World Wide Web. He wants his Web page to be bright and colorful. One way of doing this is to create a colorful background for the page. You create a background using a graphic image. Such backgrounds are called **tile-image backgrounds** because the graphic image is repeated over and over again like tiles until it covers the entire page. Not all browsers support tile-image backgrounds. This feature is part of HTML 3.0 and above and is included in extensions for some browsers like Netscape Navigator and Internet Explorer. To create a tile-image background, you must have a graphic image in either GIF or JPEG file format. You insert the file in the background by adding the background property to the <BODY> tag with the syntax:

```
<BODY BACKGROUND="Filename.gif">
```

Your friend gives you a GIF file named Diamonds.gif that contains the pattern he uses in his clown costume. He also has a GIF file named Chester.gif that shows him in his clown outfit. You already wrote the text for his Web page, and you need only add links to his graphics files.

1. Open the file Chester.htm from the Cases folder of the Tutorial.01 folder on your Student Disk in your computer's text editor.

2. Modify the <BODY> tag to read:

   `<BODY BACKGROUND="Diamonds.gif">`

3. After the <HR> tag, insert the line:

   `<P ALIGN=CENTER><IMG SRC="Chester.gif"></P>`

4. Save the file as Chester2.htm file in the Cases folder of the Tutorial.01 folder on your Student Disk, then print it and close your text editor. The Diamonds.gif and Chester.gif files should already be in the Cases folder, but make sure of this before proceeding. The HTML file and all graphics to which it refers should be in the same folder.

5. Open the Chester2.htm file with your Web browser to verify that the graphic image file, Diamonds.gif, fills the background of the page and that the photo of Chester the Jester is displayed properly. Compare your image to Figure 1-36.

Figure 1-36 ◄

6. Print the Chester2 page from your browser, and hand them in.

4. Create Your Own Resume After completing Mary Taylor's resume, you are eager to make your own. Using the techniques from this tutorial, design and create a resume for yourself. Make sure to include these features: section headers; bulleted or numbered lists; bold and/or italic fonts; paragraphs; inline graphic images; horizontal lines.

1. Create a file called MyResume.htm in the Cases folder of the Tutorial.01 folder on your Student Disk and enter the appropriate HTML code.

2. Add any other tags you think will improve your document's appearance.

3. You could take a picture of yourself to a local office services business and have them scan it. If you do, ask them to save it as a GIF file. Then place the GIF file in the Cases folder of the Tutorial.01 folder on your Student Disk. Add the appropriate code in your MyResume.htm file. If you don't have your own GIF file, use the file Kirk.gif, located in the Cases folder of the Tutorial.01 folder on your Student Disk.

4. You could use a graphics package that can store images in GIF format to create a background image that you could insert as you did in Case Problem 3. If you do, use light colors so the text you place on top is readable. Add the appropriate code to your MyResume.htm file using the steps in CP 3.

5. Test your code as you develop your resume by viewing MyResume.htm in your browser.

6. When you finish entering the code, save and print the MyResume.htm file.

7. View the final version in your browser, and print the Web page, then close your browser.

Lab Assignment

This Lab Assignment is designed to accompany the interactive Course Lab called The Internet World Wide Web. To start the Internet World Wide Web Course Lab, click the Start button on the Windows 95 taskbar, point to Programs, point to Course Labs, point to New Perspectives Applications, and click The Internet World Wide Web. If you do not see Course Labs on your Programs menu, see you instructor or technical support person.

The Internet World Wide Web Lab Assignment One of the most popular services on the Internet is the World Wide Web. This Lab is a Web simulator that teaches you how to use Web browser software to find information. You can use this Lab whether or not your school provides you with Internet access.

1. Click the Steps button to learn how to use Web browser software. As you proceed through the Steps, answer all of the Quick Check questions that appear. After you complete the Steps, you will see a Quick Check Summary Report. Follow the instructions on the screen to print this report.

2. Click the Explore button on the Welcome screen. Use the Web browser to locate a weather map of the Caribbean Virgin Islands. What is its URL?

3. A scuba diver named Wadson Lachouffe has been searching for the fabled treasure of Greybeard the pirate. A link from the Adventure Travel Web site leads to a Wadson's Web page called "Hidden Treasure." In Explore, locate the Hidden Treasure page and answer the following questions:
   a. What was the name of Greybeard's ship?
   b. What was Greybeard's favorite food?
   c. What does Wadson think happened to Greybeard's ship?

4. In the Steps, you found a graphic of Jupiter from the photo archives of the Jet Propulsion Laboratory. In the Explore section of the Lab, you can also find a graphic of Saturn. Suppose one of your friends wanted a picture of Saturn for an astronomy report. Make a list of the blue, underlined links your friend must click to find the Saturn graphic. Assume that your friend will begin at the Web Trainer home page.

5. Enter the URL *http://www.atour.com* to jump to the Adventure Travel Web site. Write a one-page description of this site. In your paper include a description of the information at the site, the number of pages the site contains, and a diagram of the links it contains.

6. Chris Thomson is a student at UVI and has his own Web pages. In Explore, look at the information Chris has included on his pages. Suppose you could create your own Web page. What would you include? Use word processing software to design your own Web pages. Make sure you indicate the graphics and links you would use.

Adding Hypertext Links to a Web Page

Developing an Online Resume with Hypertext Links

In this tutorial you will:

- Create hypertext links between elements within a document

- Create hypertext links between one document and another

- Review some basic Web page structures

- Create hypertext links to pages on the Internet

- Use and understand the difference between absolute and relative pathnames

- Learn to create hypertext links to various Internet resources, including FTP servers and newsgroups

CASE

Creating an Online Resume, continued

In Tutorial 1 you created the basic structure and content of an online resume for Mary Taylor. Since then Mary has made a few changes to the resume, and she has ideas for more content. The two of you sit down and discuss her plans. Mary notes that although the page contents reflect the paper resume, the online resume has one disadvantage: prospective employers must scroll around the document window to view pertinent facts about Mary. Mary wants to make it as easy to jump from topic to topic in her online resume as it is to scan through topics on a paper resume.

Mary also has a few references and notes of recommendation on file that she wants to make available to interested employers. She didn't include all this information on her paper resume because she wanted to limit that resume to a single page. With an online resume, Mary can still be brief, but at the same time she can make additional material readily available.

In this session you will create anchors on a Web page that let you jump to specific points in the document. After creating those anchors, you will create and then test your first hypertext link to another document.

Creating a Hypertext Document

In Tutorial 1 you learned that a hypertext document contains links that you can select, usually by clicking a mouse, to instantly view another topic or document, often called the **destination** of the link. In addition to making access to other documents easy, hypertext links provide some important organizational benefits. They indicate what points or concepts you think merit special attention or further reading. You can take advantage of these features by adding hypertext links to Mary's online resume.

At the end of Tutorial 1, the resume had three main sections: Objectives, Education, and Employment. You and Mary have made some additions and changes since then, including adding a fourth section, Other Information, that points to additional information about Mary. However, due to the document window's limited size, the opening screen does not show any of the main sections of Mary's resume. The browser in Figure 2-1 shows Mary's name, address, and photograph, but nothing about her education or employment history. Employers have to scroll through the document to find this information.

Figure 2-1 ◀
Opening screen
of Mary's
online resume

You can do little to show more of Mary's resume in the browser except remove the image file or move it to the end of the resume, which Mary doesn't want you to do. However, you could place text for the four headings (Objectives, Education, Employment, and Other Information) at the top of the document and then turn the text into hypertext links. When readers click or highlight one of the headings, they jump to that section of the document. The hypertext links that you create here point to sections within the same document. You do this in three steps:

1. Type the headings into the HTML file.

2. Mark each section in the HTML file using an anchor. (You'll learn what this is shortly.)

3. Link the text you added in Step 1 to the marks you added in Step 2.

You can accomplish the first step using techniques you learned in Tutorial 1. You need to open the Resume.htm text file in your text editor and then enter the text. You want the text to appear on the same line as Mary's photo in the browser, as in Figure 2-2.

Figure 2-2 ◀
Adding text for
links to later
sections in
resume

Objectives · Education ·   · Employment · Other Info

you'll add text here

To achieve this, you place the text within the paragraph tags that already encompass the Taylor.gif graphics file. You could type all the text into the HTML file on the same line, but to keep the HTML file as legible as possible, add the text in two lines instead. This way, when you add more tags to the text later, it will still be easy to interpret. Because you format with markup tags in HTML, putting the text on different lines does not affect its appearance in the browser.

To add text to the document describing the different sections of the resume:

1. Open your text editor.

2. Open the file **ResumeMT.htm** from the Tutorial.02 folder on your Student Disk, then save the file in the same folder as **Resume.htm** so you still have a copy of the original.

   TROUBLE? If you can't locate the ResumeMT.htm file in the Tutorial.02 folder in your text editor's Open dialog box, you might need to set the file type to All Files.

3. Before "<IMG SRC="Taylor.gif">," type **Objectives &#183 Education &#183** then press **Enter** so this new entry is on its own line.

4. Create a new line directly after "<IMG SRC="Taylor.gif">," then type **&#183 Employment &#183 Other Info** so this new entry is on its own line. See Figure 2-3. The new lines include the special character code, &#183, which inserts a bullet into the text to separate section headings.

Figure 2-3 ◀
Text that points
to each of
the section
headings

new lines

```
<BODY>
<H1 ALIGN=CENTER>Mary Taylor</H1>
<H5 ALIGN=CENTER>11 Kemper Ave. &#183 Lake View, CO 80517 &#183 (303) 555-10
<HR>

<P ALIGN=CENTER>
Objectives &#183 Education &#183
<IMG SRC="Taylor.gif">
&#183 Employment &#183 Other Info
</P>

<H2 ALIGN=CENTER>Objectives</H2>
Masters degree graduate interested in a telecommunications position in the D
```

5. Save the changes to the Resume.htm file, but leave the text editor open. You will revise this document throughout this tutorial.

6. Open your Web browser (you do not have to connect to the Internet), and view Resume.htm. See Figure 2-4.

Figure 2-4 ◀
New text with
special
characters

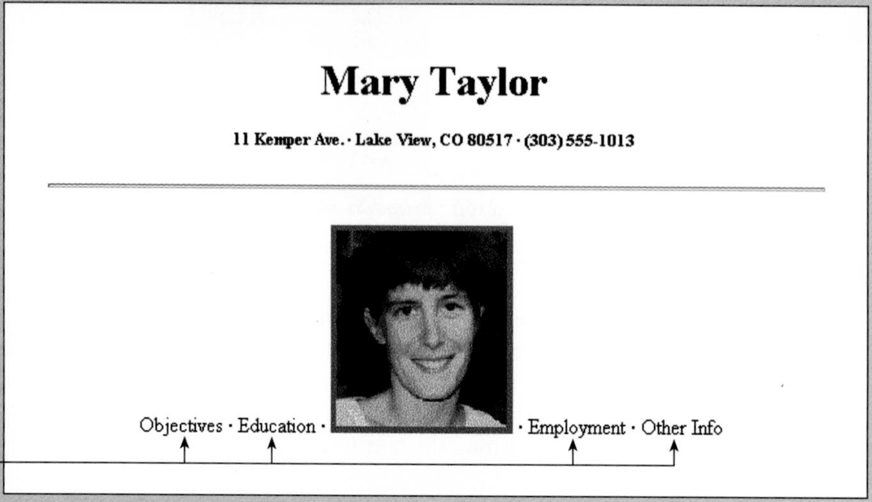

new text ———

Mary Taylor

11 Kemper Ave. · Lake View, CO 80517 · (303) 555-1013

Objectives · Education · · Employment · Other Info

You've inserted the four headings on the same line next to Mary's photo.

Creating Anchors

Now that you've created the text describing the resume's different sections, you need to locate each heading and mark the heading text in the document using the <A> tag. The **<A> tag** creates an **anchor**, text that is specially marked so you can link to it from other points in the document. You assign each anchor its own anchor name using the NAME property. For example, if you want the text "Employment" to be an anchor, you could assign it the anchor name "EMP":

```
<A NAME="EMP">Employment</A>
```

The text "Employment" becomes an anchor named "EMP." Later, when you create a link from the beginning of Mary's resume to this anchor, the link will point to this particular place in the document using the anchor name "EMP." Figure 2-5 illustrates how the anchor you create will work as a reference point to a link.

Figure 2-5 ◀
Anchoring text

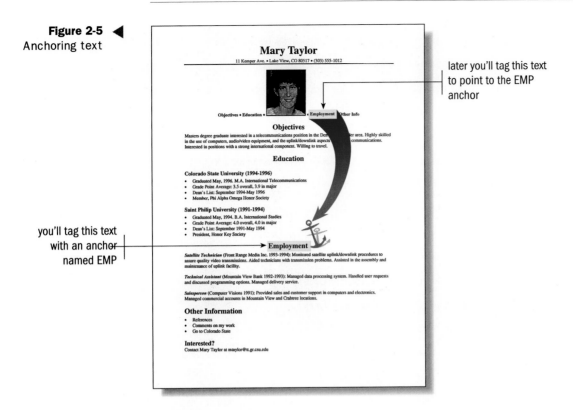

later you'll tag this text
to point to the EMP
anchor

you'll tag this text
with an anchor
named EMP

An anchor doesn't have to be just text. You can also mark an inline image using the same syntax:

```
<A NAME="PHOTO"><IMG SRC="Taylor.gif"></A>
```

In this example, you anchor a photo. You can create a link to this photo from other points in the document by using the anchor name "PHOTO."

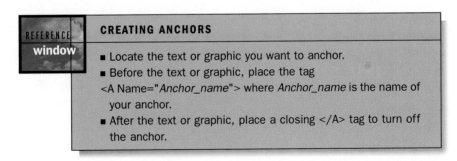

REFERENCE window

CREATING ANCHORS

- Locate the text or graphic you want to anchor.
- Before the text or graphic, place the tag
  <A Name="*Anchor_name*"> where *Anchor_name* is the name of your anchor.
- After the text or graphic, place a closing </A> tag to turn off the anchor.

As you'll see, adding an anchor does not change your document's appearance in any way. For Mary's resume file, you decide to create four anchors named "OBJ," "ED," "EMP," and "OTHER" for the Objectives, Education, Employment, and Other Information sections.

To add anchors to the resume's section headings:

1. Return to your text editor, and open the **Resume.htm file**, if it is not already open.

2. Locate the H2 heading for the Objectives section. This line currently reads:

```
<H2 ALIGN=CENTER>Objectives</H2>
```

3. Add an anchor tag around the Objectives heading so that it reads:

`<H2 ALIGN=CENTER><A NAME="OBJ">Objectives</A></H2>`

4. Locate the H2 heading for the Education section. This line currently reads:

`<H2 ALIGN=CENTER>Education</H2>`

5. Add an anchor tag around the Education heading so that it reads:

`<H2 ALIGN=CENTER><A NAME="ED">Education</A></H2>`

6. Locate the H2 heading for the Employment section, which reads:

`<H2 ALIGN=CENTER>Employment</H2>`

and add an anchor tag so that it reads:

`<H2 ALIGN=CENTER><A NAME="EMP">Employment</A></H2>`

7. Locate the H2 heading for the Other Information section, which reads:

`<H2>Other Information</H2>`

and add an anchor tag so that it reads:

`<H2><A NAME="OTHER"> Other Information</A></H2>`

8. Save the changes you made to the Resume file.

9. Open your Web browser, reload the Resume.htm file, then scroll through Resume.htm to confirm that the Resume file appears unchanged. Remember that the marks you placed in the document are reference points and should not appear in your browser.

TROUBLE? If you see a change in the document, check to make sure that you used the NAME property of the <A> tag.

You created four anchors in the Web page. The next step is to create links to those anchors from the text you added around Mary's picture.

Creating Links

After you anchor the text that will be the destination for your links, you create the links themselves. For Mary's resume, you want to link the text you entered around her photograph to the four sections in her document. Figure 2-6 shows the four links you want to create.

Figure 2-6 ◄
Links you need
to create

links ——————→

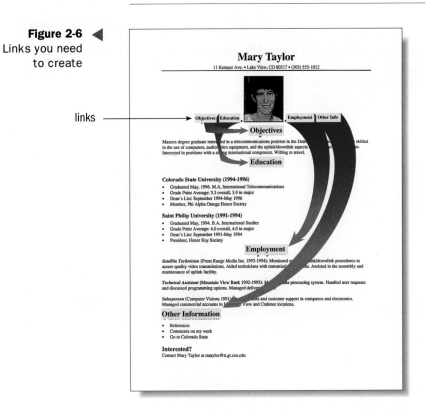

To create a link to an anchor, you use the same tag you used to create the anchor. The difference is that instead of using the NAME property to define the anchor, you use the HREF property, short for Hypertext Reference, to indicate the location to jump to. HREF can refer to an anchor that you place in the document, or, as you'll see later, a different HTML file on the Internet.

If you set up an anchor in the document with the anchor name *anchor_name*, you refer to that anchor with a pound (#) symbol. The entire reference looks like "#*anchor_name*." For example, to create a link to a location in the current document with the anchor name "EMP," you enter this HTML command:

```
<A HREF="#EMP">Employment</A>
```

In this example, the entire text, "Employment," becomes a hypertext link. Selecting any part of that text within your Web browser jumps you to the location of the EMP anchor. The pound symbol has an important role in the hypertext anchor name, as you'll see later in this tutorial. You can also designate an inline image as a hypertext link. To turn an inline image into a hypertext link, place it within link tags, as in:

```
<A HREF="#OTHER"><IMG SRC="Taylor.gif"></A>
```

Tags that create links are called **link tags**.

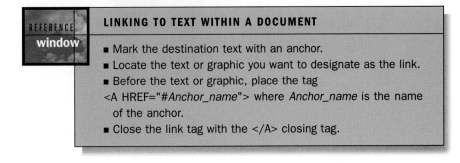

REFERENCE
window

LINKING TO TEXT WITHIN A DOCUMENT

- Mark the destination text with an anchor.
- Locate the text or graphic you want to designate as the link.
- Before the text or graphic, place the tag
  <A HREF="#*Anchor_name*"> where *Anchor_name* is the name
  of the anchor.
- Close the link tag with the </A> closing tag.

In the current HTML document you've created four anchors to which you can link. You're ready to place the link tags around the appropriate text in the HTML file.

To add link tags to the Resume.htm file:

1. Return to your text editor, and make sure the Resume.htm file is open.

2. Locate the paragraph containing the four section titles and Mary's photograph at the top of the page. Within that paragraph you need to bracket each occurrence of a section title within a link tag.

3. Change the line reading "Objectives &#183 Education &#183" to

```
<A HREF="#OBJ">Objectives</A> &#183 <A HREF="#ED">Education</A> &#183
```

4. Change the line reading "&#183 Employment &#183 Other Info" to

```
&#183 <A HREF="#EMP">Employment</A> &#183 <A HREF="#OTHER">Other Info</A>
```

5. Compare your HTML file to Figure 2-7.

Figure 2-7 ◀
Adding link
tags

link tags ⟶

```
<BODY>
<H1 ALIGN=CENTER>Mary Taylor</H1>
<H5 ALIGN=CENTER>11 Kemper Ave. &#183 Lake View, CO 80517 &#183 (303) 555-10
<HR>

<P ALIGN=CENTER>
<A HREF="#OBJ">Objectives</A> &#183 <A HREF="#ED">Education</A> &#183
<IMG SRC="Taylor.gif">
&#183 <A HREF="#EMP">Employment</A> &#183 <A HREF="#OTHER">Other Info</A>
</P>

<H2 ALIGN=CENTER><A NAME="OBJ">Objectives</A></H2>
Masters degree graduate interested in a telecommunications position in the D
```

6. Save the changes you made to Resume.htm.

7. Open your Web browser and reload the Resume.htm file. Text links appear around Mary's photo. See Figure 2-8.

TROUBLE? If text links do not appear, check your code and make sure that you are using the <A> tag around the text and the HREF property within the tag.

Figure 2-8 ◀
Text links as
they appear in
the browser

Mary Taylor

11 Kemper Ave. · Lake View, CO 80517 · (303) 555-1013

link tags usually
appear as underlined
text in a different
color ⟶ Objectives · Education   · Employment · Other Info

Before continuing, you should verify that the links work properly. To test a link, you click it.

To test your links:

1. Click each link. You should jump to the section of the document indicated by the link. If not, check your code for errors by comparing it to Figure 2-7.

2. If you are continuing to Session 2.2, you can leave your browser and text editor open. Otherwise, close them.

Sometimes a link does not work as you expect. One common source of trouble is the case of the anchor. The HREF property is case-sensitive. An anchor name "EMP" is not evaluated the same as "emp." You should also remember to make each anchor name unique within a document. If you use the same anchor name for different text, your links won't go where you expect.

If you still have problems, make sure you coded the anchor and link tags correctly. When you add an anchor to a large section of text like a section heading, make sure to place the anchor within the heading tags. For example, you should write your tag as:

```
<H2><A NAME="EMP">Employment</A></H2>
```

not as:

```
<A NAME="EMP"><H2>Employment</H2></A>
```

The latter could confuse some browsers. The general rule is to always place anchors within other tag elements. Do not insert any tag elements within an anchor, except for tags that create document objects such as inline graphics.

You show the new links to Mary. She is excited to see how they work. She thinks they will quickly inform interested employers about her resume's contents, and help them quickly find the information they want.

Quick Check

1. What is the HTML code for marking the text "Colorado State University" with the anchor name "CSU"?

2. What is the HTML code for linking the text "Universities" to an anchor with the name "CSU"?

3. What is wrong with this statement?

```
<A NAME="INFO"><H3>For more information</H3></A>
```

4. What is the HTML code for marking an inline image, Photo.jpg, with the anchor name "PHOTO"?

5. What is the HTML code for linking the inline image, Button.jpg, to an anchor with the name "LINKS"?

6. True or false: Anchor names are case-insensitive.

In the next session, you'll add links to other HTML documents.

SESSION

2.2

In Session 2.1 you created hypertext links to other points within the same document. In this session you create links to other HTML documents.

Mary wants to add two more pages to her online resume: a page of references and a page of comments about her work from former employers and teachers. She then wants to add links to her resume that point to both these pages. Figure 2-9 shows what she has in mind.

Figure 2-9 ◄
Mary's three
Web documents

Mary wants you to
create links from her
resume to her
Comments page and
her References page

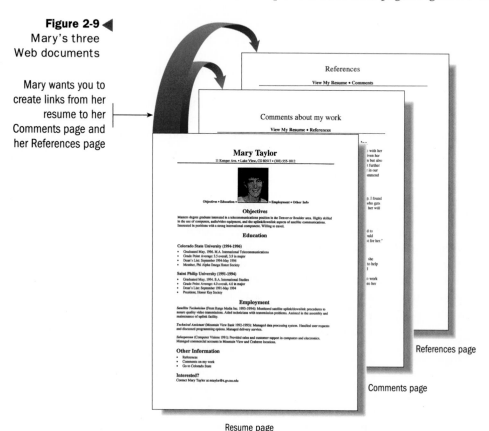

References page

Comments page

Resume page

You tell Mary that her ideas are good, but that before she starts thinking about how the documents will link to each other, she should understand the basics of Web page structures.

Web Page Structures

The three pages that will make up Mary's online resume—Resume, Comments, and References—are part of a system of Web pages. A **system** is a set of pages, usually created by the same person or group, that treat the same topic and that have the same look and feel. Before you set up links in a system of Web pages, it's worthwhile to map out exactly how you want the pages to relate, using a technique known as storyboarding. **Storyboarding** your Web pages before you create links helps you determine which structure works best for the type of information you're presenting. You want to make sure readers can navigate easily from page to page, without getting lost.

Linear Structures

You'll encounter several Web structures as you navigate the Web. Examining these structures can help you decide how to design your own system of Web pages. Figure 2-10 shows one common structure, the **linear structure**, in which each page is linked to the next and previous pages in an ordered chain of pages.

Figure 2-10 ◀
Linear
structure

in this structure you
can jump only from
one page to the next
or previous page

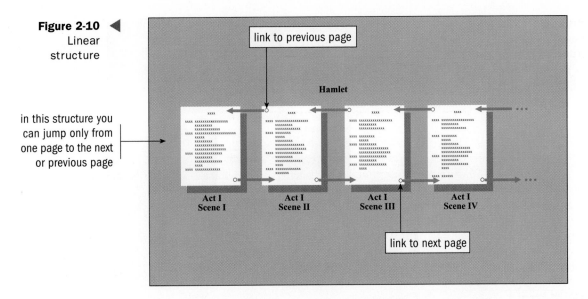

You might use this type of structure in Web pages that have a defined order. For example, you might work for a troupe that wants a single Web page for each scene from Shakespeare's *Hamlet*. If you use a linear structure for these pages, you assume that users want to progress through the scenes in order. You might, however, want to make it easier for users to return immediately to the opening scene rather than backtrack through several scenes. Figure 2-11 shows how you could include a link in each page that jumps directly back to the first page. This kind of storyboarding can reveal defects of the original structure that might otherwise be hidden.

Figure 2-11 ◀
Augmented
linear
structure

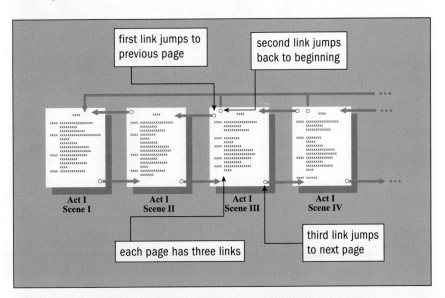

Hierarchical Structures

Another popular structure is the hierarchical structure of Web pages shown in Figure 2-12. A **hierarchical structure** starts with a general topic that includes links to more specific topics. Each specific topic includes links to yet more specialized topics, and so on. In a hierarchical structure, users can move easily from the general to the specific and back.

Figure 2-12 ◀
Hierarchical
structure

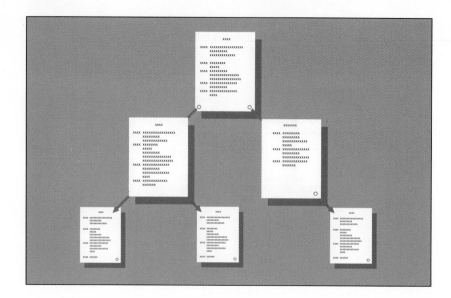

As with the linear structure, including a link to the top of the structure on each page gives users an easy path back to the beginning. Subject catalogs such as the Yahoo directory of Web pages often use this structure. Figure 2-13 shows this site, located at http://www.yahoo.com.

Figure 2-13 ◀
Hierarchical
structure on
Yahoo Web
page

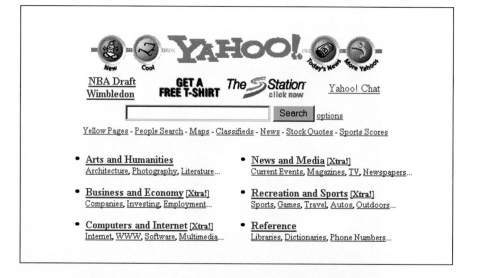

Mixed Structures

You can also combine structures. Figure 2-14 shows a hierarchical structure in which each level of pages is related in a linear structure. You might use this system for the Hamlet Web site to let the user move from scene to scene linearly, or from a specific scene to the general act to the overall play.

Figure 2-14 ◀
Combination of
linear and
hierarchical
structures

overall structure
is hierarchical

the scenes

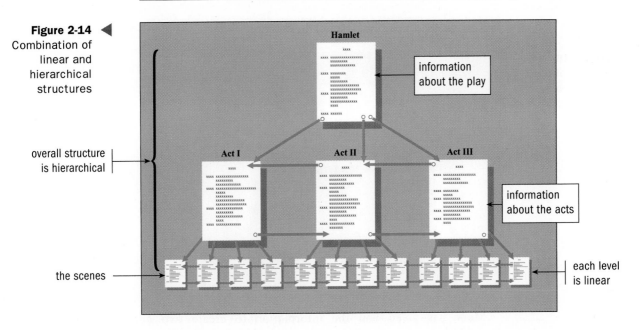

As these examples show, a little foresight can go a long way toward making your Web pages easier to use. The best time to organize a structure is when you first start creating multiple pages and those pages are small and easy to manage. If you're not careful, your structure might look like Figure 2-15.

Figure 2-15 ◀
Multi-page
document
with no
coherent
structure

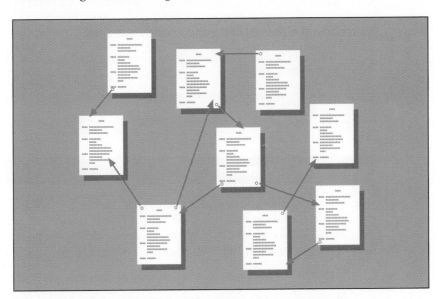

This structure is confusing because it gives users no idea of what content to expect when jumping from one link to another. Nor are users ever sure if they have viewed all possible pages.

Creating Links Between Documents

Mary and you discuss the type of structure that will work best for her online resume. She wants employers to move effortlessly between the three documents. Because there are only three pages, all focused on the same topic, you decide to include links within each document to the other two. If Mary later adds other pages to her resume, she will need to create a more formal structure involving some principles discussed in the previous sections.

For her simple three-page system, the structure shown in Figure 2-16 works just fine.

Figure 2-16 ◄
Structure of
Mary's Web
pages

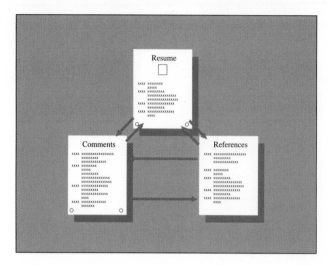

Mary has given you the information to create two additional HTML files: ReferMT.htm, a page with the names and addresses of previous employers or professors; and ComMT.htm, a page with comments from previous employers and teachers. You suggest that Mary include a graphic—a checkmark—on the Comments page. You have just the file for her, Check.gif. These three files are in the Tutorial.02 folder on your Student Disk. Save these files with new names: Refer.htm and Comments.htm.

To rename the ReferMT.htm and ComMT.htm files:

1. Using your text editor, open ReferMT.htm from the Tutorial.02 folder on your Student Disk and save it as **Refer.htm.**

2. With your text editor, open the file ComMt.htm in the Tutorial.02 folder and save it as **Comments.htm**.

Linking to a Document

You begin by linking Mary's Resume page to the References and Comments pages. You use the same <A> tag that you used earlier. For example, let's say you wanted a user to be able to click the phrase "Comments on my work" to jump back to the Comments.htm file. You could enter this HTML command in your current document:

```
<A HREF="Comments.htm">Comments on my work</A>
```

In this example, the entire text, "Comments on my work," is linked to the HTML file, Comments.htm. The only requirement is that Comments.htm must be in the same folder as the document containing the links.

REFERENCE window	**LINKING TO A DOCUMENT ON YOUR COMPUTER**
	■ Locate the link text or graphic (that is, the text or image you want to click to jump to the destination of the link).
	■ Before the text or graphic, place the tag <A HREF="*filename*"> where *filename* is the name of the document.
	■ After the text or graphic, place the tag </A>.

Unlike creating hypertext links between elements on the same page, you do not need to set an anchor in a file to link to it.

To add links in the Resume page to the References and Comments pages:

1. If you closed your text editor, reopen it and retrieve the Resume.htm file that you worked on in Session 2.1 of this tutorial.

2. Scroll down to the Other Information section of the file near the bottom of the page. Three items are listed; you want the first, References, to link to the References page, and the second, Comments on my work, to link to the Comments page.

3. Change the line reading "<LI>References" to:

`<LI><A HREF="Refer.htm">References</A>`

4. Change the line reading "<LI> Comments on my work" to read:

`<LI><A HREF="Comments.htm">Comments on my work</A>`

See Figure 2-17.

Figure 2-17 ◀
Text you want designated as links to other files

these two lines will link to other pages

```
<H2><A NAME="OTHER">Other Information</A></H2>
<UL>
<LI><A HREF="Refer.htm">References</A>
<LI><A HREF="Comments.htm">Comments on my work</A>
<LI>Go to Colorado State
</UL>

<H3> Interested? </H3>
Contact Mary Taylor at mtaylor@tt.gr.csu.edu

</BODY>
```

5. Save the changes to the Resume file.

6. Open your Web browser, if it is not open already, and view Resume.htm. The items in the Other Information section now appear as the text links shown in Figure 2-18.

Figure 2-18 ◀
New links

Technical Assistant (Mountain View Bank 1991-1993): Managed data processing system. Trained users on data entry and report generation. Managed delivery service.

Salesperson (Computer Visions 1990): Sales and customer support in computers and electronics. Managed commercial accounts in Lake View and Crabtree locations.

Other Information

links you just created

- References
- Comments on my work
- Go to Colorado State

Interested?

Contact Mary Taylor at mtaylor@tt.gr.csu.edu

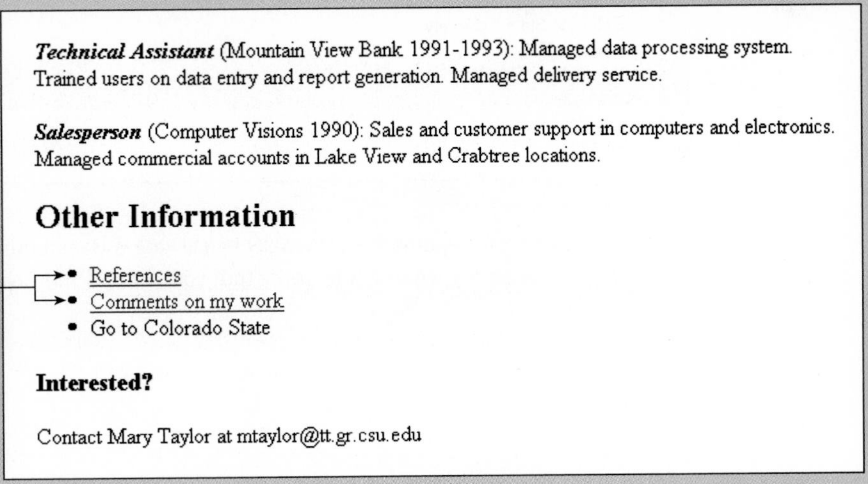

7. Click the **References** link to verify that you jump to the References page shown in Figure 2-19.

TROUBLE? If the link doesn't work, check to see that Resume.htm and Refer.htm are in the same folder.

Figure 2-19 ◀
References
page

References

View My Resume · Comments

Lawrence Gale, Telecommunications Manager

Front Range Media Inc.
1000 Black Canyon Drive
Fort Tompkins, CO 80517
(303) 555-0103

Karen Carlson, Manager

Mountain View Bank
2 North Maple St.
Lake View, CO 80517
(303) 555-8792

Trent Wu, Sales Manager

Computer Visions
24 Mall Road
Lake View, CO 80517
(303) 555-1313

Robert Ramirez, Prof. Electrical Engineering

Colorado State University
Kleindist Hall
Fort Collins, CO 80517

8. Go back to the Resume page (usually by clicking a Back button), then click the **Comments on my work** link to verify that you jump to the Comments page shown in Figure 2-20.

Figure 2-20 ◀
Comments
page

notice inline
image, Check.gif

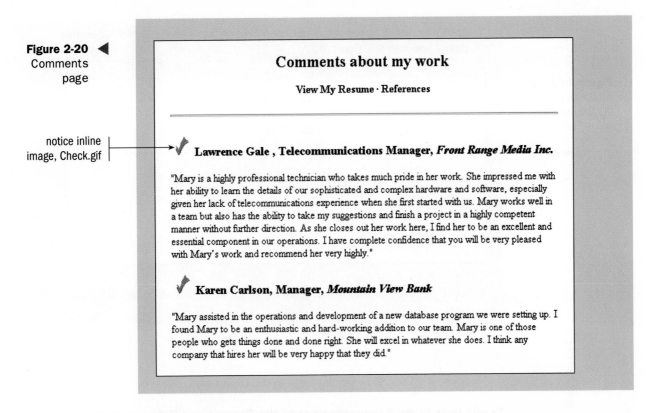

Next you want to add similar links to the Refer.htm and Comments.htm files. Each page should contain links that point to the other two pages.

To add links in the References page to the Resume and Comments pages:

1. Return to your text editor, and open the file **Refer.htm** from the Tutorial.02 folder on your Student Disk.

2. Locate the H4 heading at the top of the page.

3. Change the text "View my resume" to read:

   `<A HREF="Resume.htm">View my resume</A>`

4. Locate the text "Comments" on the same line. Change "Comments" to read:

   `<A HREF="Comments.htm">Comments</A>`

5. Compare your code to Figure 2-21.

Figure 2-21 ◀
Adding links to
the References
page

new links

```
<BODY>
<H2 ALIGN=CENTER> References</H2>

<H4 ALIGN=CENTER> <A HREF="Resume.htm">View My Resume</A> &#183
<A HREF="Comments.htm">Comments</A> </H4>
<HR>

<H4>Lawrence Gale, Telecommunications Manager</H4>
Front Range Media Inc.<BR>
1000 Black Canyon Drive<BR>
Fort Tompkins, CO 80517<BR>
(303) 555-0103
```

6. Save the changes to Refer.htm.

7. Open your Web browser, if it is not open already, and view Refer.htm. Your links should now look like Figure 2-22.

Figure 2-22 ◀
Links on
References
page

new links

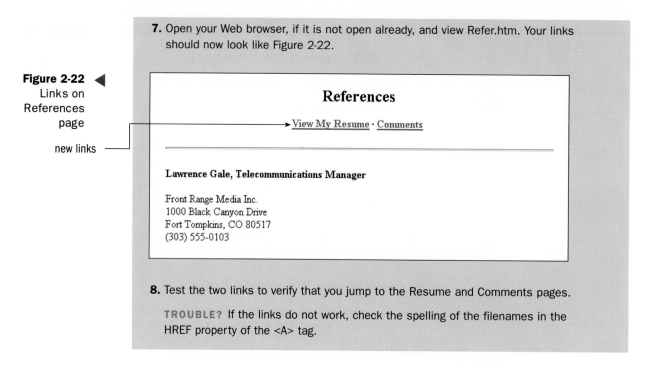

8. Test the two links to verify that you jump to the Resume and Comments pages.

TROUBLE? If the links do not work, check the spelling of the filenames in the HREF property of the <A> tag.

Now you need to follow similar steps so the Comments page links to the two other pages.

To add links in the Comments page to the Resume and References pages:

1. Return to your text editor, then open the file **Comments.htm** from the Tutorial.02 folder on your Student Disk.

2. Locate the H4 heading at the top of the page.

3. Change the text "View my resume" to read:

```
<A HREF="Resume.htm">View my resume</A>
```

4. Locate the text "References" on the same line. Change "References" to read:

```
<A HREF="Refer.htm">References</A>
```

5. Save the changes to Comments.htm.

6. Open your Web browser, if it is not open already, and view Comments.htm. You should see the links shown in Figure 2-23.

Figure 2-23 ◀
Links on the
Comments
page

new links

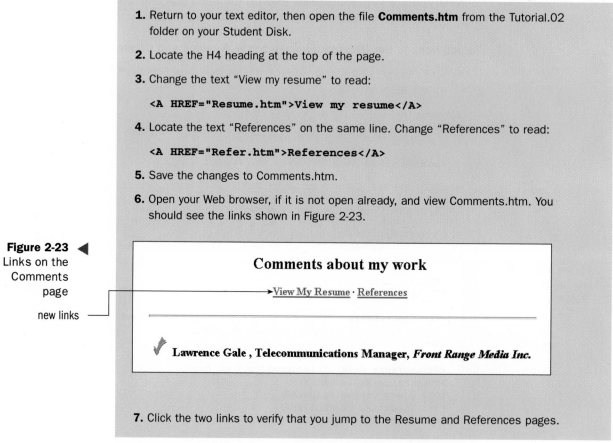

7. Click the two links to verify that you jump to the Resume and References pages.

Now that all the links between the three pages are set up, you can easily move between the three documents.

Linking to a Section of a Document

You might have noticed in testing your links that you always jump to the top of the destination page. What if you'd like to jump to a specific location later in a document, rather than the beginning? To do this, you can set anchors as you did in Session 2.1 and link to the anchor within the document. For example, to create a link to a section in the file Home.htm marked with an anchor name of "Interests," you could enter this HTML code in your current document:

```
<A HREF="Home.htm#interests">View my interests</A>
```

In this example, the entire text, "View my interests," is linked to the Interests section in the Home.htm file. Note that the pound (#) symbol in this tag distinguishes the filename from the anchor name.

Mary wants to link the positions listed in the Employment section of her resume to specific comments from employers on the Comments page. The Comments.htm file already has these anchors in place:

- "GALE" for comments made by Lawrence Gale, Mary's telecommunications manager

- "CARLSON" for comments made by Karen Carlson, manager of Mountain View Bank

- "WU" for comments made by Trent Wu of Computer Visions

Now you need to link the positions listed in the Resume file to these three anchors.

To add links to the Resume page that jump to anchors on the Comments page:

1. With your text editor, reopen the **Resume.htm** file.

2. Locate the Employment section in the middle of the Resume file. You need to bracket each job title within link tags with the reference pointing to the appropriate comment in the Comments page. Leave in place any tags that format the text such as the <P>, <EM>, and <STRONG> tags.

3. Move to the first job description, and replace the title "Satellite Technician" with:

```
<A HREF="Comments.htm#GALE">Satellite Technician</A>
```

4. Move to the next job description, and replace the title "Technical Assistant" with:

```
<A HREF="Comments.htm#CARLSON">Technical Assistant </A>
```

5. Move to the final job description, and replace the title "Salesperson" with:

```
<A HREF="Comments.htm#WU">Salesperson</A>
```

6. Save the changes to the Resume file.

7. Open your Web browser and load **Resume.htm**. The job titles in the Employment section should appear with text links as shown in Figure 2-24.

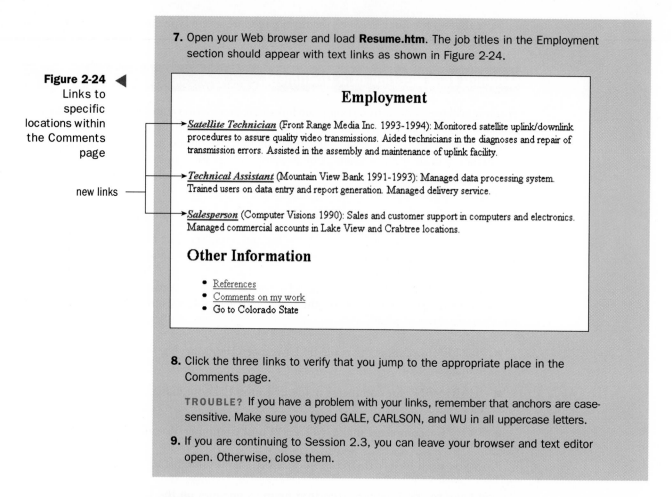

Employment

Satellite Technician (Front Range Media Inc. 1993-1994): Monitored satellite uplink/downlink procedures to assure quality video transmissions. Aided technicians in the diagnoses and repair of transmission errors. Assisted in the assembly and maintenance of uplink facility.

Technical Assistant (Mountain View Bank 1991-1993): Managed data processing system. Trained users on data entry and report generation. Managed delivery service.

Salesperson (Computer Visions 1990): Sales and customer support in computers and electronics. Managed commercial accounts in Lake View and Crabtree locations.

Other Information

- References
- Comments on my work
- Go to Colorado State

8. Click the three links to verify that you jump to the appropriate place in the Comments page.

> **TROUBLE?** If you have a problem with your links, remember that anchors are case-sensitive. Make sure you typed GALE, CARLSON, and WU in all uppercase letters.

9. If you are continuing to Session 2.3, you can leave your browser and text editor open. Otherwise, close them.

With these last hypertext links in place, you have given readers of Mary's online resume access to additional information.

Quick Check

[1] What is storyboarding? Why is it important in creating a Web page system?

[2] What is a linear structure? Draw a picture of a linear structure, and give an example how to use it.

[3] What is a hierarchical structure? Draw a picture of a hierarchical structure, and give an example how to use it.

[4] You are trying to create a system of Web pages for the play *Hamlet* in which each scene has a Web page. On each page you want to include links to the previous and next scenes of the play, as well as to the first scene of the play and the first scene of the current act. Draw a diagram of this multi-page document. (Just draw enough acts and scenes to make the structure clear.)

[5] What HTML code would you enter to link the text "Sports info" to the HTML file Sports.htm?

[6] What HTML code would you enter to link the text "Basketball news" to the HTML file Sports.htm at a place in the file with the anchor name "BBALL"?

In the next session, you learn how to point your hypertext links to documents and resources on the Internet.

In Session 2.2 you created links to other documents within the same folder as the Resume.htm file. In this session you learn to create hypertext links to documents located in other folders and in other computers on the Internet.

Mary wants to add a link to her Resume page that points to the Colorado State University home page. The link gives potential employers an opportunity to learn more about the school and the courses it offers. Before creating this link for Mary, you need to review how HTML references files in different folders and computers.

Linking to Documents in Other Folders

Until now you've worked with documents that were all in the same folder. When you created links to other files in that folder, you specified the filename in the link tag but not its location. Browsers assume that if no folder information is given, the file is in the same folder as the current document. In some situations you might want to place different files in different folders, particularly when working with large multi-document systems that span several topics, each topic with its own folder.

When referencing files in different folders in the link tag, you must include each file's location, called its **path**. HTML supports two kinds of paths: absolute paths and relative paths.

Absolute Pathnames

The **absolute path** shows exactly where the file is on the computer. In HTML you start every absolute pathname with a slash (/). Then you type the folders' names on the computer, starting with the topmost folder in the folder hierarchy and progressing through the different levels of subfolders. You separate each folder name from the next with a slash. The pathname, from left to right, leads down through the folder hierarchy to the folder that contains the file. After you type the name of the folder that contains the file, you type a final slash and then the filename.

For example, consider the folder structure shown in Figure 2-25.

Figure 2-25 ◀
Folder tree

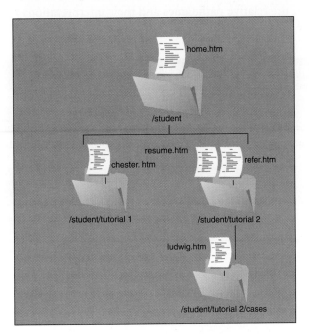

home.htm

/student

resume.htm

chester. htm

refer.htm

/student/tutorial 1

/student/tutorial 2

ludwig.htm

/student/tutorial 2/cases

Figure 2-25 shows five HTML files scattered among four folders. The topmost folder is the student folder. Beneath the student folder are the tutorial1 and tutorial2 folders, and beneath the tutorial2 folder is the cases folder. Figure 2-26 shows absolute pathnames for the five files.

Figure 2-26 ◀
Absolute path
names

Absolute pathname	Interpretation
/student/home.htm	The home.htm file in the student folder
/student/tutorial1/chester.htm	The chester.htm file in the tutorial folder, a subfolder of the student folder
/student/tutorial2/resume.htm	The resume.htm file in the tutorial2 folder, another subfolder of the student folder
/student/tutorial2/refer.htm	The refer.htm file in the same folder as the resume.htm file
/student/tutorial2/cases/ludwig.htm	The ludwig.htm file in the cases folder, a subfolder of the /student/tutorial2 folder

Even the absolute pathnames of files located on different hard disks begin with a slash. To differentiate these files, HTML requires you to include the drive letter followed by a vertical bar (|). For example, a file named "resume.htm" in the student folder on drive A of your computer has the absolute pathname "/A|/student/resume.htm."

Relative Pathnames

If a computer has many folders and subfolders, absolute pathnames can be long, cumbersome, and confusing. For that reason, most Web authors use relative pathnames in their hypertext links. A **relative path** gives a file's location in relation to the current Web document. As with absolute pathnames, folder names are separated by slashes. Unlike absolute pathnames, a relative pathname does not begin with a slash. To reference a file in a folder above the current folder in the folder hierarchy, relative pathnames use two periods(..).

For example, if the current file is resume.htm from the /student/tutorial2 folder shown in Figure 2-25, the relative pathnames and their interpretations for the other four files in the folder tree appear as in Figure 2-27.

Figure 2-27 ◀
Relative path
names

Relative pathname	Interpretation
../home.htm	The home.htm file in the folder one level up in the folder tree from the current file
../tutorial1/chester.htm	The chester.htm file in the tutorial1 subfolder of the folder one level up from the current file
refer.htm	The refer.htm file in the same folder as the current file
cases/ludwig.htm	The ludwig.htm file in the cases subfolder, one level down from the current folder

A second reason to use relative pathnames is that they make your hypertext links portable. If you have to move your files to a different computer or server, you can move the entire folder structure and still use the relative pathnames in the hypertext links. If you use absolute pathnames, you need to painstakingly revise each and every link.

Linking to Documents on the Internet

Now you can turn your attention to creating the link on Mary's resume to Colorado State University. To create a hypertext link to a document on the Internet, you need to know its URL. A **URL**, or Uniform Resource Locator, gives a file's location on the Web. The URL for Colorado State University, for example, is http://www.colostate.edu/index.html. You can find the URL of a web page in the Location box of your browser's document window. You'll learn about the parts of a URL in the next section.

After you know a document's URL, you are ready to add the code that creates the link, again the <A> code with the HREF property that creates links to documents on your computer. For example, to create a link to a document on the Internet with the URL http://www.mwu.edu/course/info.html, you use this HTML code:

```
<A HREF="http://www.mwu.edu/course/info.html">Course Information</A>
```

This example links the text "Course Information" to the Internet document located at http://www.mwu.edu/course/info.html. As long as your computer is connected to the Internet, clicking the text within the tag should make your browser jump to that document.

REFERENCE window

LINKING TO A DOCUMENT ON THE INTERNET

- Locate the text or graphic you want to designate as the link.
- Before the text or graphic, place the tag <A HREF="*URL*"> where *URL* is the URL of the Web page you want to link to.
- Close the link tag with the </A> closing tag.

In the Other Information section of Mary's resume, she wants to link the text "Colorado State University" to the CSU home page. You're ready to add that link.

To add a link to the Colorado State University page from Mary's Resume page:

1. If necessary, open your text editor, then open the **Resume.htm** file that you worked on in Session 2.2 of this tutorial.

2. Locate the **Other Information** section of the file near the bottom of the page.

3. Change the line <LI>Go to Colorado State to read:

   ```
   <LI><A HREF="http://www.colostate.edu/index.html"> Go to
      Colorado State</A>
   ```

4. Save the changes to the Resume file.

5. If necessary, open the Web browser and connect to the Internet.

6. Open the file **Resume.htm**. The Go to Colorado State entry should look like the text link shown in Figure 2-28.

Figure 2-28 ◀
Link to
another page
on the Web

link to another
Web site

Other Information

- References
- Comments on my work
- Go to Colorado State

Interested?

Contact Mary Taylor at mtaylor@tt.gr.csu.edu

7. Click the **Go to Colorado State** link. The Colorado State University home page shown in Figure 2-29 appears.

TROUBLE? If the CSU home page doesn't appear right away, it might just be loading slowly on your system because it contains a large graphic. If the CSU home page still doesn't appear, verify that your computer is connected to the Internet.

Figure 2-29 ◀
Colorado State
University
home page

8. Click the **Back** button in your browser to return to Mary's resume.

Linking to Other Internet Objects

Occasionally you see a URL for an Internet object other than a Web page. Recall that part of the World Wide Web's success is that it lets users access several types of Internet resources using the same application. The method you used to create a link to the Colorado State University home page is the same method you use to set up links to other Internet resources, ranging from FTP servers to Usenet newsgroups. Only the proper URL for each object is required.

Each URL follows the same basic format. The first part identifies the **communication protocol**, the set of rules governing how information is exchanged. Web pages use the communication protocol **HTTP**, short for Hypertext Transfer Protocol. All Web page URLs begin with the letters "http." Other Internet resources use different communication protocols. After the communication protocol there is usually a separator, like a colon followed by a slash or two (://). The exact separator depends on the Internet resource. The rest of the URL identifies the location of the document or resource on the Internet. Figure 2-30 interprets a Web page with the URL:

`http://www.mwu.edu/course/info.html#majors`

Figure 2-30 ◀
Interpreting
parts of a URL

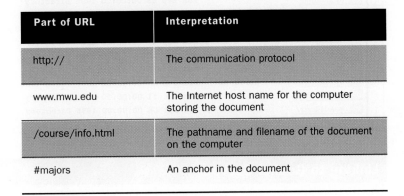

Part of URL	Interpretation
http://	The communication protocol
www.mwu.edu	The Internet host name for the computer storing the document
/course/info.html	The pathname and filename of the document on the computer
#majors	An anchor in the document

Before you walk Mary through the task of creating her final link, you take a quick detour to show her how to create links to other Internet resources if needed. You might not be familiar with all the Internet resources discussed in these next sections. This tutorial doesn't try to teach you about these resources; it just shows you how to reference them in your HTML file. Many books offer detailed information on these resources, among them CT's *The Internet Illustrated*.

Linking to FTP Servers

FTP servers store files that Internet users can download, or transfer, to their computers. **FTP,** short for File Transfer Protocol, is the communications protocol these file servers use to transfer information. URLs for FTP servers follow the same format as for Web pages, except they use the FTP protocol rather than the HTTP protocol: ftp://*FTP_Hostname*. For example, to create a link to the FTP server located at ftp.microsoft.com, you could use this HTML code:

`<A HREF="ftp://ftp.microsoft.com">Microsoft FTP server</A>`

In this example, clicking the text "Microsoft FTP server" jumps the user to the Microsoft FTP server page shown in Figure 2-31.

Figure 2-31 ◄
FTP server at
ftp.microsoft
.com

files and folders on
the FTP server

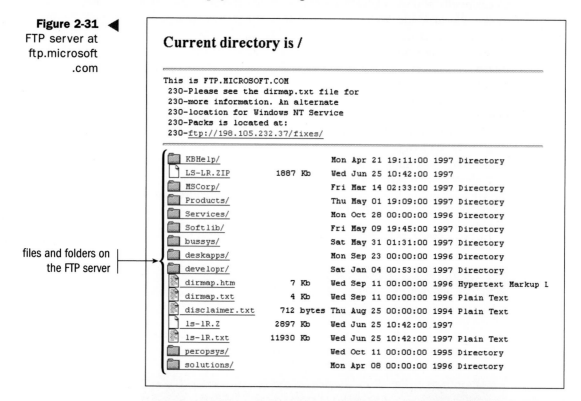

Linking to Gopher Servers

Before use of the World Wide Web became widespread, **Gopher servers** were popular tools that organized the Internet's resources. Gopher does this using hierarchical menus, from which you select the Internet resource that you want to access. The URL for a Gopher server is gopher://*Host_name*. To set up a hypertext link to the Gopher server at gopher.wisc.edu, you enter this code on your Web page:

`<A HREF="gopher://gopher.wisc.edu">Go to the Wisconsin Gopher</A>`

When a user clicks Go to the Wisconsin Gopher, the browser loads the page shown in Figure 2-32.

Figure 2-32 ◀
Gopher server
at gopher.wisc
.edu

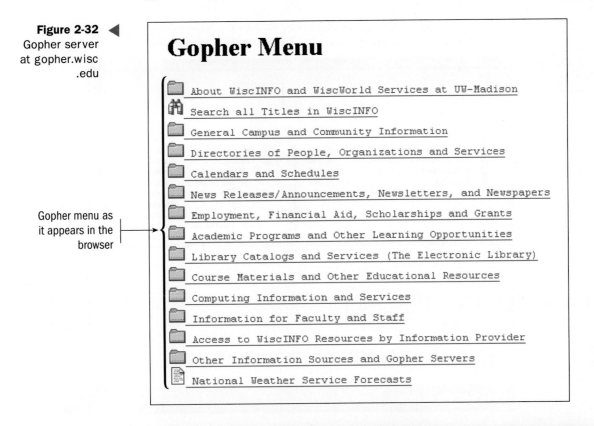

Gopher menu as
it appears in the
browser

Linking to Usenet News

Usenet is a collection of discussion forums, called **newsgroups**, that lets users send and retrieve messages on a wide variety of topics. The URL for a newsgroup is news:*newsgroup*. To access the surfing newsgroup, alt.surfing, you place this line in your HTML file:

```
<A HREF="news:alt.surfing">Go to the surfing newsgroup</A>
```

Not all browsers support the newsgroup URL. Even if your browser does, you still might need to configure your browser to access a news server that supports the newsgroup. If a user clicks the Go to the surfing newsgroup link in the Netscape Navigator browser, for example, Netscape Navigator loads its newsreader, shown in Figure 2-33. The user then works with the Netscape Navigator newsreader, not the browser, to view the latest messages from alt.surfing.

Netscape Navigator displays a newsreader when
it tries to access a newsgroup URL

Figure 2-33 ◀
Accessing
alt.surfing
newsgroup

newsgroups →

alt.surfing newsgroup →

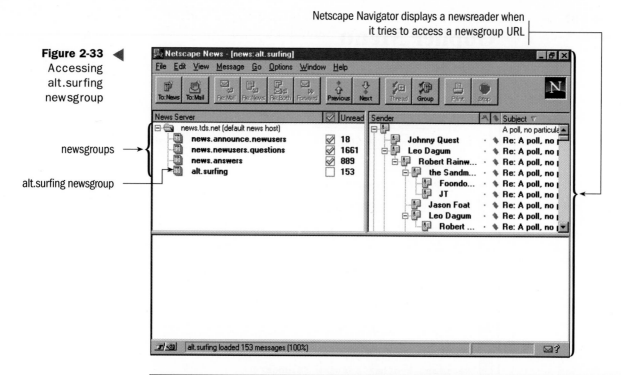

Linking to E-mail

Many Web authors include their e-mail addresses on their Web pages so users who access these pages can send feedback. Some browsers let these e-mail addresses act as hypertext links. When a user clicks the e-mail address, the browser runs a mail program and automatically inserts the author's e-mail address into the outgoing message. The user then edits the body of the message and, with a single mouse click, mails it. The URL for an e-mail address is mailto:*e-mail_address*. To create a link to the e-mail address davis@mwu.edu, for example, you enter the following into your Web document:

```
<A HREF="mailto:davis@mwu.edu">davis@mwu.edu</A>
```

If you click this link with the Netscape Navigator browser, for example, Netscape Navigator loads the Netscape mail program shown in Figure 2-34.

Netscape Navigator displays a mail program
when it tries to open a mailto URL

Figure 2-34 ◀
Sending mail to
davis@mwu
.edu

e-mail address →

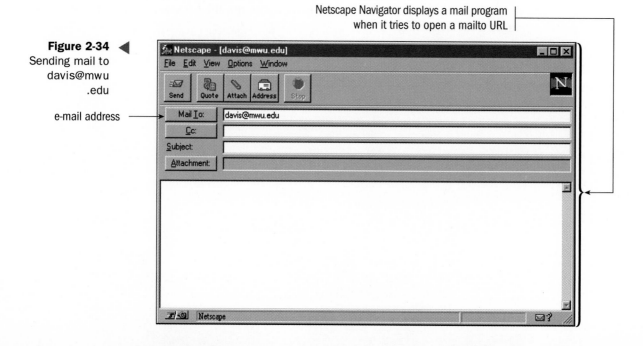

As with newsgroups, not all browsers support the e-mail hypertext link, although most popular ones like Netscape Navigator and Internet Explorer do.

Adding an E-mail Link to Mary's Resume

Mary wants a final addition to her resume: a link to her e-mail address. With this link, an interested employer can quickly send Mary a message through the Internet. Mary placed her e-mail address at the bottom of the Resume page. Now you need to designate that text as a link.

To add an e-mail link to Mary's resume:

1. Return to the **Resume.htm** file in your text editor.

2. Go to the bottom of the page.

3. Change the text "mtaylor@tt.gr.csu.edu" to

```
<A HREF="mailto:mtaylor@tt.gr.csu.edu">mtaylor@tt.gr.csu.edu</A>
```

4. Save the changes to the Resume file.

5. Return to your Web browser.

6. Reload **Resume.htm**.

7. Move to the bottom of the page. Mary's e-mail address should look like the hypertext link shown in Figure 2-35.

   TROUBLE? Some browsers do not support the mailto URL. If you use a browser other than Netscape Navigator or Internet Explorer, check to see if it supports this feature.

Figure 2-35 ◀
Mary Taylor's
e-mail address
as a text link

Mary's e-mail address ───

Interested?

Contact Mary Taylor at mtaylor@tt.gr.csu.edu

8. Click the hypertext link to Mary's e-mail address. If you are using the Netscape Navigator browser, you should see the Netscape Mail program with Mary's e-mail address inserted in the Mail To box. See Figure 2-36.

Figure 2-36 ◀
Netscape Mail
program with
Mary Taylor's
e-mail address
automatically
inserted

Mary's e-mail address ───

9. Cancel the mail message. Mary's e-mail address is fictional, so you can't send her mail anyway.

10. Close your Web browser and text editor.

You show Mary the final form of her online resume. She's really thrilled with the result. You tell her the next thing she needs to do is contact an Internet Service Provider and transfer the files to an account on their machine. When that's done, Mary's resume becomes available online to countless employers across the Internet.

Quick Check

1. What's the difference between an absolute path and a relative path?

2. Refer to the diagram in Figure 2-25: If the current file is ludwig.htm in the /student/tutorial2/cases folder, what are the relative pathnames for the four other files?

3. What HTML tag would you enter to link the text "Washington" to the FTP server at ftp.uwash.edu?

4. What HTML tag would you enter to link the text "Minnesota" to the Gopher server at gopher.umn.minn.edu?

5. What HTML tag would you enter to link the text "Boxing" to the newsgroup, rec.sports.boxing.pro?

6. What HTML tag would you enter to link the text "President" to the e-mail address president@whitehouse.com?

Tutorial Assignments

Mary Taylor decides that she wants you to add a few more items to her resume. She wants to add a link at the bottom of her resume page that returns readers to the top. In the Employment section, she wants to add that she worked as a tutor for Professor Ramirez at Colorado State University and link that to comments Professor Ramirez made about her in the Comments page. Finally she wants to add a link to the Colorado State University Gopher server.

1. Open the Resume.htm file located in the Tutorial.02 folder on your Student Disk. You worked with this file over the course of this tutorial.

2. Save the file on your Student Disk in the TAssign folder with the same name, Resume.htm.

3. Add an anchor tag around the page heading. Change the line

   ```
   <H1 ALIGN=CENTER>Mary Taylor</H1>
   ```

   to read:

   ```
   <H1 ALIGN=CENTER><A NAME="TOP">Mary Taylor</A> </H1>
   ```

4. After the HTML line at the bottom of the page containing Mary's e-mail address and before the </BODY> tag, enter a new line:

   ```
   <P><A HREF="#TOP">Go to the top of the page</A></P>
   ```

5. Move to the Employment section.

6. After the paragraph describing Mary's experience as a salesperson, insert this line: Tutor (Colorado State): "Tutored students in electrical engineering and mathematics."

7. Mark the text you entered in Step 6 with the correct code for a two-sided paragraph tag. Add the <EM> and <STRONG> tags used in other job descriptions.

8. Make "Tutor" a hypertext link to the RAMIREZ anchor in the Comments page using the tag:

   ```
   <A HREF="comments.htm#RAMIREZ">Tutor</A>
   ```

9. Move to the Other Information section.

10. Add a new list item to the unsorted list: "Go to Colorado State Gopher."

HTML

11. Make the list item you entered in Step 10 a hypertext link by adding the tag:

    ```
    <A HREF="gopher://gopher.colostate.edu/">Go to Colorado State
       Gopher</A>
    ```

12. Save the changes to your Resume.htm file, then print this file and close your text editor.

13. View the file with your Web browser. Make sure you open Resume.htm in the TAssign folder of the Tutorial.02 folder.

14. Print a copy of the page as viewed by your browser, then close your browser.

15. Give both printouts to your instructor.

Case Problems

1. Creating Links to Federal Departments As a librarian at the city library, you are creating a Web page to help people access the home pages for several federal government departments. Figure 2-37 lists each department's URL.

Figure 2-37

Department	URL
Department of Agriculture	http://www.usda.gov/
Department of Commerce	http://www.doc.gov/
Department of Defense	http://www.defenselink.mil/
Department of Education	http://www.ed.gov/
Department of Energy	http://www.doe.gov/
Department of Health and Human Services	http://www.dhhs.gov/
Department of Housing and Urban Development	http://www.hud.gov/
Department of Interior	http://www.doi.gov/
Department of Justice	http://www.usdoj.gov/
Department of Labor	http://www.dol.gov/
Department of State	http://www.state.gov/
Department of Transportation	http://www.dot.gov/
Department of Treasury	http://www.ustreas.gov/
Department of Veteran Affairs	http://www.va.gov/

Create an unsorted list containing department names. Make each name a text link to the department's home page.

1. Open the text editor on your computer and open a new document.

2. Enter the <HTML>, <HEAD>, and <BODY> tags to identify different sections of the page.

3. Within the HEAD section, insert a <TITLE> tag with the text, "Federal Government Departments."

4. Within the BODY section, create an H1 heading with the text, "A list of federal departments," and then center the heading on the page with the ALIGN property.

5. Create an unordered list using the <LI> tag for each department name in Figure 2-37. You can save yourself a lot of typing by using the Copy and Paste commands in your text editor.

6. Surround each department name in the list with a hypertext tag. For example, for the Department of Agriculture, enter the line:

```
<LI><A HREF="http://www.fie.com/www/agri.htm"> Department
  of Agriculture</A>
```

7. Save the code in a file named Depart.htm in the Cases folder of the Tutorial.02 folder on your Student Disk, then print the file and close your text editor.

8. View the file with your Web browser, and create a printout, then close your browser.

9. Give the printouts to your instructor.

2. Using Graphics as Hypertext Links You are an assistant to a professor in the Music Department who is trying to create Web pages for topics in classical music. Previously you created a Web page for her showing the different sections of the fourth movement of Beethoven's Ninth symphony. Now that you've learned to link multiple HTML files together, you have created pages for all four movements.

The four pages are in the Cases folder of the Tutorial.02 folder on your Student Disk. Their names are: Move1A.htm, Move2A.htm, Move3A.htm and Move4A.htm. You'll rename them Move1.htm, Move2.htm, Move3.htm, and Move4.htm, so you have the originals if you want to work on them later. Figure 2-38 shows the page for the third movement.

Figure 2-38 ◀
Web page for
third movement
of Beethoven's
Ninth
Symphony

> # Beethoven's Ninth Symphony
>
> ### 🖐 The Third Movement ☞
>
> ---
>
> **Sectional Form**
>
> 1. A-Section
> 2. B-Section
> 3. A-Section varied
> 4. B-Section
> 5. Interlude
> 6. A-Section varied
> 7. Coda

You now need to link the pages. You've already placed graphic elements—the hands pointing to the previous or next movement of the symphony—in each file. You decide to mark each graphic image as a hypertext link that jumps the user to the previous or next movement.

1. Open the text editor on your computer.

2. Open the Move1A.htm file in the Cases folder of the Tutorial.02 folder on your Student Disk, and save it as Move1.htm in the same folder.

3. Change the image tag <IMG SRC="LEFT.GIF"> to read:

```
<A HREF="move2.htm"><IMG SRC="LEFT.GIF"></A>
```

4. Save the Move1.htm file.

5. Open the Move2A.htm file in the Cases folder of the Tutorial.02 folder on your Student Disk, and save it as Move2.htm in the same folder. Add hypertext links to the graphics as you did in Step 3 (this time to Move1 and Move3 using the Left and Right graphics), then save the Move2.htm file.

6. Open the Move3A.htm file in the Cases folder of the Tutorial.02 folder on your Student Disk, and save it as Move3.htm in the same folder. Add hypertext links to the graphics as you did in Step 3 (this time to Move2 and Move4 using the Left and Right graphics), then save the Move3.htm file.

7. Open the Move4A.htm file in the Cases folder of the Tutorial.02 folder on your Student Disk, and save it as Move4A.htm in the same folder. Add hypertext links to the graphics as you did in Step 3 (this time to Move3), then save the Move4A.htm file.

8. Print all four HTML files, then close your text editor.

9. Open the file Move1.htm in your Web browser.

10. Verify that you can move forward and backward through the four movements of the Ninth Symphony using the graphic images on the page.

11. Print each page in the Web browser, then close your browser.

12. Give the printouts to your instructor.

3. Creating a List of FTP Servers You maintain a Web site for a small college. One of your jobs is to create a list of FTP servers for students who want to download Internet files. Figure 2-39 lists the "popular" FTP sites you've identified.

Figure 2-39 ◀

Location	Description
archive.umich.edu	Software archives for UNIX, PC, and Macintosh computers
ftp.cica.indiana.edu	Software archives for UNIX machines and PCs
ftp.cwru.edu	Full text of U.S. Supreme Court decisions
ftp.microsoft.com	Device drivers and technical support for Microsoft products
ftp.sura.net	Software archives specializing in Internet tools
nic.funet.fi	Archive of electronic documents and works of literature
rtfm.mit.edu	Internet document archives—includes tutorials about using the Internet
wuarchive.wustl.edu	Software archives for UNIX, PC, and Macintosh computers.

To make the information in Figure 2-39 more accessible to students, you decide to place it on a Web page, making each FTP server's location a hypertext link that calls the server when clicked. To make the page more readable, format it using the definition list tag discussed in Tutorial 1.

1. Open the text editor on your computer to a new document.

2. Enter the <HTML>, <HEAD>, and <BODY> tags to identify different sections of the page.

3. Within the HEAD section, insert a <TITLE> tag with the text: "Popular FTP Servers."

4. Within the BODY section, create an H1 heading with the text, "A list of popular FTP servers," and then center the heading on the page with the ALIGN property.

5. Create a definition list using the <DT> tag for each FTP servers location and the <DD> tag for each servers description.

6. For each FTP server address listed, insert a hypertext tag. For example, for the server at ftp.microsoft.com, enter the line:

```
<DT><A HREF="ftp://ftp.microsoft.com">ftp://ftp.microsoft.com</A>
```

7. Save the code in a file named FTP.htm in the Cases folder of the Tutorial.02 folder on your Student Disk, then print the file and close your text editor.

8. View the file with your Web browser, and create a printout, then close your browser.

9. Give the printouts to your instructor.

4. Create Your Own Home Page Now that you've completed this tutorial, you are ready to create your own home page. The page should include information about you and your interests. If you like, you can create a page devoted entirely to one of your favorite hobbies. Include the following elements:

- section headers

- bold and/or italic fonts

- paragraphs

- an ordered, unordered, or definition list

- an inline graphic image

- links to some of your favorite Internet pages

- a hypertext link that moves the user from one object on your page to another

1. Create a file called Myhome.htm in the Cases folder of the Tutorial.02 folder on your Student Disk, and enter the appropriate HTML code.

2. Add any other tags you think will improve your document's appearance.

3. Insert any graphic elements you think will enhance your document.

4. Use your Web browser to explore other Web pages. Record the URLs of pages that you like, and list them in your document.

5. Test your code as you develop your resume by viewing Myhome.htm in your browser.

6. When you finish entering your code, save and print the Myhome.htm file, then close your text editor.

7. View the final version in your browser, and print the Web page, then close your browser.

8. Hand in any printouts to your instructor.

Answers to Quick Check Questions

SESSION 1.1

1 Hypertext refers to text that contains points called links that allow the user to move to other places within the document, or to open other documents, by activating the link.

2 A Web server stores the files used in creating World Wide Web documents. The Web browser retrieves the files from the Web server and displays them. The files stored on the Web server are described in a very general way; it is the Web browser that determines how the files will eventually appear to the user.

3 HTML, which stands for Hypertext Markup Language, is used to create Web documents.

4 HTML documents do not exactly specify the appearance of a document; rather they describe the purpose of different elements in the document and leave it to the Web browser to determine the final appearance. A word processor like Word exactly specifies the appearance of each document element.

5 Documents are transferred more quickly over the Internet and are available to a wider range of machines.

6 Extensions are special formats supported by a particular browser, but not generally accepted by all browsers. The advantage is that people who use that browser have a wider range of document elements to work with. The disadvantage is that the document will not work for users who do not have that particular browser.

7 All you need is a simple text editor.

SESSION 1.2

1 The <HTML> tag identifies the language of the file as HTML to packages that support more than one kind of generalized markup language.

2 `<H1 ALIGN=CENTER> Heading Text </H1>`

3 `<P> Paragraph Text </P>`

4 HTML does not recognize the blank lines as a format element. A Web browser will ignore blank lines and run the paragraphs together on the page.

5 Unordered list:
```
<UL>
    <LI> List item
    <LI> List item
</UL>
```
Ordered list:
```
<OL>
    <LI> List item
    <LI> List item
</OL>
```
Definition list:
```
<DL>
    <DT> List term <DD> Term definition
    <DT> List term <DD> Term definition
</DL>
```

6 `<EM> Italicized text </EM>` and `<I> Italicized text </I>`
The advantage of using the EM tag is that it will be recognized even by browsers that do not support italics (such as a terminal connected to a UNIX machine), and those browsers will still emphasize the text in some way. The I tag, on the other hand, will be ignored by those machines. Using the I tag has the advantage of explicitly describing how you want the text to appear.

SESSION 1.3

1 &#169

2 `<HR>`

3 `<HR WIDTH=70% SIZE=4>`

4 An inline image is a GIF or JPEG file that appears on a Web document. A browser can display it without a file viewer.

5 An external image is a graphic that requires the use of a software program, called a viewer, to be displayed.

6 `<IMG ALIGN=LEFT SRC="mouse.jpg">`

7 GIFs and JPEGs

SESSION 2.1

1 `<A NAME="CSU"> Colorado State University </A>`

2 `<A HREF="#CSU"> Universities </A>`

3 Anchor tags should be placed within style tags such as the H3 heading tag.

4 `<A NAME="PHOTO"> <IMG SRC="Photo.jpg"> </A>`

5 `<A HREF="#LINKS"> <IMG SRC="Button.jpg"> </A>`

6 False. Anchor names are case-sensitive.

SESSION 2.2

1 Storyboarding is diagramming a series of related Web pages, taking care to identify all hypertext links between the various pages. Storyboarding is an important tool in creating Web presentations that are easy to navigate and understand.

2 A linear structure is one in which Web pages are linked from one to another in a direct chain. Users can go to the previous page or next page in the chain, but not to a page in a different section of the chain.

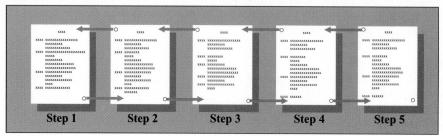

You could use a linear structure in a Web page presentation that included a series of steps that the user must follow, such as in a recipe or instructions to complete a task.

3 A hierarchical structure is one in which Web pages are linked from general to specific topics. Users can move up and down the hierarchy tree.

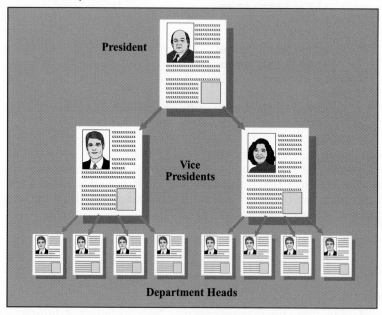

A company might use such a structure to describe the management organization.

4

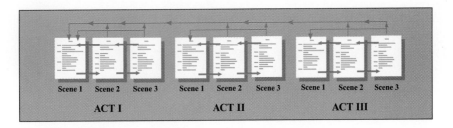

Scene 1 Scene 2 Scene 3   Scene 1 Scene 2 Scene 3   Scene 1 Scene 2 Scene 3

ACT I   **ACT II**   **ACT III**

5 `<A HREF="Sports.htm"> Sports info </A>`

6 `<A HREF="Sports.htm#BBALL"> Basketball news </A>`

SESSION 2.3

1 An absolute path gives the location of a file on the computer's hard disk. A relative path gives the location of a file relative to the active Web page.

2 ../../home.htm
../../tutorial1/chester.htm
../resume.htm
../refer.htm

3 `<A HREF= "ftp://ftp.uwash.edu> Washington </A>`

4 `<A HREF="gopher://gopher.umn.minn.edu> Minnesota </A>`

5 `<A HREF="news:rec.sports.boxing.pro"> Boxing </A>`

6 `<A HREF="mailto:president@whitehouse.com"> President </A>`

NEW
PERSPECTIVES
S E R I E S

Creating Web Pages with **HTML**

LEVEL II

TUTORIALS

Read This **Before You Begin**

STUDENT DISKS

To complete HTML Tutorials 3–5 and end-of-tutorial assignments in this book, you need two Student Disks. Your instructor will either provide you with Student Disks or ask you to make your own.

If you are supposed to make your own Student Disks, you will need two blank, formatted high-density disks. You will need to copy a set of folders from a file server or standalone computer onto your disks. Your instructor will tell you which computer, drive letter, and folders contain the files you need. The following table shows you which folders go on each of your disks, so that you will have enough disk space to complete all the tutorials, Tutorial Assignments, and Case Problems:

Student Disk	Write this on the disk label	Put these folders on the disk
1	Student Disk 1: Tutorials 3 and 4	Tutorial.03 and Tutorial.04
2	Student Disk 2: Tutorial 5	Tutorial.05

When you begin each tutorial, be sure you are using the correct Student Disk. See the inside front or inside back cover of this book for more information on Student Disk files, or ask your instructor or technical support person for assistance.

USING YOUR OWN COMPUTER

If you are going to work through this book using your own computer, you need:

■ **Computer System** A text editor and a Web browser (preferably Netscape Navigator or Internet Explorer, versions 3.0 or above) must be installed on your computer. If you are using a non-standard browser, it must support frames and HTML 3.2 or above.

■ **Student Disks** Ask your instructor or lab manager for details on how to get the Student Disks. You will not be able to complete the tutorials or end-of-tutorial assignments in this book using your own computer until you have the Student Disks. The Student Files may also be obtained electronically over the Internet. See the inside front or inside back cover of this book for more details.

VISIT OUR WORLD WIDE WEB SITE

Additional materials designed especially for you are available on the World Wide Web. Go to **http://www.course.com**. For example, see our Student Online Companion that contains additional coverage of selected topics in the text. These topics are indicated in the text by an online companion icon located in the left margin.

To complete HTML Tutorials 3–5 and end-of-tutorial assignments in this book, your students must use a set of student files on two Student Disks. These files are included in the Instructor's Resource Kit, and they may also be obtained electronically over the Internet. See the inside front or inside back cover of this book for more details. Follow the instructions in the Readme file to copy the files to your server or standalone computer. You can view the Readme file using WordPad.

Once the files are copied, you can make Student Disks for the students yourself, or you can tell students where to find the files so they can make their own Student Disks. Make sure the files get correctly copied onto the Student Disks by following the instructions in the Student Disks section above, which will ensure that students have enough disk space to complete all the tutorials and end-of-tutorial assignments.

COURSE TECHNOLOGY STUDENT FILES

You are granted a license to copy the Student Files to any computer or computer network used by students who have purchased this book.

Designing a Web Page

Working with Color and Graphics

In this tutorial you will:

- Learn how HTML handles color

- Create a color scheme for a Web page

- Insert a background image into a Web page

- Create spot color

- Learn about different image formats

- Learn how to control the placement and appearance of images on a Web page

- Work with client-side image maps

CASE

Announcing the 1999 Space Expo

MidWest University has one of the top departments in the country for the study of astronomy and astrophysics. The university is also home to the Center for Space Science and Engineering, which works with the government and with industry to create products to be used on the Space Shuttle, space probes, and communications and weather satellites. Tom Calloway is the director of public relations for the center.

One of the major events of the year is the Space Expo, held in late April, at which professors and graduate students showcase their research. The purpose of the Expo is to allow representatives from industry, academia, and the government to meet and discuss new ideas and emerging trends. In recent years, the Expo has caught the imagination of the general public, and Tom has made a major effort to schedule events for schools and families to attend. The Expo has become not only an important public relations event, but also an important fund-raiser for the department and the center.

It is early March, less than two months before the Expo, and Tom would like you to create a page advertising the Space Expo on the World Wide Web. The page should provide all the necessary information about Expo events, and it should also catch the eye of the reader through the use of interesting graphics and color.

In this session you will explore how HTML handles and defines color. You'll learn how to add color to a Web page's background and text. You'll also see how to liven up your page with a background image.

Working with Color in HTML

The time of the 1999 Space Expo is drawing close, and Tom has called you to discuss the appearance of the Web page advertising the event. Tom has already written the text of the page, as shown in Figure 3-1.

Figure 3-1 ◄
The 1999
Space Expo
Web page

The 1999 Space Expo

More than 60 exhibits and events await visitors at the 1999 Space Expo,
Looking Towards the Future
Friday-Sunday, April 24-26

The 1999 Space Expo is an annual, student-run event that showcases recent developments in astronomy and space sciences and demonstrates how these developments can be applied to everyday life. The event includes student, government and industrial exhibits, and features presentations from NASA, Ball Aerospace, Rockwell, and IBM.

The 1999 Space Expo will feature activities for the kids, including *Creating a Comet, Building a Model Rocket,* and *The Inter-Galactic Scavenger Hunt.* Friday is Students' Day, with school children in grades K-8 displaying astronomy and space science projects and competing for individual and school achievement awards.

Professor Greg Stewart's famous astronomy show is also coming to the Space Expo. Professor Stewart will show the wonders of the night sky and discuss the nature of quasars, exploding stars, and black holes. Presentations will be at the Brinkman Planetarium at 1 p.m. and 3 p.m., Friday through Sunday.

Please check out these other events:

- Bryd Hall   Rockwell representatives and graduate students will display some of the latest advances in robotics for use in the Space Shuttle missions.
- Mitchell Theatre   Famous astronomer and popular science writer, Kathy White, will present a talk, "Forward to Mars and Beyond," on Saturday at 7 p.m. Tickets for this very special event are $12. Seating is limited.
- Astronomy Classrooms   Graduate students and professors display the results of their research in atmospherics, satellite technology, climatology, and space engineering.

The 1999 Space Expo is located on the engineering and physics campus, north of Granger Stadium, and is open to the public on April 24 (Students' Day) from 10 a.m.-5 p.m., April 25 from 9 a.m.-7 p.m. and April 26 from 11 a.m.-5 p.m. Admission is $4.00 for the general public and $3.00 for senior citizens and students. Children four and under will be admitted free.

Sponsored by the Department of Astronomy and the Center for Space Science and Engineering.

Tom is satisfied with the page's content, but he wants you to work on the design of the page. For example, he'd like you to add a colorful background or background image to the page for visual interest, and modify the appearance of some of the text as well. He also would like you to add some graphics to the document, including the official logo of this year's Expo, as well as photographs of the Space Center. As the public relations director, he wants the Web page to be as visually appealing as possible so that it catches the viewer's eye.

Tom leaves you with a list of files, images, and photos to work with. You'll begin working on a color scheme for the page. But before doing that, you must first learn how to handle color within HTML.

Using Color Names

If you've worked with color in a graphics or desktop publishing program, you've probably selected and identified your color choices without much difficulty, because those packages usually have graphical interfaces. When working with color in HTML files, however, you have to create color schemes using text-based HTML tags. Trying to describe a color in textual terms can be a challenge.

HTML identifies a color in one of two ways: either by the color's name or by a description of the color's appearance. Both methods have their advantages and disadvantages. You'll first learn about color names.

There are 16 color names that are recognized by all versions of HTML. These color names are shown in Figure 3-2.

Figure 3-2 ◀
The 16 basic
color names

Aqua	Gray	Navy	Silver
Black	Green	Olive	Teal
Blue	Lime	Purple	White
Fuchsia	Maroon	Red	Yellow

As you can see, the list of color names is fairly basic: red, blue, green, black, white, and so forth. As long as you keep to simple color combinations, you can rely solely upon these color names to set up color schemes for your Web pages, and those color schemes will be understood by all graphical browsers.

However, a list of 16 color names is limiting, so some browsers (Netscape Navigator and Internet Explorer) now support an extension to this list of color names. Figure 3-3 shows a partial list of these additional color names. The extended color name list allows you to create color schemes with greater color variation. A fuller list is provided in the appendices.

Figure 3-3 ◀
Partial list
of extended
color names

Blueviolet	Gold	Orange	Seagreen
Chocolate	Hotpink	Paleturquoise	Sienna
Darkgoldenrod	Indigo	Peachpuff	Snow
Firebrick	Mintcream	Salmon	Tan

One problem with using a color name list is that, while it's easy to specify a blue background, "blue" might not be specific enough for your purposes. How do you specify a "light blue background with a touch of green"? To do so, you would have to look through a long list of color names before finding that Paleturquoise is close to the color you want. Even so, some users might try to access your page with older browsers that do not support the long list of color names. In that situation you would lose control over your page's appearance, and it might end up being unreadable on those browsers.

In cases where you want to have more control and more choices over the colors in your Web page, you must use a color value.

Using Color Values

A **color value** is a numerical expression that exactly describes a color's appearance. To understand how HTML uses numbers to represent colors, you have to examine some of the basic principles of color theory.

In classical color theory, any color can be thought of as a combination of three primary colors: red, green, and blue. You are probably familiar with the color diagram shown in Figure 3-4, in which the colors yellow, magenta, cyan, and white are produced by combining the three primary colors. By varying the intensity of each primary color, you can create any color and any shade of color that you want. This principle allows your computer monitor to combine pixels of red, green, and blue light to create the array of colors you see on your screen.

Figure 3-4 ◄
Combining
the three
primary colors

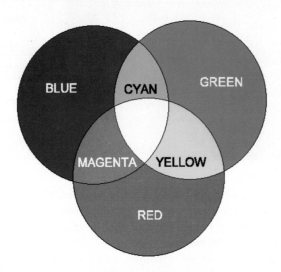

Software programs, like your Web browser, use a mathematical approach to define color. The intensity of each of the three primary colors is assigned a number from 0 (absence of color) to 255 (highest intensity). In this way, 255^3, or more than 16.7 million, distinct colors can be defined—more combinations than the human eye can distinguish. Each color is represented by a triplet of numbers, called an **RGB triplet**, based on its **R**ed, **G**reen, and **B**lue components. For example, white has a triplet of (255,255,255), indicating that red, green, and blue are equally mixed at the highest intensity. Gray is defined with the triplet (192,192,192), indicating an equal mixture of the primary colors with less intensity than white. Yellow has the triplet (255,255,0) because it is an equal mixture of red and green with no presence of blue. In most programs, you make your color choices with visual clues, usually without being aware of the underlying RGB triplet. Figure 3-5 shows a typical Colors dialog box in which you would make color selections based on the appearance of the color, rather than on the RGB values.

Figure 3-5 ◄
A typical Colors
dialog box

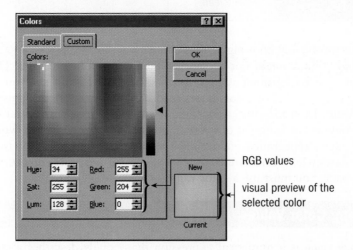

It is these RGB triplets that you have to enter into your HTML code if you want to express the exact appearance of a color. HTML requires that such color values be entered as hexadecimals. A **hexadecimal** is a number that is represented using 16 as a base rather than 10. In base 10 counting, you use combinations of 10 characters (0 through 9) to represent all of the integers, whereas hexadecimals include 6 extra characters: A (for 10), B (for 11), C (for 12), D (for 13), E (for 14), and F (for 15). For values above 15, you use a combination of the 16 characters; 16 is expressed as "10," 17 is expressed as "11," and so forth. To represent a number in hexadecimal, you convert the value to multiples of 16 plus a remainder. For example, twenty-one is equal to (16 x 1) + 5, so its hexadecimal representation is 15. The number 255 is equal to (16 x 15) + 15, or FF in hexadecimal format (remember that F=15 in hexadecimal). In the case of the number 255, the first F represents the number of times 16 goes into 255 (which is 15), and the second F represents the remainder of 15.

Once you know the RGB triplet of a color you want to use in your Web page, you need to convert that triplet to hexadecimal format and express it in a single string of six characters. For example, the color yellow has the RGB triplet (255,255,0), which is represented by the hexadecimal string FFFF00. Figure 3-6 shows the RGB triplets and hexadecimal equivalents for the 16 basic color names presented earlier.

Figure 3-6 ◀
Color names,
RGB triplets,
and
hexadecimal
values

Color Name	RGB Triplet	Hexadecimal	Color Name	RGB Triplet	Hexadecimal
Aqua	(0,255,255)	00FFFF	Navy	(0,0,128)	000080
Black	(0,0,0)	000000	Olive	(128,128,0)	808000
Blue	(0,0,255)	0000FF	Purple	(128,0,128)	800080
Fuchsia	(255,0,255)	FF00FF	Red	(255,0,0)	FF0000
Gray	(128,128,128)	808080	Silver	(192,192,192)	C0C0C0
Green	(0,128,0)	008000	Teal	(0,128,128)	008080
Lime	(0,255,0)	00FF00	White	(255,255,255)	FFFFFF
Maroon	(128,0,0)	800000	Yellow	(255,255,0)	FFFF00

At this point you might be wondering if you have to become a math major before you can even start adding color to your Web pages. In practice, Web authors rely on several tools to generate HTML code for specific colors. Some of the resources you can use on the World Wide Web are shown in Figure 3-7. You might also choose to create your initial code with an HTML editor, defining your color scheme with a Colors dialog box similar to the one shown earlier. Once that code is generated, you can further modify it within your text editor.

Figure 3-7 ◀
Color selection
resources
available on the
World Wide Web

Title	URL	Description
The Color Center	http://www.hidaho.com/colorcenter/	A Web page that allows you to interactively select page colors and textures and fragments of HTML code
Thalia's Color Page	http://www.sci.kun.nl/thalia/ guide/color/	A Web page containing color databases, an application to interactively select your color scheme, and additional information on HTML and color issues
Color Browser	http://www.maximized.com/ shareware/colorbrowser/	A Windows program to view and select colors
HTML-Color Pickers	http://tucows.hunterlink.net.au/mac/ colormac.html	An overview of various color pickers for Windows and Macintosh computers.

However you decide to work with color in your Web pages, it's important to understand how HTML handles color, if for no other reason than to be able to interpret the source code of HTML files you'll find on the Web.

Specifying a Color Scheme for Your Page

After reviewing the issues surrounding color and HTML, you are ready to add color to the Web page that Tom has given you. Web browsers have a default color scheme that they apply to the background and text of the pages they retrieve. In most cases this scheme will involve black text on a white or gray background, with hypertext highlighted in purple and blue. You can override the default color scheme of the browser by specifying one of your own for your Web page. To do this, you'll need to modify the properties of the page using the <BODY> tag.

REFERENCE window	**DEFINING A COLOR SCHEME**
	■ Locate the <BODY> tag in your HTML file.

	■ Edit the <BODY> tag to read:
	  <BODY BGCOLOR=*color* TEXT=*color* LINK=*color*
	  VLINK=*color*>
	  where BGCOLOR is the background color property, TEXT is the text color property, LINK is the color of hypertext links, and VLINK is the color of hypertext links that have been previously visited.
	  For *color*, enter either the color name or the hexadecimal value formatted as "#hexadecimal_number".

In your work with HTML, you've used the <BODY> tag to identify the section of the HTML file containing the content that users would see in their browsers. At that point, the <BODY> tag had no purpose other than to separate the content of the Web page from other items such as the page's title and file heading. But the <BODY> tag can also be used to indicate the colors on your page. The syntax for controlling a page's color scheme through the <BODY> tag is:

```
<BODY BGCOLOR=color TEXT=color LINK=color VLINK=color>
```

Here, the BGCOLOR property sets the background color, the TEXT property controls text color, the LINK property defines the color of hypertext links, and the VLINK property defines the color of links that have been previously visited by the user. The value of *color* will be either one of the accepted color names or the color's hexadecimal value. If you use the hexadecimal value, you must preface the hexadecimal string with the pound symbol (#) and enclose the string in double quotation marks. For example, the HTML tag to create a background color with the hexadecimal value FFCO88 is:

```
<BODY BGCOLOR="#FFCO88">
```

After viewing various color combinations, Tom has decided that he'd like you to use a color scheme of white text on a dark green background. He also wants the hypertext links to appear in red, with previously visited links appearing in turquoise. Using color values he retrieved from a graphics program, Tom has learned that the RGB triplet for the dark green background is (0,102,0), which you'll enter as "#006600" in the <BODY> tag.

To change the color scheme of the Expo Web page:

1. Open your text editor.

2. Open the file **Expotext.htm** from the Tutorial.03 folder on your Student Disk, and then save the file in the same folder as **Expo1999.htm**.

3. Within the <BODY> tag at the top of the file, type **BGCOLOR="#006600" TEXT=WHITE LINK=RED VLINK=TURQUOISE**.

Your file should appear as displayed in Figure 3-8.

Figure 3-8 ◀
Modified
<BODY> tag

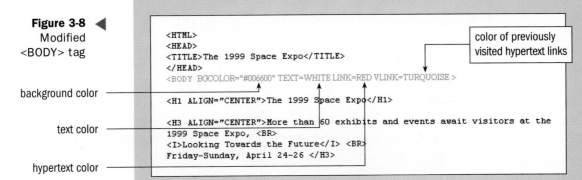

color of previously
visited hypertext links

background color

text color

hypertext color

```
<HTML>
<HEAD>
<TITLE>The 1999 Space Expo</TITLE>
</HEAD>
<BODY BGCOLOR="#006600" TEXT=WHITE LINK=RED VLINK=TURQUOISE >

<H1 ALIGN="CENTER">The 1999 Space Expo</H1>

<H3 ALIGN="CENTER">More than 60 exhibits and events await visitors at the
1999 Space Expo, <BR>
<I>Looking Towards the Future</I> <BR>
Friday-Sunday, April 24-26 </H3>
```

4. Save the changes to the Expo1999.htm file, but leave the text editor open. You'll be revising this file throughout this session.

5. Open your Web browser and view the Expo1999.htm file. See Figure 3-9.

Figure 3-9 ◀
The 1999
Space Expo
page with the
new color
scheme

white text

dark green
background

hypertext links
appear in red

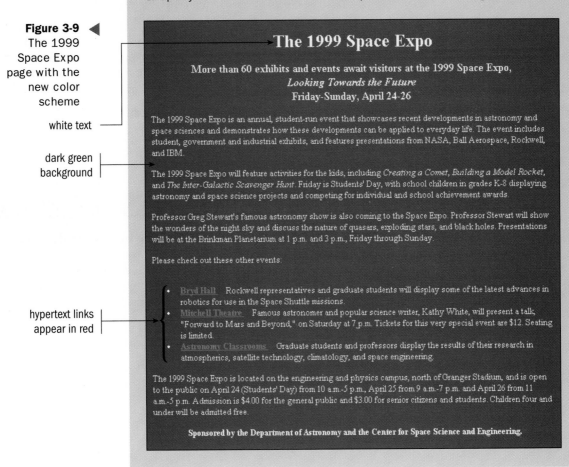

The Expo page now appears with white text on a dark green background. Hypertext links will show up in red and turquoise (you'll need to scroll the window to see the hypertext links). By adding the color scheme to the <BODY> tag of the HTML file, you've superceded the browser's default color scheme with one of your own.

Modifying Text with the <FONT> Tag

Specifying the text color in the <BODY> tag of your Web page changed the color of all the text on the page. Occasionally you will want to change the color of individual words or characters within the page. Color that affects only a few sections of a page is called **spot color**. HTML allows you to create incidences of spot color using the <FONT> tag.

REFERENCE window

MODIFYING TEXT APPEARANCE WITH THE <FONT> TAG

- In your Web page, locate the text whose appearance you want to modify.
- Place the text within the <FONT> tag as follows:
  <FONT SIZE=*sizevalue* COLOR=*color* FACE=*fontname*> Revised Text </FONT>
  where SIZE is the actual size of the text or the amount by which you want to increase or decrease the size of the text, in points; COLOR is the color name or color value you want to apply to the text; and FACE is the name of the font you want to use for the text.

You've already worked with some character tags that allow you to bold or italicize individual characters. The <FONT> tag gives you even more control by allowing you to specify the color, the size, and even the font to be used for the text on your page. The syntax for the <FONT> tag is:

```
<FONT SIZE=size COLOR=color FACE=font> Revised Text </FONT>
```

The <FONT> tag has three properties: size, color, and face. Your only concern right now is to use the <FONT> tag to change text color, but it's worthwhile exploring the other properties of the tag at this time.

Changing the Font Size

The SIZE property allows you to specify the font size of the revised text. The SIZE value can be expressed in either absolute or relative terms. For example, if you want your text to have a size of 2 points, you enter SIZE=2 in the <FONT> tag. On the other hand, if you want to increase the font size by 2 points relative to the surrounding text, you enter SIZE=+2 in the tag. Figure 3-10 shows the various point sizes as they appear in the browser.

Figure 3-10 ◀
Examples
of different
point sizes

This is 1 point text
This is 2 point text
This is 3 point text
This is 4 point text
This is 5 point text
This is 6 point text
This is 7 point text

For comparison, text formatted with the <H1> tag corresponds by default to bold, 6 point text; the <H2> tag is equivalent to bold, 5-point text, and so forth. Figure 3-11 presents a complete comparison of header tags and point sizes.

Figure 3-11 ◀
Header tags
and point sizes

Tag	Format
<H1>	6 point, bold
<H2>	5 point, bold
<H3>	4 point, bold
<H4>	3 point, bold
<H5>	2 point, bold
<H6>	1 point, bold
Normal text (no <H*i*> tag)	3 point, not bold

So, if you use the property SIZE=+1 to increase the size of text enclosed within an <H3> tag, the net effect will be to produce text that is 5 points in size and bold. Note that the largest font size supported by browsers is 7 points.

Changing the Font Color

The COLOR property allows you to change the color of individual characters or words. As when creating a color scheme, you specify the color by using either an accepted color name or the color value. For example, to change the color of the word "Expo" to the color value 8000C0, you would enter the following HTML tag:

```
<FONT COLOR="#8000C0"> Expo </FONT>
```

The text surrounding the word "Expo" would still be formatted in the color scheme specified in the <BODY> tag, or in the default scheme used by the Web browser.

Changing the Font Face

The final property of the <FONT> tag is the FACE property. You use the FACE property to indicate the font the text should be displayed in. This property is a bit of a departure from earlier versions of HTML, in which the browser alone determined the font used in the Web page. With the FACE property you can override the browser's choice. For this to work, you must specify a font that is installed on the user's computer. But, because you have no way of knowing which fonts have been installed, the FACE property allows you to specify a list of potential font names. The browser will attempt to use the first font in the list; if that fails, it will try the second font, and so on to the end of the list. If none of the fonts listed matches a font installed on the user's computer, the browser will ignore this property and use the default font. For example, to display the word "Expo" in a font without serifs, you could enter the following HTML tag:

```
<FONT FACE="ARIAL, HELVETICA, SANS SERIF"> Expo </FONT>
```

In this example, each of the three specified fonts is a non-serif font. The browser will first attempt to display the word "Expo" in the Arial font. If that fails, it will try the Helvetica font, and after that it will try the Sans Serif font. If none of these fonts are installed on the user's computer, the browser will use the default font.

DESIGN window	**WORKING WITH TEXT** ■ Do not overwhelm your page with different font sizes, colors, and font faces. Using a minimal number of font styles gives your page a uniform appearance that is easy to read. ■ Avoid using the same color for normal text as you do for hypertext links, so that you do not confuse the reader. ■ If you use a particular font face for your text, specify a list of alternate font names to accommodate different operating systems.

Using the <FONT> Tag for Spot Color

As you can see, the <FONT> tag gives you a lot of control over the appearance of individual blocks of text. At this point, though, you are only interested in using the <FONT> tag for spot color. Tom wants the name of this year's event, "Looking Towards the Future," to stand out on the page. To accomplish this, you'll format the line of text so that the title appears in yellow.

To change the appearance of the Expo title:

   1. Return to your text editor and the Expo1999.htm file.

   2. Enclose the title within the <FONT> tag as follows:

   <FONT COLOR=YELLOW> Looking Towards the Future </FONT>

The Expo1999.htm file should now appear as shown in Figure 3-12.

Figure 3-12 ◀
Using the
<FONT> tag
to create
spot color

text will appear
in yellow

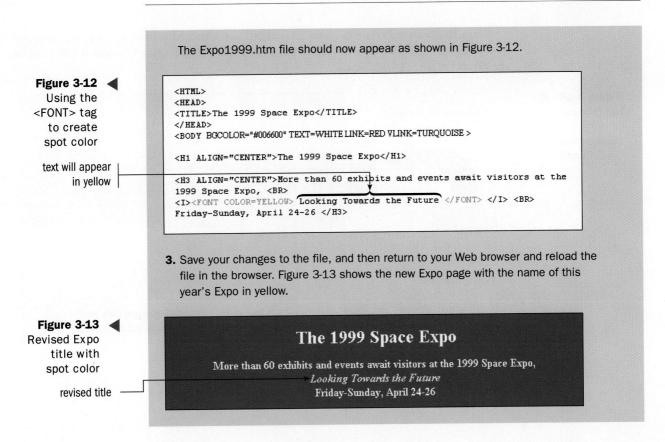

```
<HTML>
<HEAD>
<TITLE>The 1999 Space Expo</TITLE>
</HEAD>
<BODY  BGCOLOR="#006600" TEXT=WHITE LINK=RED VLINK=TURQUOISE >

<H1 ALIGN="CENTER">The 1999 Space Expo</H1>

<H3 ALIGN="CENTER">More than 60 exhibits and events await visitors at the
1999 Space Expo, <BR>
<I><FONT COLOR=YELLOW> Looking Towards the Future </FONT> </I> <BR>
Friday-Sunday, April 24-26 </H3>
```

3. Save your changes to the file, and then return to your Web browser and reload the file in the browser. Figure 3-13 shows the new Expo page with the name of this year's Expo in yellow.

Figure 3-13 ◀
Revised Expo
title with
spot color

revised title

> ## The 1999 Space Expo
>
> More than 60 exhibits and events await visitors at the 1999 Space Expo,
> *Looking Towards the Future*
> Friday-Sunday, April 24-26

You show the revised page to Tom. He likes the use of color in the page and the spot color, but feels that the background needs work. He's seen Web pages that have graphic images used for backgrounds, and he'd like you to try something similar.

Inserting a Background Image

Another property of the <BODY> tag is the BACKGROUND property. With this property you can use a graphic file as a background image for your page. The syntax for inserting a background image is:

```
<BODY BACKGROUND="image">
```

Here, *image* is the name or URL of the graphic file you want to use. For example, to use a graphic file named "Bricks.gif" as your background image, you would enter:

```
<BODY BACKGROUND="Bricks.gif">
```

REFERENCE window	**INSERTING A BACKGROUND IMAGE**
	■ Locate the <BODY> tag in your HTML file.
	■ Edit the <BODY> tag as follows:
	<BODY BACKGROUND="*image*">
	where *image* is the filename or URL of the graphic image you want to use for your page's background.

When the browser retrieves your graphic file, it repeatedly inserts the image into the page's background, in a process called **tiling**, until the entire display window is filled up, as shown in Figure 3-14.

Figure 3-14 ◀
The process
of tiling the
background
image

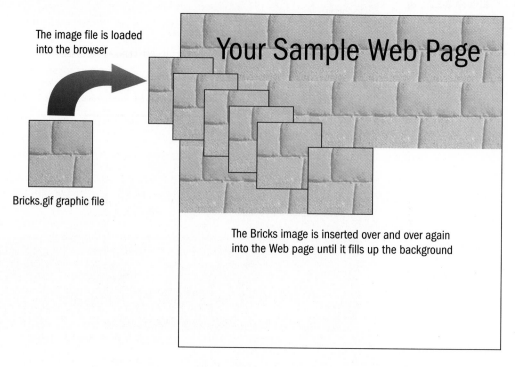

The image file is loaded
into the browser

Bricks.gif graphic file

Your Sample Web Page

The Bricks image is inserted over and over again
into the Web page until it fills up the background

In choosing a background image, you should remember the following:

■ Use an image that will not detract from your page's text, making it hard to read.

■ Do not use a large image file (more than 20 kilobytes). Large and complicated backgrounds will cause your page to take a long time to load, and no matter how attractive the page's background is, it won't impress people who won't wait around to see it.

■ The background should appear seamless to the user. Use images that will not show boundaries and grids when tiled.

Figure 3-15 shows examples of well-designed and poorly designed Web page backgrounds.

Figure 3-15 ◀
Examples of
Web page
backgrounds

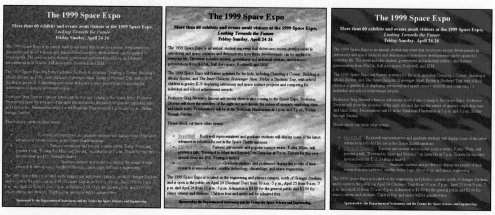

Background overwhelms the text
in the foreground

Background shows distracting
seams between image tiles

Background does not show seams
or overwhelm the foreground text

Finding the right background image is a process of trial and error. You won't know for certain whether a background image works well until you actually view it in a browser. There are numerous collections of background images available on the Web. You can copy many of these and use them on your own pages for free. The only restriction is that you cannot sell or distribute the images in a commercial product. Figure 3-16 provides a short list of these collections.

Figure 3-16 ◀
Places on the Web to get background images

Title	URL	Description
3D Netscape Backgrounds	http://www.sonic.net/~lberlin/new/3dnscape.html	A collection of heavily textured and colored backgrounds
Founder's Background Samplers	http://www.mei-web.de/backgrounds/back_main.shtml	A collection of background images from around the world
Netscape's Background Sampler	http://www.netscape.com/assist/net_sites/bg/backgrounds.html	A collection of backgrounds from Netscape
SBN Image Gallery	http://www.microsoft.com/gallery/images/default.asp	A collection of images and backgrounds from the Microsoft Site Builder Network
Cool Archive	http://www.coolarchive.com/	An archive of images, backgrounds, buttons and icons
The Design Shoppe	http://www.thedesign-shoppe.com/	Free, original graphics for Web pages

After searching, Tom has found a graphic he thinks will work well for the Expo. The image, named Space.jpg, is shown in Figure 3-17.

Figure 3-17 ◀
Space.jpg background image

Next, you'll add this image to the 1999 Space Expo background.

To add the Space.jpg graphic file to the background:

1. Return to your text editor and the Expo1999.htm file.

2. Modify the <BODY> tag, replacing the BGCOLOR property with:
   BACKGROUND="Space.jpg"

The revised <BODY> tag should now appear as shown in Figure 3-18.

Figure 3-18 ◀
Specifying the
Space.jpg
graphic as a
background
image

the background
image property

```
<HTML>
<HEAD>
<TITLE>The 1999 Space Expo</TITLE>
</HEAD>
<BODY BACKGROUND="Space.jpg" TEXT=WHITE LINK=RED VLINK=TURQUOISE >

<H1 ALIGN="CENTER">The 1999 Space Expo</H1>

<H3 ALIGN="CENTER">More than 60 exhibits and events await visitors at the
1999 Space Expo, <BR>
<I><FONT COLOR=YELLOW> Looking Towards the Future </FONT> </I> <BR>
Friday-Sunday, April 24-26 </H3>
```

3. Save your changes to Expo1999.htm, and then view the page in your Web browser. Figure 3-19 shows the new background for the Expo page.

Figure 3-19 ◀
Space Expo
Web page with
the background
image

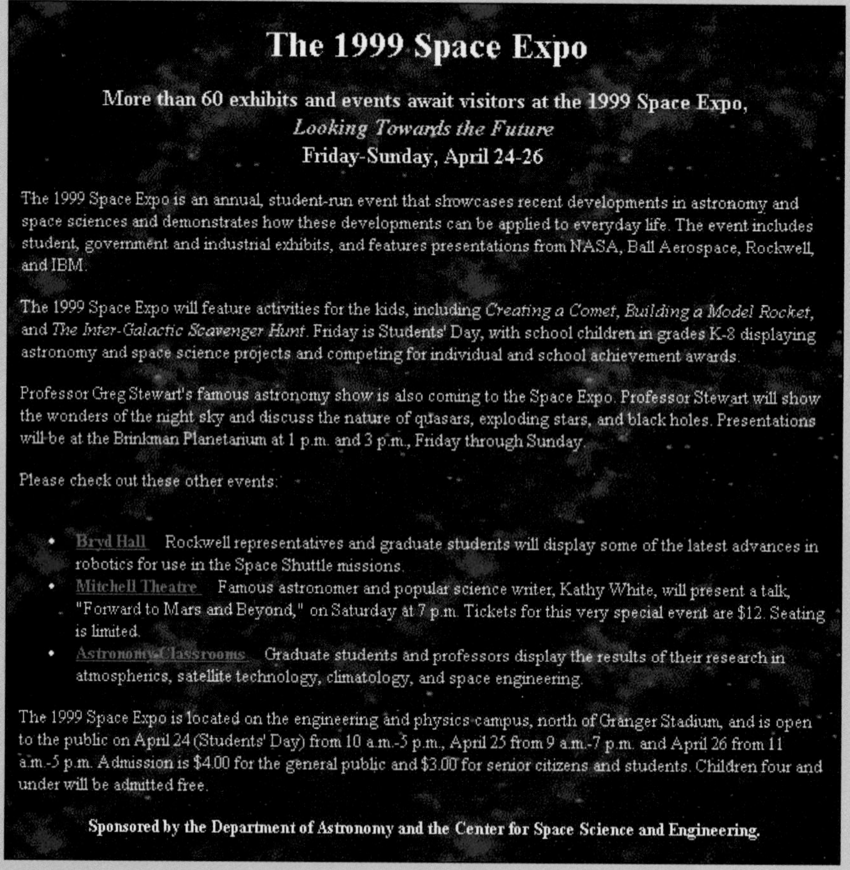

Tom is pleased with the impact of the new page background. He notes that the size of the image file is not too large (only 6 kilobytes) and that it does not show any obvious seams between the image tiles. Also, the background does not overwhelm the content of the Web page, and it fits in well with the theme of the Space Expo.

Quick Check

1. What are the two ways of specifying a color in an HTML file? What are the advantages and disadvantages of each?

2. What tag would you enter in your HTML file to use a color scheme of red text on a gray background, with hypertext links displayed in blue, and previously visited hypertext links displayed in yellow?

3. What is spot color?

4. What tag would you enter to format the words "Major Sale" in red, with a font size 5 points larger than the surrounding text?

5. What tag would you enter to display the text "Major Sale" in the Times New Roman font and, if that font is not available, in the MS Serif font?

6. What tag would you enter to use the graphic file "Stars.gif" as the background image for a Web page?

7. Name three things you should avoid when using a background image for your Web page.

In the next session, you'll learn more about handling graphics with HTML as you add inline images to the Expo1999.htm file.

SESSION

3.2

In this session you will learn about different graphic file formats and how you can use them to add special effects to your Web page. You'll explore the advantages and disadvantages of each format. Finally, you'll learn how to control the size, placement, and appearance of your page's inline images.

Understanding Image Formats

Having finished adding color to the Expo Web page, you now turn to the task of adding graphics. The two image formats supported by most Web browsers are GIF and JPEG. Choosing the appropriate image format for your graphics is an important part of Web page design. You have to balance the goal of creating an interesting and attractive page against the need to keep the size of your page small and easy to retrieve. Each graphic format has its advantages and disadvantages, and you will probably use a combination of both in your Web page designs. First you'll look at the advantages and disadvantages of GIF image files.

Working with GIF Files

GIF (Graphics Interchange Format) is the most commonly used image format on the Web. Web pages with GIF image files should be compatible with any graphical browser users have. GIF files are limited to displaying 256 colors, so they are more often used for graphics requiring fewer colors, such as clip art images, line art, logos, and icons. Images that require more color depth, such as photographs, often appear grainy when saved as GIFs. There are actually two GIF file formats: GIF87 and GIF89a. The GIF89a format, the newer standard, includes enhancements such as interlacing, transparent colors, and animation. You'll explore these enhancements now, and learn how to use them in your Web page design. First you'll look at interlacing.

Interlaced and Noninterlaced GIFs

Interlacing refers to the way the GIF file is saved by the graphics software. Normally, with a **noninterlaced** GIF the image is saved one line at a time, starting from the top of the graphic and moving downward. The graphic image is retrieved as it was saved: starting from the top of the image and moving down. Figure 3-20 shows how a noninterlaced GIF appears as it is slowly retrieved by the Web browser. If the graphic is large, it might take several minutes for the entire image to appear. People who access your page might find this annoying if the part of the image that interests them is located at the bottom.

Figure 3-20
Noninterlaced image as the browser retrieves it

top appears first

image appears one line at a time

entire image is retrieved

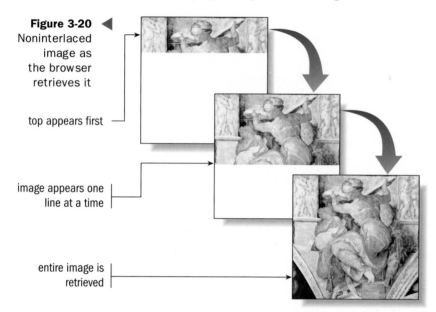

With **interlaced** GIFs, the image is saved and retrieved "stepwise." For example, every fifth line of the image might appear first, followed by every sixth line, and so forth through the remaining rows. As shown in Figure 3-21, the effect of interlacing is that the graphic starts out as a blurry representation of the final image, then gradually comes into focus—unlike the noninterlaced graphic, which is always a sharp image as it's being retrieved, although an incomplete one.

Figure 3-21
Interlaced
image as
the browser
retrieves it

a rough image
appears first

image starts to show
more detail

final image is crisp
and detailed

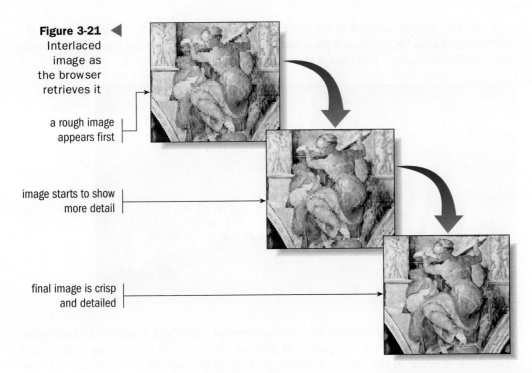

Interlacing is an effective format if you have a large graphic and want to give users a preview of the final image. They get an idea of what the image looks like and can decide whether to wait for it to come into focus. The downside of interlacing is that it increases the size of the GIF file—anywhere from 3 to 20 kilobytes, depending on the image.

Transparent GIFs

Another enhancement of the GIF89a format is the ability to create transparent colors. A **transparent color** is a color from the image that is not displayed when the image appears in the browser. In place of that color, the browser will display whatever happens to appear on the page background. This effect integrates inline images with the page background. The process by which you create a transparent color depends on your graphics software. Many packages include extra options you can select when saving images in GIF89a format. One of these is to designate a particular color from the image as transparent. Other packages include a transparent color tool, which you use to click the color from the image that you want saved as transparent.

Tom has a graphic created in the GIF89a format that displays the official logo for the 1999 Space Expo. He wants you to replace the text heading from the Expo1999.htm file with the graphic image. The logo is shown in Figure 3-22.

Figure 3-22 ◀
The 1999
Space Expo
logo

the red background
color will appear
transparent when
displayed in
the browser

When the graphic was created, the red background color was designated as transparent. This means that when you insert the graphic into your Web page, the background image you inserted in the previous session will show through in places where red now appears. To see how this works, you'll replace the text heading with the logo.

To insert the logo in your HTML file:

1. If you took a break after the previous session, start your text editor and reopen the Expo1999.htm file from the Tutorial.03 folder of your Student Disk.

2. Go to the top of the page and replace the text within the <H1> tag with the following <IMG> tag:

   <IMG SRC="Logo.gif">

   Figure 3-23 shows the modified section of the Expo1999.htm file.

Figure 3-23 ◀
Inserting the
logo image into
the page
heading

the logo image file —

```
<HTML>
<HEAD>
<TITLE>The 1999 Space Expo</TITLE>
</HEAD>
<BODY BACKGROUND="Space.jpg" TEXT=WHITE LINK=RED VLINK=TURQUOISE >

<H1 ALIGN="CENTER"> <IMG SRC="Logo.gif"> </H1>

<H3 ALIGN="CENTER">More than 60 exhibits and events await visitors at the
1999 Space Expo, <BR>
<I><FONT COLOR=YELLOW> Looking Towards the Future </FONT> </I> <BR>
Friday-Sunday, April 24-26 </H3>
```

3. Save your changes, and then load the file in your Web browser. The browser displays the revised page with the logo, as shown in Figure 3-24.

Figure 3-24
Space Expo
logo in the
Web page

logo background
is transparent

Note that the background image is visible beneath the graphic in those locations
where red text appeared in the original image.

Animated GIFs

One of the most popular uses of GIF files in recent years has been to create animated
images. Compared to video clips, animated GIFs are easier to create and smaller in size.
An animated GIF is composed of several graphic images, each one slightly different. When
the GIF image is displayed in the Web browser, the images are displayed one after another
in rapid succession, creating the animated effect. To create animated GIFs, you need special software. Figure 3-25 provides a list of such programs available on the Web.

Figure 3-25
Software to
create
animated GIFs

Title	URL	Platform
GifBuilder	http://iawww.epfl.ch/Staff/ Yves.Piguet/clip2gif-home/ GifBuilder.html	Macintosh
Gif.glf.giF	http://www.cafe.net/peda/ggg/	Windows, Macintosh
GIF Construction Set	http://www.mindworkshop.com/ alchemy/gifcon.html	Windows
AniMagic	http://rtlsoft.com/ animagic/	Windows

Animated GIF software allows you to control the rate at which the animation plays (in
number of frames per second) and to determine the number of times the animation will be
repeated before halting. You can also set the animation to loop continuously. Most of these
packages will import and combine individual GIF files, but some also provide tools to create special transitions between one GIF image and another. For example, you could use the
software to gradually fade from one image into another, in a process called **morphing**.

If you don't want to take the time to create your own animated GIFs, many animated GIF collections are available on the Web. Figure 3-26 lists a few of them.

Figure 3-26 ◀
Animated GIF
collections

Title	URL
Netscape Animated GIFs	http://www.netscape.com/assist/net_sites/starter/samples/animate.html
Yahoo! List of Animated GIF Collections	http://dir.yahoo.com/Arts/Visual_Arts/Animation/Computer_Animation/Animated_GIFs/
Gallery of GIF Animation	http://members.aol.com/royalef1/galframe.htm
GIF World	http://www.gifworld.com/

Because an animated GIF is much larger than the corresponding static GIF image, overusing animated GIFs can greatly increase the size of your page. You should also be careful not to overwhelm the user with animated images. Animated GIFs can quickly become a source of irritation to the user once the novelty has worn off, especially because there is no way for the user to turn them off! As with other GIF files, animated GIFs are limited to 256 colors, which makes them ideal for small icons and logos, but not for larger images.

To see whether an animated GIF will enhance the appearance of your Web page, you'll replace the existing Space 1999 Expo logo with an animated version of the logo.

To insert the animated logo in your HTML file:

1. Return to your text editor and the Expo1999.htm file.

2. Replace "Logo.gif" in the <IMG> tag at the top of the document with the filename **"LogoAnim.gif"**.

3. Save your changes, and then reload the file in your Web browser.

   As shown in Figure 3-27, the revised logo now shows a spinning Earth superimposed on the Space Expo title. Note as well that animated GIFs, like static GIFs, can use transparent colors.

Figure 3-27 ◀
Animated
GIF logo

animated globe —

transparent
background

Not all Web browsers support animated GIFs. If a user tries to access your page with an older browser, only a static image of the first frame of the animation will be displayed.

Tom likes the new animated logo you've added. The next image you'll add to the page is a photo in the JPEG format.

Working with JPEG Files

The other important image format supported by most Web browsers is the JPEG format. **JPEG** stands for **Joint Photographic Experts Group**. The JPEG format differs from the GIF format in several ways. With JPEG files you can create graphics that use the full 16.7 million colors available in the color palette. Because of this, JPEG files are most often used for photographs and images that cover a wide spectrum of color.

Another feature of JPEG files is that they can be compressed, yielding image files that are usually (though not always) smaller than their GIF counterparts. For example, in the previous session you used the JPEG file Space.jpg as your background image. The file itself is only 6 Kb; however, if that image is converted to a GIF file, the size increases to 23 Kb. There are also situations in which the GIF format creates a smaller and better-looking image, such as when the image has large sections covered with a single color.

Compressing a graphic reduces the file size, but it might do so at the expense of image quality. Figure 3-28 shows the effect of increasing a compression on a JPEG file. As you can see, the increased compression cuts the file size to one-sixth of the original, but leaves much of the image blurry.

Figure 3-28 ◄
The effects of compression on JPEG file size and image quality

Minimal compression
File size=23 kb

Moderate compression
File size=11 kb

Medium compression
File size=7 kb

Heavy compression
File size=4 kb

By testing different compression levels with your graphics software, you can reduce the size of your JPEG files while maintaining an attractive image. Note that a smaller file size does not always mean that your page will load faster. The browser has to decompress the JPEG image when it retrieves it, and for a heavily compressed image this can take more time than retrieving and displaying a less-compressed file.

There are some other differences between JPEGs and GIFs. You cannot use transparent colors or animation with JPEG files, and standard JPEG files are not interlaced, which means that they do not "fade in" gradually as do interlaced GIFs. In recent years a new format called **Progressive JPEG** has been introduced, which allows for interlacing without increasing the size of the graphic file. Not all graphics programs and Web browsers support progressive JPEGs, however.

Tom wants you to add a photograph of the Center for Space Science and Engineering to the Expo Web page. The photo has been saved as a JPEG file named Center.jpg on your Student Disk. You will insert the image directly below the Expo logo.

To insert the Center photograph into your Web page:

1. Return to your text editor and the Expo1999.htm file.

2. Locate the paragraph that begins "The 1999 Space Expo is an annual, student-run event …" and then insert the following <IMG> tag after the paragraph's <P> tag:

   <IMG SRC="Center.jpg">

   Figure 3-29 shows the revised HTML code.

Figure 3-29 ◄
Adding the
Center JPEG
image to the
Expo Web page

```
<H1 ALIGN="CENTER"> <IMG SRC="LogoAnim.gif"> </H1>

<H3 ALIGN="CENTER">More than 60 exhibits and events await visitors at the
1999 Space Expo, <BR>
<I><FONT COLOR=YELLOW> Looking Towards the Future </FONT> </I> <BR>
Friday-Sunday, April 24-26 </H3>

<P> <IMG SRC="Center.jpg"> The 1999 Space Expo is an annual, student-run eve:
developments in astronomy and space sciences and demonstrates how these
developments can be applied to everyday life. The event includes student,
government and industrial exhibits, and features presentations from NASA,
Ball Aerospace, Rockwell, and IBM.</P>
```

image tag for the
Center JPEG file

3. Save your changes, and then reload the Expo1999.htm file in your Web browser. Figure 3-30 shows the revised page with the newly inserted JPEG graphic.

Figure 3-30 ◄
Space Center
inline image

the Space
Center photo

TROUBLE? If the graphic appears blurry or grainy, it could be because your monitor is capable of displaying only 256 colors and not the full palette of 16.7 million colors.

CHOOSING GRAPHIC IMAGE TYPES

DESIGN
window

Use GIF images when you want to:
- create animated graphics
- use transparent colors
- display logos or clip art containing up to 256 colors

Use JPEG images when you want to:
- display photographs
- use images that contain more than 256 colors
- reduce the size of your images through file compression

Using the ALT Property

One of the properties available with the <IMG> tag is the ALT property. The ALT property allows you to specify text that will appear in place of your inline images. Alternate image text is important because it allows users who have nongraphical browsers to learn the content of your graphics. Alternate image text also appears as a placeholder for the graphic while the page is loading. This is particularly important for users accessing your page through a slow dial-up connection.

SPECIFYING ALTERNATE TEXT FOR AN INLINE IMAGE

REFERENCE
window

- Locate the <IMG> tag for the inline image.
- Edit the <IMG> tag as follows:
  <IMG SRC="*image*" ALT="*alternate text*">
  where *image* is the filename or URL of the graphic image and
  alternate text is the text you want to have displayed in place
  of the image.

The syntax for specifying alternate text is:

```
<IMG SRC="image" ALT="alternate text">
```

You'll add the ALT property to the two <IMG> tags in your Expo Web page now.

To insert alternate image text into your Web page:

1. Return to the Expo1999.htm file in your text editor.

2. Within the <IMG> tag for the Expo logo, insert the text: **ALT="The 1999 Space Expo"**.

3. After the <IMG> tag for the Center photograph, insert the text: **ALT="The MWU Center for Space Science and Engineering"**.

Figure 3-31 shows the revised <IMG> tags for the Expo1999.htm file.

Figure 3-31 ◀
Specifying
alternate text
for the inline
images

alternate text ──

```
<HTML>
<HEAD>
<TITLE>The 1999 Space Expo</TITLE>
</HEAD>
<BODY BACKGROUND="Space.jpg" TEXT=WHITE LINK=RED VLINK=TURQUOISE >

<H1 ALIGN="CENTER"> <IMG SRC="LogoAnim.gif" ALT="The 1999 Space Expo" > </H1>

<H3 ALIGN="CENTER">More than 60 exhibits and events await visitors at the
1999 Space Expo, <BR>
<I><FONT COLOR=YELLOW> Looking Towards the Future </FONT> </I> <BR>
Friday-Sunday, April 24-26 </H3>

<P> <IMG SRC="Center.jpg" ALT="The MWU Center for Space Science and Engineering" >
The 1999 Space Expo is an annual, student-run event that showcases recent
developments in astronomy and space sciences and demonstrates how these
developments can be applied to everyday life. The event includes student,
government and industrial exhibits, and features presentations from NASA,
Ball Aerospace, Rockwell, and IBM.</P>
```

4. Save your changes to the file. Figure 3-32 shows the appearance of your Web page with the alternate text replacing the image. (You can create this effect by turning off the display of inline images within your browser, or by interrupting the retrieval of the Expo page before the two images are rendered.)

Figure 3-32 ◀
Alternate text
as it appears in
the Web page

alternate text ──

Now that you've entered the images on the page, your next task is to control their placement and appearance.

Controlling Image Placement and Size

You show Tom the progress you've made on the Web page. Although he's pleased with the graphic image of the Center, he wants you to modify the placement of the image on the page. With the image's current placement, the page now has a large blank space to the upper right of the image. Tom wonders if you could control the way text flows around the image so that there is less blank space. You can, using the ALIGN property of the <IMG> tag.

REFERENCE
window

ALIGNING TEXT AROUND AN IMAGE

- Locate the <IMG> tag for the inline image.
- Edit the <IMG> tag as follows:
  <IMG SRC="*image*" ALIGN=*alignment*>
  where *image* is the filename or URL of the graphic image, and *alignment* specifies how surrounding text should be aligned with the graphic (top, middle, bottom, left, or right).

Controlling Image Alignment

As you know, the ALIGN property can be used to control the alignment of paragraph tags. The ALIGN property fulfills a similar function in the <IMG> tag. The syntax for the ALIGN property is:

```
<IMG SRC="image"ALIGN=alignment>
```

Here, *alignment* is a value that indicates how you want the image aligned with the surrounding text. Different versions of HTML support different values for the ALIGN property. The three values for the ALIGN property accepted in all versions of HTML are Top, Middle, and Bottom. With ALIGN set to Top, the surrounding text aligns with the top of the image; the Middle setting aligns the text with the middle of the image; and the Bottom setting aligns the text with the bottom of the image.

Figure 3-33 shows the effect of each of these on text surrounding the Space Center image.

Figure 3-33 ◀
Effects of the
ALIGN property

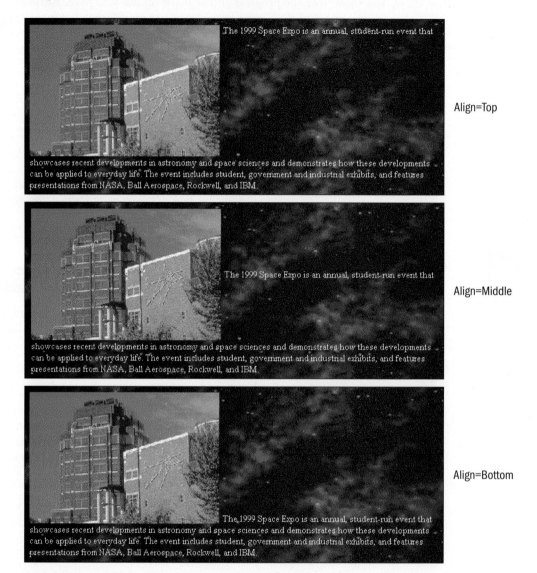

Inserting an image works fine if you have only one line of text, or if the image itself is very small. However, if you are trying to integrate a large image with several lines, you will invariably create a lot of blank space, as illustrated in Figure 3-33.

Versions of HTML 3.0 and above, as well as the Netscape Navigator and Internet Explorer browsers, support an extension to the <IMG> tag that aligns the image with either the left or right margin of the page and wraps text around the image. By using the values LEFT and RIGHT for the ALIGN property, you can remove the blank space problem that Tom was concerned about.

Next, you'll align the Center image with the left side of the page, wrapping the surrounding text around the image.

To align the Center photograph on the left side of the page:

1. In the <IMG> tag for the Center photograph, insert the following text after the ALT property: **ALIGN=LEFT**.

Your revised <IMG> tag should appear as shown in Figure 3-34.

Figure 3-34 ◀
Using
the ALIGN
property in an
<IMG> tag

aligning the
image with the left
page margin

```
<P> <IMG SRC="Center.jpg" ALT="The MWU Center for Space Science and
Engineering" ALIGN=LEFT >
The 1999 Space Expo is an annual, student-run event that showcases recent
developments in astronomy and space sciences and demonstrates how these
developments can be applied to everyday life. The event includes student,
government and industrial exhibits, and features presentations from NASA,
Ball Aerospace, Rockwell, and IBM.</P>
```

2. Save your changes, and then reload the Expo page in your browser. Figure 3-35 shows the new page with the text wrapped around the Center photograph.

Figure 3-35 ◀
Space Center
image aligned
with the left
page margin

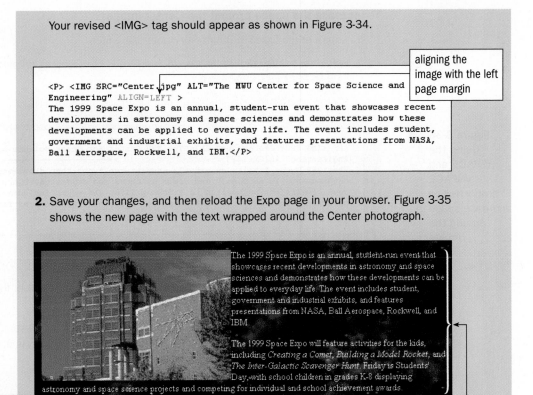

The 1999 Space Expo is an annual, student-run event that showcases recent developments in astronomy and space sciences and demonstrates how these developments can be applied to everyday life. The event includes student, government and industrial exhibits, and features presentations from NASA, Ball Aerospace, Rockwell, and IBM.

The 1999 Space Expo will feature activities for the kids, including *Creating a Comet*, *Building a Model Rocket*, and *The Inter-Galactic Scavenger Hunt*. Friday is Students' Day, with school children in grades K-8 displaying astronomy and space science projects and competing for individual and school achievement awards.

text wraps around
the right side

Because the LEFT and RIGHT alignment values are not supported by all browsers, some older browsers might not display your page correctly. However, almost all of the newer browsers should be able to render the page properly.

Controlling Vertical and Horizontal Space

Wrapping the text around the image has solved one problem: the large blank space has been removed. A second problem now exists, however—there's not enough space separating the image and the surrounding text, which makes the page appear crowded. You can increase the horizontal and vertical space around the image with the HSPACE and VSPACE properties, as follows:

```
<IMG SRC="image"VSPACE=value HSPACE=value>
```

The HSPACE property increases the space to the left and right of the image, and the VSPACE property increases the space above and below the image. The value of the VSPACE and HSPACE properties is measured in pixels. As with the ALIGN property, the HSPACE and VSPACE properties might not be supported by older browsers, but all new browsers should support them.

REFERENCE
window

INCREASING THE SPACE AROUND AN IMAGE

■ Locate the <IMG> tag for the inline image.
■ Edit the <IMG> tag as follows:
  <IMG SRC="*image*" HSPACE=*value* VSPACE=*value*>
  where *image* is the filename or URL of the graphic image,
  HSPACE is the space to the left and right of the image (in pixels),
  and VSPACE is the space above and below the image (in pixels).

You need to use the VSPACE and HSPACE properties to increase the space between the Center image and the surrounding text.

To increase the space around the Center image:

1. Return to the Expo1999.htm file in your text editor.

2. Within the <IMG> tag for the Center image, add the following properties and values: **VSPACE=5 HSPACE=10**.

   Your revised <IMG> tag should appear as shown in Figure 3-36.

Figure 3-36 ◄
Using the
HSPACE and
VSPACE
properties to
increase space
around the
image

```
<P> <IMG SRC="Center.jpg" ALT="The MWU Center for Space Science and
Engineering" ALIGN=LEFT VSPACE=5 HSPACE=10 >
The 1999 Space Expo is an annual, student-run event that showcases recent
developments in astronomy and space sciences and demonstrates how these
developments can be applied to everyday life. The event includes student,
government and industrial exhibits, and features presentations from NASA,
Ball Aerospace, Rockwell, and IBM.</P>
```

properties to increase
the vertical and
horizontal space

These property values will increase the gap to the left and right of the image to 10 pixels, and the gap above and below to 5 pixels.

3. Save your changes, and then reload the Expo page in your browser. The revised page shows an increased gap between the image and the surrounding text. See Figure 3-37. The page does not seem so crowded now.

Figure 3-37 ◄
Increased
vertical and
horizontal
space around
the Space
Center image

more space
around the image

Controlling Image Size

The final properties you'll be setting for the image are the HEIGHT and WIDTH properties, which tell the browser how large to make the image. You can use these properties to increase or decrease the size of the image on your page. Generally, if you want to decrease the size of an image, you should do so in a graphics package, because then you will also be reducing the size of the graphics file. Changing the size of the image within the <IMG> tag does not affect the file size. The syntax for setting the HEIGHT and WIDTH properties is:

```
<IMG SRC="image" HEIGHT=value WIDTH=value>
```

REFERENCE
window

SPECIFYING THE SIZE OF AN INLINE IMAGE

- Locate the <IMG> tag for the inline image.
- Edit the <IMG> tag as follows:
  <IMG SRC="image" HEIGHT=value WIDTH=value>
  where "image" is the filename or URL of the graphic image, and
  HEIGHT and WIDTH are the dimensions of the image (in pixels).

Specifying the height and width of an image is a good idea, even if you're not trying to change the image's dimensions. Why? Because of the way browsers work with inline images. When a browser encounters an inline image, it has to calculate the image size, and then use this information to format the page. If you include the dimensions of the image, the browser does not have to perform that calculation, and the page will be displayed that much faster. To determine the size of an image, use your graphics software and record the dimension of each graphic on your page in pixels.

The LogoAnim image is 414 pixels wide by 209 pixels high, and the Space Center image is 280 pixels wide by 186 pixels high. You'll enter this information into the <IMG> tags for each image.

To specify the width and height of the two images:

1. Return to your text editor.

2. Within the <IMG> tag for the LogoAnim image, add the following properties and values: **WIDTH=414 HEIGHT=209**.

3. Within the <IMG> tag for the Space Center image, add the following properties and values: **WIDTH=280 HEIGHT=186**.

   The revised Expo1999.htm file should appear as shown in Figure 3-38.

Figure 3-38 ◄
Specifying the width and height of the inline images

width and height properties

```
<H1 ALIGN="CENTER"> <IMG SRC="LogoAnim.gif" ALT="The 1999 Space Expo"
WIDTH=414 HEIGHT=209 > </H1>

<H3 ALIGN="CENTER">More than 60 exhibits and events await visitors at the
1999 Space Expo, <BR>
<I><FONT COLOR=YELLOW> Looking Towards the Future </FONT> </I> <BR>
Friday-Sunday, April 24-26 </H3>

<P> <IMG SRC="Center.jpg" ALT="The MWU Center for Space Science and
Engineering" ALIGN="LEFT" VSPACE=5 HSPACE=10 WIDTH=280 HEIGHT=186 >
The 1999 Space Expo is an annual, student-run event that showcases recent
developments in astronomy and space sciences and demonstrates how these
developments can be applied to everyday life. The event includes student,
government and industrial exhibits, and features presentations from NASA,
Ball Aerospace, Rockwell, and IBM.</P>
```

4. Save your changes, and then reload the Expo page in your browser. Confirm that the layout is the same as the last time you viewed the page, because you have not changed the dimensions of the inline images—you've simply included their dimensions in the HTML file.

General Tips for Working with Color and Images

You've completed much of the layout of the 1999 Space Expo page. When working with color and images in your Web page, keep in mind that the primary purpose of the page is to convey information. "A picture is worth a thousand words," and if an image can convey an idea quickly, by all means use it. If an image adds visual interest to your page and makes the user interested in what you have to say, include it. However, always be aware that overusing graphics can make your page difficult to read and cumbersome to display. With that in mind, this section provides some tips to remember as you work with color and images in your Web pages.

Reduce the Size of Your Pages

You should strive to make your page quick and easy to retrieve. If users will be accessing your page over a dial-up connection, the amount of material they can retrieve in a given time will be limited. For example, a user with a 14.4 kbps modem can retrieve information at a rate of about 1 kilobyte per second. If you have more than 30k of graphics on your page, that user will wait, on average, half a minute to see it. If you have more than 100k of graphics, the user might have to wait from 1½ to 2 minutes. Even with a 28.8 kbps modem, such a page could take a minute to load. A general rule of thumb is that the total amount of graphics on your Web page should be no more than 40 to 50 kilobytes. There are several ways to achieve this:

- Reduce the size of the images using your graphics software (not by simply changing the WIDTH and HEIGHT properties in the <IMG> tag).

- Reduce the number of colors used. Instead of saving an image in a 16.7 million color format, reduce it to 256 colors.

- Experiment with different graphic format types. Is the file size smaller with the JPEG format or the GIF? Can you compress the JPEG graphic without losing image quality?

- Use **thumbnails**—pictures that are reduced versions of your graphic images. Place the thumbnail image within a hypertext link to the larger, more detailed image, so that clicking the reduced image loads the better image. This gives users who really want to view the more well-defined image the option to do so.

- Reuse your images. If you are creating a Web presentation covering several pages, consider using the same background image for each page. Once a browser has retrieved the image file, it will store the image locally on the user's computer and will be able to retrieve it quickly to display it again, if necessary.

Finally, you should provide an alternate, text-only version of your Web page for those users who are either using a text-based browser or want to quickly load the information stored on your page without viewing inline images.

Manage Your Colors

Color can add a lot to your page, but it can also detract from it. Make sure that you have enough contrast between the text and the background. In other words, don't put dark text on a dark background or light text on a light background. Avoid clashing colors. A green text on a red background is not only difficult to read, it's an eyesore. Color is handled differently on different browsers, so you should try to view your page in most of the popular browsers. Certainly you should check to see how Netscape Navigator and Internet Explorer render your page.

You should also check to see how your page appears under different color depths. Your monitor might be capable of displaying 16.7 million colors, but users viewing your page might not be so lucky. View your page with your display set to 256 colors to see how it is rendered. When a 16.7 million color image is displayed at 256 colors, the browser must go through a process called **dithering**, in which the appearance of increased color depth is approximated. As shown in Figure 3-39, dithered images can sometimes appear grainy. Even if your computer is capable of displaying full-color images, you might want to consider creating all your images in 256 colors to control the effect of dithering.

Figure 3-39 ◀
Image dithering

original image   dithered image

To completely eliminate dithering, some Web authors recommend that you use the Safety Palette. The **Safety Palette** is a palette of 211 colors that are guaranteed to be displayed accurately on all browsers without dithering.

By limiting your color selections to the colors of the Safety Palette, you can be assured that your images will appear the same in the users' Web browsers as they do in your graphics software. You can learn more about the Safety Palette at http://www.microsoft.com/workshop/design/default.asp.

Quick Check

1. Discuss three reasons for using the GIF image format instead of the JPEG format.
2. Discuss three reasons for using the JPEG image format instead of the GIF format.
3. What HTML tag would you enter to display the alternate text "MidWest University" in place of the graphic image mwu.jpg?
4. What tag would you enter to align the mwu.jpg image with the top of the surrounding text?
5. What tag would you enter to wrap the surrounding text around the left side of the mwu.jpg image? For which browsers would this tag not work?
6. What tag would you enter to increase the horizontal and vertical space around the mwu.jpg image to 10 pixels?
7. The mwu.jpg image is 120 pixels wide by 85 pixels high. Using this information, what would you enter into your HTML file to increase the speed at which the page is rendered by the browser?
8. What is dithering? What is the Safety Palette?

You're finished working with the inline images on your Web page. You've learned about the different image formats supported by most browsers and their advantages and disadvantages. You've also seen how to control the appearance and placement of images on your Web page. In the next session you'll learn how to create an image that links to other Web pages.

SESSION 3.3

In this session you will learn about different types of image maps, and you'll create an image map and test it for the Space Expo Web page.

Introducing Image Maps

Tom has reviewed your Space Expo Web page and is pleased with the progress you're making. He's decided that the page should also include a map of the center's floor plan (shown in Figure 3-40) so that visitors will know where to go for different exhibits.

Figure 3-40 ◄
Map of the Center for Space Science and Engineering

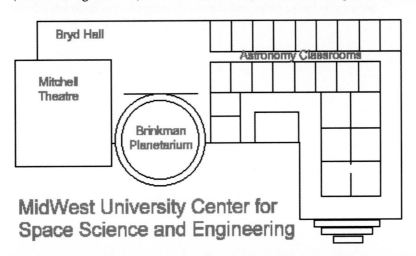

Tom wants the graphic of the map to be interactive, so that when a user clicks Mitchell Theatre on the floor plan, a page displaying events at the theatre will appear. If a user clicks the Brinkman Planetarium, a page about the planetarium will be displayed, and so forth. Figure 3-41 shows how these links will work on the map.

Figure 3-41 ◄
Linking the map to different Web pages

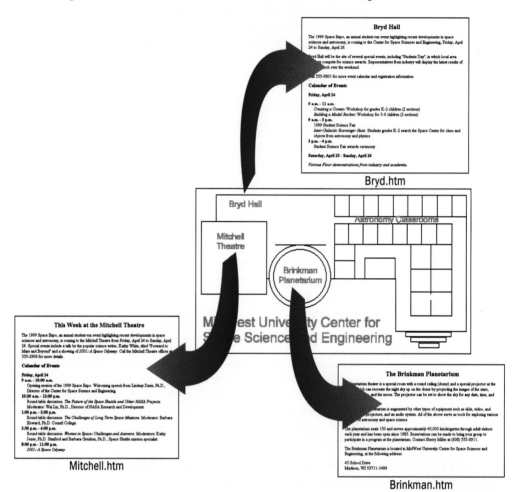

To use a single graphic to access multiple targets, you must set up hotspots within the image. A **hotspot** is a defined area of the image that acts as a hypertext link. One such hotspot for the floor plan of the Space Center would be the circular area that defines the location of the Brinkman Planetarium.

You define hotspots through the use of image maps. **Image maps** list the coordinates on the image that define the boundaries of the hotspots. Anytime a user clicks inside those boundaries, the hyperlink is activated. As a Web author, you can use two types of image maps: server-side image maps and client-side image maps. Each has advantages and disadvantages.

Server-Side Image Maps

In a **server-side image map**, the server, which is the computer that stores the Web page, controls the image map. As shown in Figure 3-42, the Web author includes the coordinates of the hotspots within the Web page, these coordinates are sent to a program running on the server whenever a user clicks the inline image, and the program uses them to activate the appropriate hyperlink.

Figure 3-42 ◀
Server-side
image map

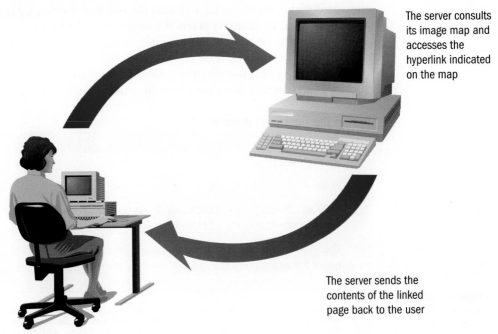

The server consults
its image map and
accesses the
hyperlink indicated
on the map

The server sends the
contents of the linked
page back to the user

The user clicks a hotspot on
the image

Server-side image maps are supported by most, if not all, graphical browsers. There are limitations to server-side image maps. Because a program on the server must process the image map, you cannot test your HTML code using local files. Also, server-side image maps can be slow to operate, because every time a user clicks the inline image, the request has to be processed by the Web server. On most Web browsers the target of a hyperlink is indicated in the browser's status bar, giving valuable feedback to the user but this is not done with the hotspots of a server-side image map. Because it is the server and not the Web browser that handles the hotspots, no feedback is given to the user regarding the location of the hotspots and their targets. These limitations can be overcome through the use of client-side image maps.

Client-Side Image Maps

In a **client-side image map**, you insert the image map into the HTML file, and the image map is processed locally by the Web browser. Because all of the processing is done locally, and not on the Web server, you can easily test your Web pages using the HTML files stored on your computer. Another advantage of client-side image maps is that they tend to be more responsive than server-side maps, because the information does not have to be sent over the network or dial-up connection. Finally, when a user moves the pointer over the inline image, the browser's status bar will display the target of each hotspot. The downside of client-side image maps is that older browsers do not support them.

As you become more experienced with HTML, you will probably want to support both server-side and client-side image maps in your Web pages. For now, however, you will concentrate solely on working with client-side image maps.

Before creating the image map, you'll add the floor plan graphic to the Expo1999.htm file. In addition to the graphic, you'll add a note that describes what the user should do to activate hyperlinks within the graphic's image map. This note should appear directly above the image. To achieve this, you can use the <BR> tag, which creates a line break and forces the following image or text to appear on its own line. The CLEAR property is often used within the <BR> tag to create the effect of starting a paragraph below the inline image. The CLEAR property starts the next line at the first point at which the page margin is clear of text or images. For example, using <BR CLEAR=LEFT> starts the next line when the left page margin is clear.

In this case, you'll use just the <BR> tag to force the floor plan graphic to appear directly below the text describing how to activate the hyperlinks in the graphic.

To add the floor plan graphic:

1. If you took a break after the previous session, open the Expo1999.htm file in your text editor.

2. At the bottom of the file, directly above the <H5> tag, enter the following HTML code:

   ```
   <H5 ALIGN=CENTER> Click each location for a list of events <BR>
   <IMG SRC="Layout.gif"> </H5>
   ```

   The <BR> tag creates a line break, causing the Layout.gif image to appear directly below the explanatory text. Your revised file should appear as shown in Figure 3-43.

Figure 3-43 ◀
Inserting the
floor plan image

```
<P>The 1999 Space Expo is located on the engineering and physics campus,
north of Granger Stadium, and is open to the public on April 24 (Students'
Day) from 10 a.m.-5 p.m., April 25 from 9 a.m.-7 p.m. and April 26 from
11 a.m.-5 p.m. Admission is $4.00 for the general public and $3.00 for
senior citizens and students. Children four and under will be admitted
free. </P>

<H5 ALIGN=CENTER > Click each location for a list of events <BR>
<IMG SRC="Layout.gif"> </H5>

<H5 ALIGN="CENTER">Sponsored by the Department of Astronomy and the Center
for Space Science and Engineering.</H5>

</BODY>
</HTML>
```

creates a new line
below the text

center floor plan

3. Save your changes to the Expo1999.htm file, and then open the file in your Web browser. Figure 3-44 shows the Layout image as it appears in the Web page.

Figure 3-44 ◀
Center floor
plan as it
appears in the
Web page

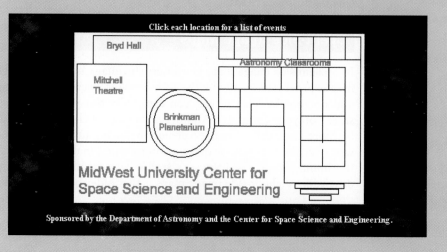

HTML

Now that you've inserted the floor plan image into the Web page, your next task is to turn this image into an image map.

Defining Image Map Hotspots

To create the image map, you could open the image in a graphics program and record the coordinates of the points corresponding to the hotspot boundaries. In practice, this is difficult and time-consuming, so you'll typically use a special program to create image map coordinates for you. There are several different programs available for this purpose, some of which are listed in Figure 3-45.

Figure 3-45 ◀
Software to create image maps

Title	URL	Platform
Web Hotspots 3.0 S Edition	http://www.concentric.net/~automata/hotspots.shtml	Windows
LiveImage	http://www.mediatec.com/	Windows
Mac-ImageMap	http://weyl.zib-berlin.de/imagemap/Mac-ImageMap.html	Macintosh
Mapedit	http://www.boutell.com/mapedit/	Windows, UNIX
MapServe	http://www.spub.ksu.edu/other/machttp_tools/mapserve/mapserve.html	Macintosh

Most image map programs generate the coordinates for hotspots as well as the necessary HTML tags. To help you understand the syntax of image maps better, you'll be given the coordinates and then use that information to create your own HTML code.

REFERENCE
window

DEFINING A CLIENT-SIDE IMAGE MAP

- Create the <MAP> tag that defines the different hotspots on the image as follows:
  <MAP NAME="*mapname*">
  <AREA SHAPE="*shape*" COORDS=*coordinates* HREF=*URL*>
  ...
  </MAP>
  where *mapname* is the name of the image map, *shape* is the type of hotspot (rectangle, circle, or polygon), *coordinates* are the locations of points that define the shape, and *URL* is the target of the hypertext link. You can have multiple <AREA> tags for each image map.
- Once the image map is created, add the USEMAP property to the <IMG> tag for the inline image as follows:
  <IMG SRC="*image*" USEMAP="#*mapname*">
  where *image* is the filename of the graphic, and *mapname* is the name of the image map defined in the <MAP> tag.

The general syntax for an image map tag is:

```
<MAP NAME="mapname">
<AREA SHAPE=shape COORDS="coordinates" HREF="URL">
</MAP>
```

The <MAP> tag gives the name of the image map. You can create different image maps for each inline image in your HTML file. Within the <MAP> tag, you use the <AREA>

tag to specify the areas of the image that will act as hotspots. You can include as many <AREA> tags as you need for the image map.

The <AREA> tag has three properties: SHAPE, COORDS, and HREF. The SHAPE property refers to the shape of the hotspot: RECT for a rectangular hotspot, CIRCLE for a circular hotspot, and POLY for irregular polygons.

In the COORDS property you enter coordinates to specify the hotspot's location. The values you enter depend on the shape of the hotspot. As you'll see, you need to enter different coordinates for a rectangular hotspot than you would for a circular one. Coordinates are expressed as a point's distance in pixels from the left and the top edges of the image. For example, the coordinates (123,45) refer to a point 123 pixels from the left edge and 45 pixels down from the top. If the coordinates of your <AREA> tags overlap, the browser uses the first tag in the list.

In the HREF parameter, you enter the URL for the hypertext link that the hotspot points to. You can use the value "NOHREF" in place of a URL if you do not want the hotspot to activate a hypertext link. This is a useful technique when you are first developing your image map, without all the hypertext links in place. The <AREA> tag then acts as a placeholder until the time when you have the hypertext links ready for use.

REFERENCE window

DEFINING IMAGE MAP HOTSPOTS

- Locate the <MAP> tag that defines the hotspots on the image.
- Within the <MAP> tag, enter the code for the type of hotspot(s).
  The syntax for a rectangular hotspot is:
  <AREA SHAPE=RECT COORDS="x_left, y_upper, x_right, y_lower"HREF="URL">
  where x_left, y_upper are the coordinates of the upper-left corner of the rectangle, and x_right,y_lower are the coordinates of the lower-right corner.
  The syntax for a circular hotspot is:
  <AREA SHAPE=CIRCLE COORDS="x_center, y_center, radius" HREF="URL">
  where x_center, y_center is the center of the circle, and radius is the circle's radius.
  The syntax for a polygonal hotspot is:
  <AREA SHAPE=POLY COORDS="x1, y1, x2, y2, x3, y3, ... " HREF="URL" >
  where x1, y1, x2, y2, x3, y3, ... are the coordinates of the vertices of the polygon.

Before creating your <AREA> tags, you'll add the <MAP> tag to the Expo1999.htm file and assign the name "Layout" to the image map.

To insert the <MAP> tag:

1. Return to the Expo1999.htm file in your text editor.

2. Go to the bottom of the file and enter the following directly above the </BODY> tag:

```
<MAP NAME="Layout">
</MAP>
```

With the <MAP> tag in place, you must next determine what kinds of areas the image map will require. Tom wants the image to include hotspots for the Mitchell Theatre, the Brinkman Planetarium, and Bryd Hall. The locations of these three hotspots are shown in Figure 3-46.

Figure 3-46 ◀
Hotspots
for the floor
plan image

Bryd Hall hotspot

Mitchell Theatre
hotspot

Brinkman
Planetarium hotspot

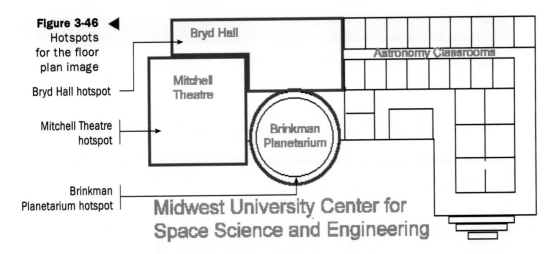

You'll define the hotspot for the Mitchell Theatre first. The hotspot for the Mitchell Theatre will be a rectangle.

Creating a Rectangular Hotspot

Two points define a rectangular hotspot: the upper-left corner and the lower-right corner. These points for the Mitchell Theatre hotspot are located at (5,45) and (108,157). In other words, the upper-left corner is 5 pixels to the left and 45 pixels down from the left and top edges of the image, respectively, and the lower-right corner is 108 pixels to the left and 157 pixels down. The hotspot will link to the file Mitchell.htm, a page with information on events at the Mitchell Theatre.

To insert the Mitchell Theatre <AREA> tag:

1. Insert a new blank line between the opening and closing <MAP> tags you just entered.
2. Type the following in the new blank line:

   `<AREA SHAPE=RECT COORDS="5,45,108,157" HREF="Mitchell.htm">`

   Note that the coordinates are entered as a series of four numbers separated by commas. Because this is a rectangular hotspot, HTML expects that the first two numbers represent the coordinates for the upper-left corner of the rectangle, and the second two numbers indicate the location of the lower-right corner.

Next you'll enter the <AREA> tag for the Brinkman Planetarium, a circular hotspot.

Creating a Circular Hotspot

The coordinates required for a circular hotspot differ from those of a rectangular hotspot. A circular hotspot is defined by the locations of its center and its radius. The circle representing the Brinkman Planetarium is centered at the coordinates (161,130), and it has a radius of 49 pixels. The hotspot will link to the file Brinkman.htm. You need to enter this <AREA> tag into the Expo1999.htm file.

To insert the Brinkman Planetarium <AREA> tag:

1. Insert a new blank line directly below the Mitchell Theatre <AREA> tag.
2. Type the following in the new blank line:

   `<AREA SHAPE=CIRCLE COORDS="161,130,49" HREF="Brinkman.htm">`

The final hotspot you have to define is for Bryd Hall. Because of its irregular shape, you have to create a polygonal hotspot.

Creating a Polygonal Hotspot

When you want to specify an irregular shape for a hotspot, you must use the POLY value for the SHAPE property. To create a polygonal hotspot, you enter the coordinates for each vertex in the shape.

The coordinates for the vertices of the Bryd Hall hotspot are (29,4), (29,41), (111,41), (111,78), (213,78), and (213,4). See Figure 3-47. The HREF for this hotspot is the file Bryd.htm.

Figure 3-47 ◄
Coordinates for the Bryd Hall hotspot

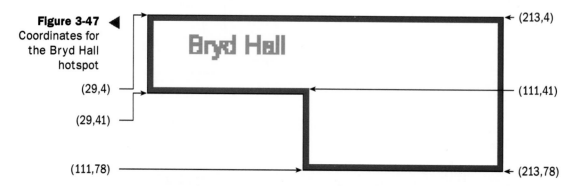

With the coordinate information in hand, you can create the final <AREA> tag for your image map.

To insert the Bryd Hall <AREA> tag:

1. Insert a new blank line directly below the Brinkman Planetarium <AREA> tag.

2. Type the following in the new blank line:

   ```
   <AREA SHAPE=POLY COORDS="29,4,29,41,111,41,111,78,213,78,213,4"
   HREF="Bryd.htm">
   ```

   Figure 3-48 shows the completed list of <AREA> tags for the Layout image map. Compare these values with the ones you've entered, to confirm that you entered them correctly.

Figure 3-48 ◄
Layout image map and hotspots

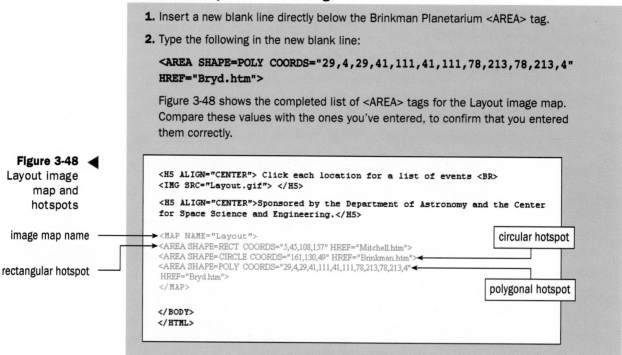

With all of the <AREA> tags in place, you're finished defining the image map. Your next task is to instruct the browser to use the Layout image map with the Layout inline image. Then you'll test the image to confirm that it works properly.

Using an Image Map

The final step in adding an image map to a Web page is to add the USEMAP property to the <IMG> tag for the image map graphic. The USEMAP property tells the browser the name of the image map to associate with the inline image. The syntax for accessing an image map is:

```
<IMG SRC="image" USEMAP="#mapname">
```

Here, *mapname* is the name assigned to the NAME property in the <MAP> tag. Note that you have to place a pound sign (#) before the image map name. You named your image map "Layout" and you inserted the Layout.gif into your Web page. Now you have to add the USEMAP property to the <IMG> tag to associate Layout.gif with the Layout image map.

To assign the Layout image map to the Layout graphic and test the image map:

1. Locate the Layout.gif <IMG> tag in the Expo1999.htm file.

2. Add the following property to the tag: **USEMAP="#Layout"**.

   The completed <IMG> tag should appear as shown in Figure 3-49.

Figure 3-49 ◄
the image map
specified

the image
map specified

```
<H5 ALIGN=CENTER> Click each location for a list of events <BR>
<IMG SRC="Layout.gif" USEMAP="#Layout"> </H5>

<H5 ALIGN="CENTER">Sponsored by the Department of Astronomy and the Center
for Space Science and Engineering.</H5>

<MAP NAME="Layout">
<AREA SHAPE=RECT COORDS="5,45,108,157" HREF="Mitchell.htm">
<AREA SHAPE=CIRCLE COORDS="161,130,49" HREF="Brinkman.htm">
<AREA SHAPE=POLY COORDS="29,4,29,41,111,41,111,78,213,78,213,4"
 HREF="Bryd.htm">
</MAP>

</BODY>
</HTML>
```

3. Save the changes to the Expo1999.htm file.

   Now that you've created the image map, you're ready to test it in your Web browser.

4. Reload the Space Expo Web page in your Web browser.

5. Scroll down to the Layout graphic and place the pointer over the graphic. Note that the pointer changes to a hand 🖑 when it is positioned over a hotspot. Note as well that the status bar displays the URL for that particular hotspot. See Figure 3-50.

Figure 3-50 ◄
Placing the
pointer over the
Mitchell
Theatre
hotspot

pointer changes to a
hand as it passes
over a hotspot

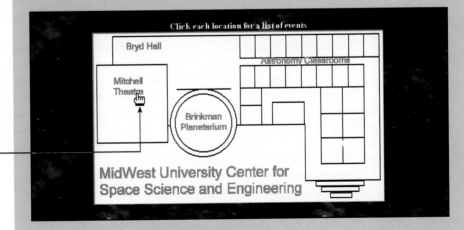

TROUBLE? If your image does not have a red border around it, don't worry. The border is created by Netscape Navigator and will be discussed in the section that follows.

6. Click within the Mitchell Theatre hotspot in the floor plan graphic. Your Web browser displays the page listing the events at the Mitchell Theatre over the Expo weekend.

7. Click the **Back** button in your Web browser to return to the 1999 Space Expo page.

8. Test the other hotspots in the graphic and confirm that they jump to the appropriate page of events. When you're finished working with those pages, return to the Expo page.

If you are using Netscape Navigator, you will notice that the floor plan image is surrounded by a red border that is not displayed when you view the image in a graphics program. Where did this border come from? The border is placed around the image by the Netscape Navigator browser to identify the image as a hyperlink to other Web pages. (*Note:* If you are using Internet Explorer, you will not see this border.) The border color is red because that is the color you specified earlier for hyperlinks. You can remove the border with the BORDER property.

Using the BORDER Property

The BORDER property allows you to create a border to surround your inline images. The syntax for changing the border width is:

```
<IMG SRC="image" BORDER=value>
```

where *value* is the width of the border in pixels. An inline image that does not contain hyperlinks to other documents will, by default, not contain a border. However, if the image does contain hyperlinks to other documents, Netscape Navigator will create a border 2 pixels wide (Internet Explorer will not). If you want to either create a border (for an image that does not have one) or remove a border, you can do so by specifying the appropriate border width.

Tom thinks that the floor plan image would look better without a border, so you'll remove it from the floor plan by specifying a border width of 0 pixels. (*Note:* You should complete the following steps even if you're not using Netscape Navigator, to ensure that your page would look good if a user accessed it using Netscape Navigator.)

To remove the border from the layout graphic:

1. Return to the Expo1999.htm file in your Web browser.

2. Go to the <IMG> tag for the Layout.gif inline image.

3. Insert the property **BORDER=0** within the <IMG> tag.

4. Save your changes to the file, and then reload it in your Web browser.

   If you are running Netscape Navigator, you should see that the border has been removed. If you are running Internet Explorer, you won't notice a difference in your page.

This example illustrates an important principle of page design: you should examine your page in different browsers. If you had used only Internet Explorer to view your page, you would not have learned of the border issue for Netscape Navigator.

The BORDER property works for both Internet Explorer and Netscape Navigator, although it is used differently with Internet Explorer. In the case of Internet Explorer, applying the BORDER property to an image without hyperlinks will create an invisible border around the image, whereas for images that contain hyperlinks, the border color will be the same as the link color.

Tom reviews the completed 1999 Space Expo page. He's pleased with the work you've done and will get back to you with any changes he wants you to make. For now you can close your browser and text editor.

To close your work:

1. Close your Web browser.

2. Return to your text editor, and then close the Expo1999.htm file.

Figure 3-51 shows the finished Web page, and Figure 3-52 shows the complete text of the Expo1999.htm file.

Figure 3-51 ◀
Completed
1999 Space
Expo Web page

More than 60 exhibits and events await visitors at the 1999 Space Expo,
Looking Towards the Future
Friday-Sunday, April 24-26

The 1999 Space Expo is an annual, student-run event that showcases recent developments in astronomy and space sciences and demonstrates how these developments can be applied to everyday life. The event includes student, government and industrial exhibits, and features presentations from NASA, Ball Aerospace, Rockwell, and IBM.

The 1999 Space Expo will feature activities for the kids, including *Creating a Comet*, *Building a Model Rocket*, and *The Inter-Galactic Scavenger Hunt*. Friday is Students' Day, with school children in grades K-8 displaying astronomy and space science projects and competing for individual and school achievement awards.

Professor Greg Stewart's famous astronomy show is also coming to the Space Expo. Professor Stewart will show the wonders of the night sky and discuss the nature of quasars, exploding stars, and black holes. Presentations will be at the Brinkman Planetarium at 1 p.m. and 3 p.m., Friday through Sunday.

Please check out these other events:

- Bryd Hall   Rockwell representatives and graduate students will display some of the latest advances in robotics for use in the Space Shuttle missions.
- Mitchell Theatre   Famous astronomer and popular science writer, Kathy White, will present a talk, "Forward to Mars and Beyond," on Saturday at 7 p.m. Tickets for this very special event are $12. Seating is limited.
- Astronomy Classrooms   Graduate students and professors display the results of their research in atmospherics, satellite technology, climatology, and space engineering.

The 1999 Space Expo is located on the engineering and physics campus, north of Granger Stadium, and is open to the public on April 24 (Students' Day) from 10 a.m.-5 p.m., April 25 from 9 a.m.-7 p.m. and April 26 from 11 a.m.-5 p.m. Admission is $4.00 for the general public and $3.00 for senior citizens and students. Children four and under will be admitted free.

Click each location for a list of events

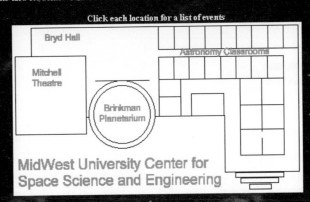

Sponsored by the Department of Astronomy and the Center for Space Science and Engineering.

Figure 3-52 ◀

Complete
Expo1999.htm
file

```
<HTML>
<HEAD>
<TITLE>The 1999 Space Expo</TITLE>
</HEAD>
<BODY BACKGROUND="Space.jpg" TEXT=WHITE LINK=RED VLINK=TURQUOISE>

<H1 ALIGN="CENTER"><IMG SRC="LogoAnim.gif" ALT="The 1999 Space Expo"
 WIDTH=414 HEIGHT=209></H1>

<H3 ALIGN="CENTER">More than 60 exhibits and events await visitors at the
1999 Space Expo, <BR>
<I><FONT COLOR=YELLOW>Looking Towards the Future</FONT></I> <BR>
Friday-Sunday, April 24-26 </H3>

<P><IMG SRC="Center.jpg" ALT="The MWU Center for Space Science and
Engineering" ALIGN=LEFT VSPACE=5 HSPACE=10 WIDTH=280 HEIGHT=186>
The 1999 Space Expo is an annual, student-run event that showcases recent
developments in astronomy and space sciences and demonstrates how these
developments can be applied to everyday life. The event includes student,
government and industrial exhibits, and features presentations from NASA,
Ball Aerospace, Rockwell, and IBM.</P>

<P>The 1999 Space Expo will feature activities for the kids, including
<I>Creating a Comet</I>, <I>Building a Model Rocket</I>, and <I>The
Inter-Galactic Scavenger Hunt</I>. Friday is Students' Day, with school
children in grades K-8 displaying astronomy and space science projects and
competing for individual and school achievement awards.</P>

<P>Professor Greg Stewart's famous astronomy show is also coming to the
Space Expo. Professor Stewart will show the wonders of the night sky and
discuss the nature of quasars, exploding stars, and black holes.
Presentations will be at the Brinkman Planetarium at 1 p.m. and 3 p.m.,
Friday through Sunday. </P>

<P>Please check out these other events:</P>

<UL>
<B><LI> <A HREF="Bryd.htm"> Bryd Hall </A> </B>     Rockwell
representatives and graduate students will display some of the latest
advances in robotics for use in the Space Shuttle
missions.</LI>

<B><LI> <A HREF="Theatre.htm"> Mitchell Theatre </A> </B>    
Famous astronomer and popular science writer, Kathy White, will present a
talk, "Forward to Mars and Beyond," on Saturday at 7 p.m. Tickets for this
very special event are $12. Seating is limited.</LI>

<B><LI> <A HREF="Classes.htm"> Astronomy Classrooms </A> </B>    
Graduate students and professors display the results of their research in
atmospherics, satellite technology, climatology, and space engineering.</LI>
</UL>

<P>The 1999 Space Expo is located on the engineering and physics campus,
north of Granger Stadium, and is open to the public on April 24 (Students'
Day) from 10 a.m.-5 p.m., April 25 from 9 a.m.-7 p.m. and April 26 from
11 a.m.-5 p.m. Admission is $4.00 for the general public and $3.00 for
senior citizens and students. Children four and under will be admitted
free. </P>

<H5 ALIGN=CENTER> Click each location for a list of events <BR>
<IMG SRC="Layout.gif" USEMAP="#Layout" BORDER=0> </H5>

<H5 ALIGN="CENTER">Sponsored by the Department of Astronomy and the Center
for Space Science and Engineering.</H5>

<MAP NAME="Layout">
<AREA SHAPE=RECT COORDS="5,45,108,157" HREF="Mitchell.htm">
<AREA SHAPE=CIRCLE COORDS="161,130,49" HREF="Brinkman.htm">
<AREA SHAPE=POLY COORDS="29,4,29,41,111,41,111,78,213,78,213,4"
 HREF="Bryd.htm">
</MAP>

</BODY>
</HTML>
```

Quick Check

1 What is a hotspot? What is an image map?

2 What are the two types of image maps? List the advantages and disadvantages of each.

3 What HTML tag would you enter to define a rectangular hotspot with the upper-left edge of the rectangle at the point (5,20) and the lower-right edge located at (85,100)? Assume that if the user clicks the hotspot, the file Oregon.htm will be displayed.

4 What tag would you enter for a circular hotspot centered at (44,81), with a radius of 23 pixels, and linked to the LA.htm file?

5. What tag would you enter for a hotspot that connects the points (5,10), (5,35), (25,35), (30,20), and (15,10) and is linked to the Hawaii.htm file?

6. What HTML tag would you enter to assign an image map named States to the graphics file WestCoast.gif?

7. What HTML tag would you enter to increase the border around the WestCoast graphic to 5 pixels?

You've finished enhancing the 1999 Space Expo page with graphics. You've seen how to create an image map so that a single graphic can link to several different Web pages. You've also learned about some of the design issues involved in adding graphics to a Web page, and how to choose the correct graphic type for a particular image. Using the knowledge you've gained, you're ready to work on new design challenges that Tom has for you.

Tutorial Assignments

After reviewing the finished 1999 Space Expo Web page, Tom made a few changes to its contents. He also has a few additional suggestions for you to implement. He would like you to add a hotspot to the Layout image that points to a page listing the talks given in various classrooms. He also would like you to work with the other Web pages to improve their appearance.

To implement Tom's suggestions:

1. In your text editor, open the Mitchtxt.htm file in the TAssign folder of the Tutorial.03 folder on your Student Disk, and then save the file as Mitchell.htm in the same folder.

2. Use the Stars.jpg file as your background image for this page. Change the color of the text on the page to white.

3. Change the font of the heading "This Week at the Mitchell Theatre" to use the hexadecimal color value 00CC00. Use the Arial font to display the heading. In case a user's computer does not have Arial, specify that Helvetica and then, finally, Sans Serif should be used instead.

4. Change the color of the "Calendar of Events" line to the hexadecimal color value 00CC00.

5. Change the color of the day and date lines (for example Friday, April 24) to the RGB triplet (255,0,0).

6. Save your changes to the Mitchell.htm file.

7. Repeat Steps 2 through 5 for the Brydtxt.htm file in the TAssign folder, saving the file as Bryd.htm in the same folder.

8. Open the Brinktxt.htm file in the TAssign folder of the Tutorial.03 folder on your Student Disk, and then save the file as Brinkman.htm in the same folder.

9. Change the background color value to (0,153,204). (*Hint:* You will have to convert this RGB triplet to hexadecimal, using one of the resources mentioned in Figure 3-7.) Change the text color value to white.

10. Change the color of the heading "The Brinkman Planetarium" to (255,255,204).

11. Insert an inline image from the Equip.jpg file at the beginning of the first paragraph. Align the image with the right edge of the page. Increase the horizontal and vertical space to 5 pixels. Enter "The Planetarium Projector" as alternate text for the image.

12. The inline image is 326 pixels wide by 201 pixels high. With this information, how could you increase the speed at which your Web browser loads this page? Implement your response to increase the speed. Save your changes to the file.

13. Open the Expotxt.htm file in the TAssign folder of the Tutorial.03 folder on your Student Disk, and then save the file as Expo1999.htm in the same folder.

14. Add a polygonal hotspot to the Layout image map that connects to the Class.htm file. The coordinates of the hotspot are (215,4), (215,132), (311,132), (311,213), (424,213), and (424,4).

15. Load the Expo1999.htm file into your Web browser and confirm that the hotspot to the Class.htm file works correctly. Examine the appearances of the other Web pages for any errors.

16. Save your work, and then close your Web browser and text editor.

Case Problems

1. Creating a New Products Page for Jackson Electronics Paul Reichtman is a sales manager at Jackson Electronics in Seattle, Washington. He wants you to create a Web presentation that advertises three new products released in the last month: the ScanMaster scanner, the LaserPrint 5000 printer, and the Print/Scan 150 combination printer-scanner-copier.

The press releases for the three products and the general announcement have already been put into HTML files for you. The general announcement is shown in Figure 3-53.

Figure 3-53 ◀

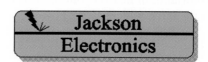

**Jackson Electronics Introduces
a New Line of Products**

Jackson Electronics announced this month a new line of small business printers, copiers and scanners. Designed to meet the growing need for economical scanning and printing solutions, the new products do not sacrifice quality or dependability.

The ScanMaster continues Jackson Electronics' leadership in the field of flatbed scanners. With the patented "Single-Pass" technology, the ScanMaster is fast, with image quality better than multiple-pass scanners.

Building on its popular line of laser printers, Jackson Electronics introduces the LaserPrint 5000. The LaserPrint 5000 prints b&w text at 12 ppm. and its memory expands up to 24 megabytes for graphic-intensive print jobs.

The new Print/Scan 150 combines the benefits of a printer, copier and scanner - all in one! And all without sacrificing quality. Save money (and space) with this three-in-one product.

Interested? Click one of the product names to the left for more information.

Paul would like you to enhance the appearance of this page and the other pages with special color and graphics. The pages should also be linked through an image map. A preview of the page you'll create is shown in Figure 3-54.

Figure 3-54 ◀

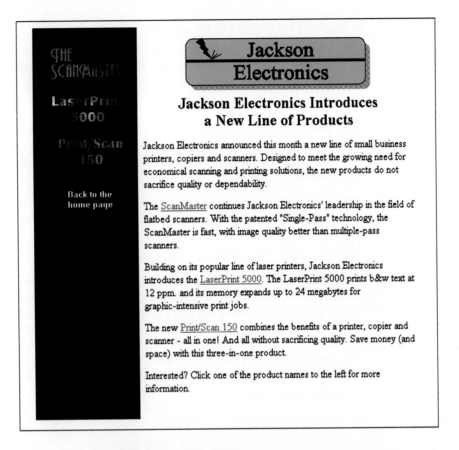

You'll create the left bar effect shown in the figure by using a background image consisting of a single line that is 1 pixel high and 1600 pixels wide. The first 180 pixels of the line are black, and the remainder of the line is white. The browser repeatedly inserts this image into the page background, but because the image is so wide, the bar is not repeated across the width of the page, only down the length of it. An inline image with a black background is placed on the left edge of the page to complete the effect. You'll use this background and image combination for all four of the documents that Paul gives you.

To create Paul's Web presentation:

1. In your text editor, open the Newtext.htm file in the Cases folder of the Tutorial.03 folder on your Student Disk, and then save the file as Jackson.htm in the same folder.

2. Change the background image to the Bars.gif file.

3. Insert the file Product.gif as an inline image at the top of the page. Align the image with the left edge of the page. Increase the space around the image to 5 pixels in all directions. Set the border width of the inline image to 0 pixels.

4. Create an image map named "Product_List."

5. Add four rectangular hotspots to the Product_List image map. The first rectangle has the coordinates (4,2) and (143,66) and is linked to the Scanner.htm file. The second has the coordinates (4,68) and (143,137) and is linked to the Printer.htm file. The third has coordinates at (4,139) and (143,208) and is linked to the PS150.htm file. The final hotspot has the coordinates (4,210) and (143,278) and is linked to the Jackson.htm file.

6. Add to the Product.gif <IMG> tag the property that uses the Product_List image map.

7. Link the first occurrences of the words "ScanMaster," "LaserPrint 5000," and "Print/Scan 150" in the body of the press release to the files Scanner.htm, Printer.htm, and PS150.htm, respectively.

8. Save your changes to the Jackson.htm file.

9. Open the files Scantext.htm, Printext.htm, and PStext.htm, and then save them as Scanner.htm, Printer.htm, and PS150.htm, respectively, in the Cases folder of the Tutorial.03 folder.

10. For each of the three files, repeat Steps 2 through 6.

11. At the bottom of each of the three files, insert a single line with the text "Return to the Jackson Electronics home page." in the <H5> heading tag. Specify that the line of text should be centered and linked to the Jackson.htm file. Save your changes to the file.

12. Load the Jackson.htm file in your Web browser and confirm that the hypertext links in the image map work properly. Confirm that the hypertext links in the main text also work correctly.

13. Close your Web browser and your text editor.

2. Announcing the SFSF '99 You are in charge of publicity for the 1999 San Francisco Science Fiction Convention (also known as SFSF '99). One of your jobs is to create a Web presentation announcing the three guests of honor for the convention. You've decided to create a home page with three thumbnail photos of the guests combined into a single image map, which will then be linked to separate biography pages for each person. The biography pages will also contain the photos, but in a larger and more detailed format. A preview of the home page is shown in Figure 3-55, and a preview of one of the biography pages is shown in Figure 3-56.

Figure 3-55 ◀

SF SF '99

Welcome to the 1999 San Francisco Science Fiction Convention

The SFSF '99 committee welcomes you to the annual San Francisco Science Fiction convention. The convention starts Thursday, August 19th at 8 p.m. with the Get-Together party in Derleith Hall. The fun doesn't stop until Sunday morning on August 22nd. Be sure to attend Friday's costume party and *"You Don't Know Jack"* trivia contest.

The guests of honor at this year's convention are: Philip Forrest, famous fan and fiction follower; Karen Chamas, author of the award-winning novel *The Unicorn Express*, and Jeffrey Unwin, critic and editor of *The Magazine of Speculative Fiction*.

Click the images above for guest biographies

Registration is $35 at the door, $30 in advance. It's worth it!

For more information and a calendar of events, contact:

SF SF '99
301 Howlitze Lane
San Francisco, CA 94201
(311)555-2989

Figure 3-56 ◀

Biography

Name: Philip Forrest
Age: 68
Occupation: Professional fan and editor of *Horizons*
Favorite Fish: Huh? What? Fried, I guess.
Comments: I'm thrilled to be selected fan guest of honor. I look forward to seeing everyone at SFSF '99

Phil has been a fan favorite for forty years. His knowledge of science fiction is legendary and anyone who has seen his immense magazine collection knows where that knowledge came from! As editor of *Horizons*, Phil has won two Tucker awards for best fanzine of year.

To create the SFSF '99 Web presentation:

1. In your text editor, open the Forsttxt.htm file in the Cases folder of the Tutorial.03 folder on your Student Disk, and then save the file as Forrest.htm in the same folder.

2. Change the background color to the RGB triplet (255, 255, 204).

3. At the top of the page, before the <H2> Biography heading, insert the Forrest.jpg inline image aligned with the left margin. Specify 10 pixels of horizontal space and 5 pixels of vertical space.

4. After the Comments line, change the <BR> tag so that it starts the next line below the inline image you inserted in Step 3. What would happen if you left the <BR> tag in its original condition?

5. Save your changes.

6. Open the file Charntxt.htm in the Cases folder of the Tutorial.03 folder, and then repeat Steps 2 through 5. Save the file as Charnas.htm in the same folder. Then open the file Unwintxt.htm in the Cases folder and repeat Steps 2 through 5. Save the file as Unwin.htm.

7. Open the SFSFtxt.htm file in the Cases folder of the Tutorial.03 folder on your Student Disk, and then save the file as SFSF.htm in the same folder.

8. Change the background color value to (255, 255, 204).

9. Within the <H2> heading at the top of the page, insert the inline image SFSF.gif. Place a <BR> tag after the image so that it resides on its own line. Color the heading text blue.

10. After the description of the guests of honor, insert a centered <H4> tag with the inline image Guests.jpg on one line, followed by a <BR> tag and then the text "Click the images above for guest biographies" on the second line. Color the text blue.

11. Create an image map named "Guests" with three rectangular hotspots. The first hotspot has the coordinates (0,0) and (70,70) and points to the Forrest.htm file; the second has coordinates at (71,0) and (140,70) and points to the Charnas.htm file; and the third has coordinates at (141,0) and (210,70) and points to the Unwin.htm file. Apply this image map to the Guests.jpg inline image.

12. For the first occurrences of the names of the guests of honor, create hypertext links that point to their biography pages.

13. Save your changes.

14. Open the SFSF.htm file in your Web browser and check all hypertext links to verify that they work properly.

15. Close your Web browser and your text editor.

3. Creating an Online Menu for Kelsey's Diner You've been asked to create an online menu for Kelsey's Diner, a well-established restaurant in Worcester, Massachusetts, so that patrons can order carry-out dishes from the Web. The manager, Cindy Towser, shows you a text file with the current carry-out breakfast menu, displayed in Figure 3-57. She wants you to spice it up with colors and graphics. She also wants you to create hyperlinks to the lunch and dinner carry-out menus. A preview of the page that you'll create is shown in Figure 3-58.

Figure 3-57 ◄

Breakfast Menu
Served 6:30 a.m. - 11:00 a.m.

Smoked Trout
   Fluffy scrambled eggs with smoked trout, goat cheese & scallions served with oven-roasted potatoes & toast. 5.45
French Toast
   Three thick slices of French bread dipped in egg batter and served crisp & golden brown with syrup. 3.25
Belgian Waffle
   Crisp malt Belgian waffle & syrup. 3.95
Breakfast Fruit Plate
   Fresh seasonal fruit with yogurt or cottage cheese & Kelsey's famous Bran Muffin. 3.95
Huevos Rancheros
   Two eggs on a flour tortilla with thick chili sauce, shredded Monterey Jack & homemade salsa. 4.95
Eggs
   Any style with oven-roasted potatoes & toast. 2.95
Lox & Bagels
   Nova lox, cream cheese, onion, cucumber & tomatoes. 5.95

Figure 3-58 ◄

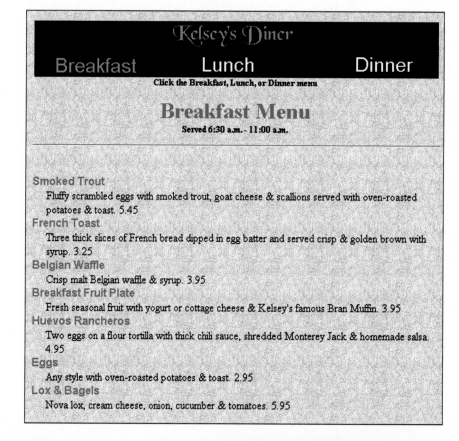

To create the Web menu for Kelsey's Diner:

1. In your text editor, open the Breaktxt.htm file in the Cases folder of the Tutorial.03 folder on your Student Disk, and then save the file as Breakfst.htm in the same folder.

2. Use the graphic file Tan.jpg as a background image for this page.

3. Insert the graphic Breakfst.gif at the top of the page within a set of <H5> tags. Center the image on the page. Directly below the image, after a line break, insert the text "Click the Breakfast, Lunch, or Dinner menu" (within the <H5> tags used for the inline image).

4. Change the text of the title "Breakfast Menu" to green and increase the point size of the text by three points.

5. For the name of each dish in the menu, bold the text, change the color of the text to green, and specify that the text should appear in either the Arial, Helvetica, or Sans Serif font (in that order).

6. At the bottom of the page, insert an image map named "Menu." The image map should have three rectangular hotspots. The first hotspot has the coordinates (20,40) and (156,77) and points to the Breakfst.htm file; the second has coordinates at (241,40) and (336,77) and points to the Lunch.htm file; the third has coordinates at (464,40) and (568,77) and points to the Dinner.htm file. Apply this image map to the Breakfst.gif inline image.

7. Repeat Steps 2 through 6 with the Lunchtxt.htm file in the Cases folder of the Tutorial.03 folder, but place the Lunch.gif image at the top of the page, and save the file as "Lunch.htm."

8. Repeat Steps 2 through 6 with the Dinnrtxt.htm file in the Cases folder of the Tutorial.03 folder, but place the Dinner.gif image at the top of the page, and save the file as "Dinner.htm."

9. Open the Breakfst.htm file in your browser and test the hyperlinks. Verify that the pages look correct and that the inline image changes to reflect the change in the menu.

10. Print a copy of the Breakfast menu, and then print the source code for all three files.

11. Close your Web browser and your text editor.

EXPLORE   **4. Creating a Listing for Tri-State Realty** Tri-State Realty is in the process of putting their listings on the World Wide Web. You've been asked to create some pages for their Web site. You've been given the following information for your first page, a listing describing property located at 22 Northshore Drive:

"This is a must see. Large waterfront home overlooking Mills Lake. It comes complete with three bedrooms, a huge master bedroom, hot tub, family room, large office or den, and three-car garage. Wood boat ramp. Great condition!"

In addition, the owners of the property have included the following main points they want to be emphasized in the Web page:

- 2900 sq. feet

- 15 years old

- updated electrical, plumbing, and heating systems

- central air conditioning

- near school, park, and shopping center

- nice, quiet neighborhood

- asking price: $280,000

Finally, you've been given the following files (in the Cases folder of the Tutorial.03 folder on your Student Disk):

- House.jpg, which contains a photo of the property; size is 243 × 163

- Tristate.gif, the company logo; size is 225 × 100

- Listings.gif, a graphic image showing the various listing categories; size is 600 × 100

- TSBack.gif, the background texture used on all Tri-State Web pages

Using this information, you'll create a Web page for the property at 22 Northshore Drive. The design of the page is up to you, but it should include the following:

- an appropriately titled heading

- a paragraph describing the house

- a bulleted list of the main points of interest

- the photo of the house, the company logo, and the graphic of the different listing categories (use the company background file as your page's background)

- at least one example of spot color

- at least one example of a font displaying a different face and size from the surrounding text

- alternative text for the logo and house photo images

- height and width information for all inline images

- the listings graphic converted to an image map, with the following hotspots (target files are not included):

  - rectangular hotspot at (5,3) (182,44) that points to the Newhome.htm file

  - rectangular hotspot at (12,62) (303,95) that points to the Mansions.htm file

  - rectangular hotspot at (210,19) (374,60) that points to the Business.htm file

  - rectangular hotspot at (375,1) (598,44) that points to the Family.htm file

  - rectangular hotspot at (378,61) (549,96) that points to the Apartmnt.htm file

- appropriately labeled hypertext links that point to the same files as indicated in the image map

- your name, as Web page author, in italics

Save the page as Tristate.htm in the Cases folder of the Tutorial.03 folder on your Student Disk, and then print a copy of your page and the HTML code. Close your Web browser and your text editor when finished.

TUTORIAL 4

Designing a Web Page with Tables

Creating a Products Page

OBJECTIVES

In this tutorial you will:

- Create a text table

- Create a graphical table using the <TABLE>, <TR>, and <TD> tags

- Create table headers and captions

- Control the appearance of a table and table text

- Create table cells that span several rows or columns

- Use nested tables to enhance page design

- Learn about Internet Explorer extensions for use with tables

Middle Age Arts

Middle Age Arts is a company that creates and sells replicas of historic European works of art for home and garden use. The company specializes in sculpture, tapestries, prints, friezes, and busts that evoke the artistic styles of the Middle Ages and the Renaissance.

Nicole Swanson, an advertising executive at Middle Age Arts, is directing the effort to create Web pages for the company. She hopes that a Web page can improve the company's visibility, as well as make it easier for customers to place orders. The type of information she wants to provide on the Web includes a description of the company, contact information for individuals who want to place an order over the phone, a list of stores that distribute Middle Age Arts products, and a display of the company's merchandise.

Nicole has asked you to work on creating Web pages for the Gargoyle Collection, a new line of Middle Age Arts products featuring gargoyles recreated from the walls and towers of Gothic buildings and churches. The page should display the product name, item number, description, and price. Information of this type is best displayed in a table, so to create the page, you'll have to learn how to work with tables in HTML.

SESSION

4.1

In this session you will learn how to add tables to a Web page, starting with simple text tables and then moving to graphical tables, and you'll learn the advantages of each approach. You'll also learn how to define table rows, cells, and headings with HTML tags. Finally, you'll add a caption to your table and learn how to control the caption's placement on the page.

Tables on the World Wide Web

Nicole has been considering the prototype page she wants you to create for the Gargoyle Collection. She wants you to start out small. The page will eventually have to display more than 50 separate items, but for now she is only interested in a small sample of that number. With that in mind, Nicole has selected three products, shown in a table format in Figure 4-1, that she wants you to place on the Web page.

Figure 4-1
Nicole's
products table

Name	Item #	Type	Finish	Price
Bacchus	48059	Wall Mount	Interior Plaster	$95
Praying Gargoyle	48159	Garden Figure	Gothic Stone	$125
Gargoyle Judge	48222	Bust	Interior Plaster	$140

There are two ways to insert a table of information on a Web page: you can create either a text table or a graphical table. A **text table**, like the one shown in Figure 4-2, contains only text, evenly spaced out on the page in rows and columns. Text tables use only standard typewriter characters, so that even a line in a text table is created by repeating a typographical character, such as a hyphen, underline, or equals sign.

Figure 4-2
A text table

all table elements are
created using
typewriter characters

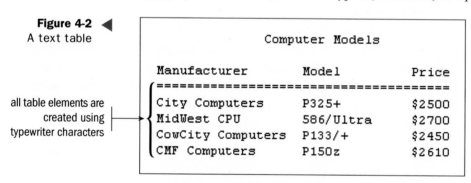

```
                 Computer Models

Manufacturer          Model           Price
=============================================
City Computers        P325+           $2500
MidWest CPU           586/Ultra       $2700
CowCity Computers     P133/+          $2450
CMF Computers         P150z           $2610
```

A **graphical table**, as shown in Figure 4-3, appears as a graphical element on the Web page. A graphical table allows you to include design elements such as color, shading, and borders in a table. Because of this, you have greater control over the table's appearance. You can control the size of individual table cells and text alignment. You can even create cells that span several rows or columns.

Figure 4-3
A graphical
table

color background

a table cell

graphical borders
and shading

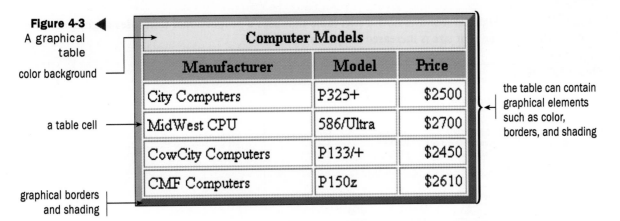

the table can contain
graphical elements
such as color,
borders, and shading

Graphical tables are more flexible than text tables and are more attractive. However, there are some situations in which you will want to use a text table. Some browsers, such as the text-based Lynx browser used on many UNIX systems, can display only text characters. Also, working with the tags for graphical tables can be complicated and time-consuming. For these reasons, you might want to create two versions of your Web page: one that uses only text elements and text tables, and another that takes advantage of graphical elements. This is the approach Nicole suggests that you take. First you'll create a text table of the products in the Gargoyle Collection, and then you'll start to work on the graphical version of the table.

Creating a Text Table

The beginning of the file you'll use for the text table version of the products page has already been created for you and is stored on your Student Disk as MAA.htm. To begin, you'll open this file and save it with a new name.

To open the MAA.htm file and then save it with a new name:

1. Start your text editor.

2. Open the file **MAA.htm** from the Tutorial.04 folder on your Student Disk, and then save the file in the same folder as **MAAtext.htm**.

The page consists of two headings formatted with the <H1> and <H3> tags followed by a paragraph of text that describes the Gargoyle Collection. You'll add the text table below the paragraph.

Using Fixed-Width Fonts

To create a text table you have to control the type of font that is used. A text table relies on spaces and the characters that fill those spaces to create its column boundaries. You have to use a font that allots the same amount of space to each character and to the empty spaces between characters. This type of font is called a **fixed-width font** or a **typewriter font.**

Most typeset documents (such as the one you're reading now) use **proportional fonts**— that is, fonts in which the width of each character differs with the character's shape. For example, the character "m" is wider than the character "l."

Proportional fonts are more visually attractive than fixed-width fonts, so you might be tempted to use them for your text tables. The distinction between the fixed-width and proportional font is important, however, because if you use a proportional font in a text table, the varying width of the characters and the spaces between characters might cause errors when the page is rendered in the user's browser.

Figure 4-4 shows how a text table that uses a proportional font loses alignment when the font size is increased or decreased.

Figure 4-4 ◄
Column
alignment
problems with
proportional
font

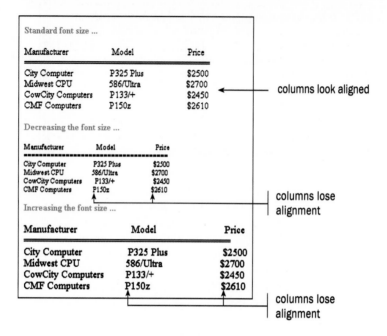

By contrast, the table shown in Figure 4-5 uses fixed-width fonts. Note that the columns remain aligned regardless of font size.

Figure 4-5 ◄
Column
alignment with
fixed-width font

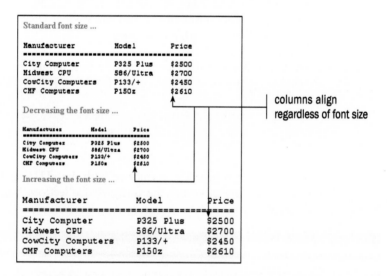

Different browsers use different font sizes to display text, so you should always use a fixed-width font to ensure that the columns in your text tables remain in alignment. You can accomplish this using the <PRE> tag.

Using the <PRE> Tag

The <PRE> tag is used to display preformatted text, which is text formatted in ways that you want retained in your Web page. HTML ignores extra blank spaces, blank lines, or tabs unless you've inserted a tag or special character for those features. Any text formatted with the <PRE> tag retains those extra blank spaces and blank lines. The <PRE> tag also displays text using a fixed-width font, which is what you want for your text table.

REFERENCE
window

CREATING A TEXT TABLE USING THE <PRE> TAG

- Type <PRE> to use the preformatted text tag.
- Enter the table text, aligning the columns of the table by inserting blank spaces as appropriate.
- Type </PRE> to turn off the preformatted text tag.

You'll use the <PRE> tag to enter the table data from Figure 4-1 into the MAAtext.htm file. When you use this tag, you insert blank spaces by pressing the spacebar to align the columns of text in the table.

To create the text table with the <PRE> tag:

1. Place the insertion point in the blank line directly above the </BODY> tag.

2. Type **<PRE>** and then press the **Enter** key to create a new blank line.

3. Type **Name** and then press the **spacebar** 15 times.

4. Type **Item #** and then press the **spacebar** 5 times.

5. Type **Type** and then press the **spacebar** 15 times.

6. Type **Finish** and then press the **spacebar** 15 times.

7. Type **Price** and then press the **Enter** key.

   Next you'll enter a series of equals signs to create an underline that will separate the column headings from the text of the table.

8. Type a line of **=** signs to underline the column headings you just entered. End the line below the "e" in "Price," and then press the **Enter** key.

9. Complete the table by entering the following text aligned with the left edge of the column headings:

```
Bacchus            48059 Wall Mount     Interior Plaster $95

Praying Gargoyle 48159 Garden Figure  Gothic Stone        $125

Gargoyle Judge     48222 Bust          Interior Plaster $140
```

10. Press the **Enter** key after entering the last row of table text, and then type **</PRE>** to turn off the preformatted text tag. Figure 4-6 shows the complete preformatted text as it appears in the file.

Figure 4-6 ◀
Text table
created with
the <PRE> tag

text appears in
the browser as it
appears here

```
<P>Throughout Europe, countless gargoyles peer down from the towers and
parapets of medieval cathedrals. In honor of these fascinating creations,
Middle Age Arts presents an exclusive line of gargoyle replicas. Choose
representations from the most famous cathedrals in the world, including
the popular gargoyles of Notre Dame. Select from the following list of
our most popular gargoyles.</P>
<PRE>
Name             Item #    Type           Finish            Price
====================================================================
Bacchus          48059     Wall Mount     Interior Plaster  $95
Praying Gargoyle 48159     Garden Figure  Gothic Stone      $125
Gargoyle Judge   48222     Bust           Interior Plaster  $140
</PRE>
</BODY>
</HTML>
```

11. Save your changes, and then close the MAAtext.htm file.

12. Open the MAAtext.htm file in your Web browser. Figure 4-7 displays the page as it appears in the browser.

Figure 4-7 ◀
Text table as it
appears in the
Web browser

text appears in a
fixed-width font

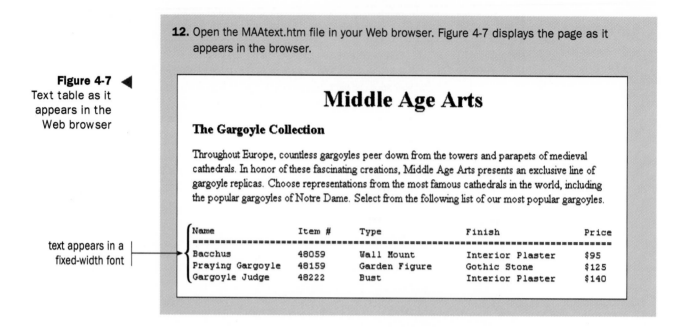

Middle Age Arts

The Gargoyle Collection

Throughout Europe, countless gargoyles peer down from the towers and parapets of medieval cathedrals. In honor of these fascinating creations, Middle Age Arts presents an exclusive line of gargoyle replicas. Choose representations from the most famous cathedrals in the world, including the popular gargoyles of Notre Dame. Select from the following list of our most popular gargoyles.

```
Name               Item #      Type            Finish              Price
===========================================================================
Bacchus            48059       Wall Mount      Interior Plaster    $95
Praying Gargoyle   48159       Garden Figure   Gothic Stone        $125
Gargoyle Judge     48222       Bust            Interior Plaster    $140
```

By using the <PRE> tag, you've created a text table that can be displayed by all browsers, and you've ensured that the columns will retain their alignment no matter what font the browser is using.

You show the completed table to Nicole. She's pleased with your work and would like you to create a similar page using a graphical table. To create that table, you'll start by learning how HTML defines table structures.

Defining a Table Structure

Creating tables with HTML can be a complicated process because you have to enter a lot of information to define the layout and appearance of your table. The first step is to specify the table structure: the number of rows and columns, the location of column headings, and the placement of a table caption. Once you have the table structure in place, you can start populating the cells of the table with text and data.

As with the text table page, the beginning of the page for the graphical table has already been created and stored on your Student Disk as MAA2.htm. You need to open that file in your text editor and save it with a new name.

To open the MAA2.htm file and then save it with a new name:

1. Return to your text editor.

2. Open the file **MAA2.htm** from the Tutorial.04 folder on your Student Disk, and then save the file in the same folder as **MAAtable.htm**.

Using the <TABLE>, <TR>, and <TD> Tags

To create a graphical table with HTML, you start with the <TABLE> tag. The <TABLE> tag identifies where the table structure begins, and the </TABLE> tag indicates where the table ends. After you've identified the location of the table, you identify the number of rows in the table by inserting a <TR> (for table row) tag at the beginning of each table row, starting with the top row of the table and moving down. The end of the table row is indicated by a </TR> tag. Finally, within the <TR> tags you must indicate the location of each table cell with <TD> (for table data) tags.

HTML does not provide a means of specifying the number and placement of table columns. Columns are determined by how many cells are inserted within each row. For example, if you have four <TD> tags in each table row, that table has four columns. So if you want to make sure that the columns in your table line up correctly, you must be careful about the placement and number of <TD> tags within each row. The general syntax of a graphical table is:

```
<TABLE>
     <TR>
             <TD> First Cell </TD>
             <TD> Second Cell </TD>
     </TR>
     <TR>
             <TD> Third Cell </TD>
             <TD> Fourth Cell </TD>
     </TR>
</TABLE>
```

This example creates a table with two rows and two columns, displaying a total of four cells. Figure 4-8 shows the layout of a table with this HTML code.

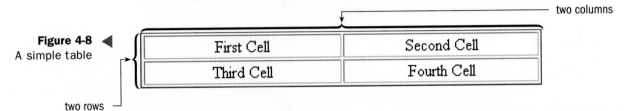

Figure 4-8
A simple table

two columns

two rows

Strictly speaking, the </TR> tag is not necessary, because the presence of the next <TR> tag will signal the browser to go to the next table row. However it is good practice to use the </TR> tag, at least until you become comfortable with the way HTML creates tables.

REFERENCE window	DEFINING THE TABLE STRUCTURE WITH HTML
	■ Enter the <TABLE> and </TABLE> tags to identify the beginning and end of the table. ■ Enter <TR> and </TR> tags to identify the beginning and end of each table row. ■ Enter <TD> and </TD> tags to identify the beginning and end of each table cell. ■ Enter <TH> and </TH> tags to identify text that will act as table headers.

Look at the table that Nicole outlined in Figure 4-1. Notice that the table requires four rows and five columns. However, one of the rows consists of column titles, called **table headers**. HTML provides a special tag for table headers, which you'll learn about shortly, leaving three rows and five columns for the body of the table. You'll create the basic table structure first and then enter the table text.

To create the structure for the products table:

1. Place the insertion point in the blank line directly above the </BODY> tag.

2. Press the **Enter** key, type **<TABLE>** to identify the beginning of the table structure, and then press the **Enter** key again.

3. Type the entries for the first row of the table as follows:

```
<TR>
   <TD></TD>
   <TD></TD>
   <TD></TD>
   <TD></TD>
   <TD></TD>
</TR>
```

Note that you do not need to indent the <TD> tags, but you might find it easier to interpret your code if you do indent them and place them on separate lines.

4. Press the **Enter** key, and then repeat Step 3 twice to create the final two rows of the table. You might want to use the copy and paste functions of your text editor to save time.

5. Press the **Enter** key, and then type **</TABLE>** to complete the code for the table structure. See Figure 4-9.

Figure 4-9 ◀
Structure of the products table in HTML

beginning of the table structure

beginning of the first table row

five table cells per table row

end of the first table row

end of the table structure

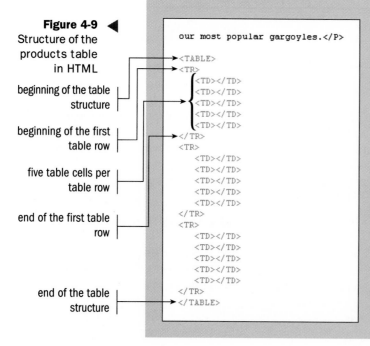

```
our most popular gargoyles.</P>

<TABLE>
<TR>
    <TD></TD>
    <TD></TD>
    <TD></TD>
    <TD></TD>
    <TD></TD>
</TR>
<TR>
    <TD></TD>
    <TD></TD>
    <TD></TD>
    <TD></TD>
    <TD></TD>
</TR>
<TR>
    <TD></TD>
    <TD></TD>
    <TD></TD>
    <TD></TD>
    <TD></TD>
</TR>
</TABLE>
```

With the table structure in place, you're ready to add the text for each cell, inserted within the <TD> tags in each table row.

To insert the table text:

1. Go to the first <TD> tag in the table structure.

2. Within the first set of <TD> tags, type **Bacchus**.

3. Within the next four <TD> tags, enter the remaining entries for the first row of the table as follows:

<TD> 48059 </TD>
<TD> Wall Mount </TD>
<TD> Interior Plaster </TD>
<TD> $95 </TD>

4. Continue entering the text for the cells in the remaining two rows of the table. Figure 4-10 shows the completed text for the body of the table.

Figure 4-10 ◄
Completed
table text

text for the first
cell in the first row
of the table

```
<TABLE>
<TR>
    <TD>Bacchus</TD>
    <TD>48059</TD>
    <TD>Wall Mount</TD>
    <TD>Interior Plaster</TD>
    <TD>$95</TD>
</TR>
<TR>
    <TD>Praying Gargoyle</TD>
    <TD>48159</TD>
    <TD>Garden Figure</TD>
    <TD>Gothic Stone</TD>
    <TD>$125</TD>
</TR>
<TR>
    <TD>Gargoyle Judge</TD>
    <TD>48222</TD>
    <TD>Bust</TD>
    <TD>Interior Plaster</TD>
    <TD>$140</TD>
</TR>
</TABLE>
```

With the text for the body of the table entered, you'll next add the table headers.

Creating Headers with the <TH> Tag

HTML provides a special tag for cells that will act as table headers (or column headings): the <TH> tag. Like the <TD> tag, the <TH> tag is used with cells within the table. The difference between the <TH> and <TD> tags is that text formatted with the <TH> tag is centered within the cell and displayed in a boldface font. A table can have several rows of table headers. In fact, because the <TH> tag is a replacement for the <TD> tag, you can use the <TH> tag for any cell containing text that you want to be displayed in centered boldfaced type.

In the gargoyle products table, Nicole has specified a single row of table headers. You'll enter them now using the <TH> tag.

To insert the table headers:

1. Go to the <TABLE> tag line and press the **Enter** key to create a new blank line below it.

2. Type the following:

<TR>
<TH> Name </TH>
<TH> Item # </TH>
<TH> Type </TH>
<TH> Finish </TH>
<TH> Price </TH>
</TR>

Figure 4-11 shows the <TH> tags as they appear in your file.

Figure 4-11 ◀
Creating table
headers with
<TH> tags

table headers ──────

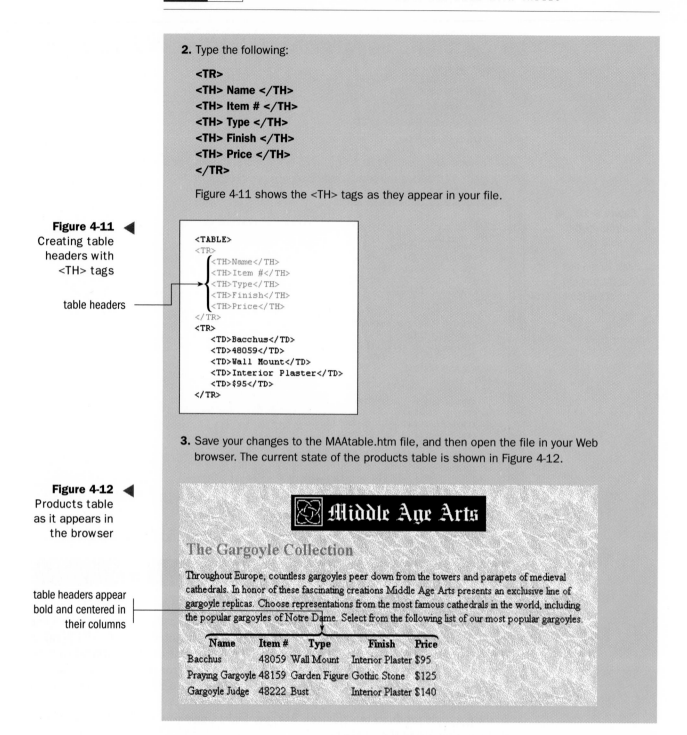

```
<TABLE>
<TR>
    <TH>Name</TH>
    <TH>Item #</TH>
    <TH>Type</TH>
    <TH>Finish</TH>
    <TH>Price</TH>
</TR>
<TR>
    <TD>Bacchus</TD>
    <TD>48059</TD>
    <TD>Wall Mount</TD>
    <TD>Interior Plaster</TD>
    <TD>$95</TD>
</TR>
```

3. Save your changes to the MAAtable.htm file, and then open the file in your Web browser. The current state of the products table is shown in Figure 4-12.

Figure 4-12 ◀
Products table
as it appears in
the browser

table headers appear
bold and centered in
their columns ──────

Middle Age Arts

The Gargoyle Collection

Throughout Europe, countless gargoyles peer down from the towers and parapets of medieval cathedrals. In honor of these fascinating creations Middle Age Arts presents an exclusive line of gargoyle replicas. Choose representations from the most famous cathedrals in the world, including the popular gargoyles of Notre Dame. Select from the following list of our most popular gargoyles.

Name	Item #	Type	Finish	Price
Bacchus	48059	Wall Mount	Interior Plaster	$95
Praying Gargoyle	48159	Garden Figure	Gothic Stone	$125
Gargoyle Judge	48222	Bust	Interior Plaster	$140

Note that the cells formatted with the <TH> tag appear in boldface and centered above each table column. Your next task is to add a table caption.

Creating a Table Caption

You create a table caption using the <CAPTION> tag. The syntax for the <CAPTION> tag is:

```
<CAPTION ALIGN=value>caption text</CAPTION>
```

where *value* indicates the caption placement—either TOP (above the table) or BOTTOM (below the table). In either case, the caption will be centered in relation to the table. Because the <CAPTION> tag works only with tables, the tag must be placed within the <TABLE> tags.

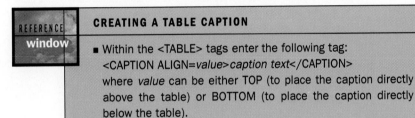

REFERENCE window

CREATING A TABLE CAPTION

■ Within the <TABLE> tags enter the following tag:
<CAPTION ALIGN=*value*>*caption text*</CAPTION>
where *value* can be either TOP (to place the caption directly above the table) or BOTTOM (to place the caption directly below the table).

Nicole asks you to add the caption "Here is a sample of our products" centered above the table.

To add the caption to the products table:

1. Return to the MAAtable.htm file in your text editor.

2. Insert a blank line below the <TABLE> tag.

3. In the new line type **<CAPTION ALIGN=TOP>Here is a sample of our products</CAPTION>**. See Figure 4-13.

Figure 4-13 ◄
Inserting a
caption above
the table

caption will be placed
above the table

<CAPTION> tag

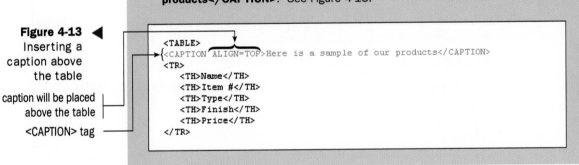

```
<TABLE>
<CAPTION ALIGN=TOP>Here is a sample of our products</CAPTION>
<TR>
    <TH>Name</TH>
    <TH>Item #</TH>
    <TH>Type</TH>
    <TH>Finish</TH>
    <TH>Price</TH>
</TR>
```

4. Save your changes to the MAAtable.htm file, and then reload the file in your Web browser. Figure 4-14 shows the table with the newly added caption.

Figure 4-14 ◄
Products table
with the table
caption

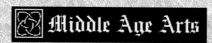

The Gargoyle Collection

Throughout Europe, countless gargoyles peer down from the towers and parapets of medieval cathedrals. In honor of these fascinating creations Middle Age Arts presents an exclusive line of gargoyle replicas. Choose representations from the most famous cathedrals in the world, including the popular gargoyles of Notre Dame. Select from the following list of our most popular gargoyles.

table caption ──────────────────────► Here is a sample of our products

Name	Item #	Type	Finish	Price
Bacchus	48059	Wall Mount	Interior Plaster	$95
Praying Gargoyle	48159	Garden Figure	Gothic Stone	$125
Gargoyle Judge	48222	Bust	Interior Plaster	$140

Captions are shown as normal text without special formatting. As with other tags in your HTML file, you can format table text by embedding the text within the appropriate tags. For example, placing the caption text within a pair of <B> and <I> tags will cause the caption to appear in a bold italicized font.

Quick Check

1. What are the two kinds of tables you can place in a Web page? What are the advantages and disadvantages of each?

2. What is the difference between a proportional font and a fixed-width font? Which should you use in a text table, and why?

3. What tag can you use to create a text table?

4. Name the purpose of the following tags in defining the structure of a table:
   <TABLE>
   <TR>
   <TD>
   <TH>

5. How do you determine the number of rows in a graphical table? How do you determine the number of columns?

6. How does the <TH> tag differ from the <TD> tag?

7. What HTML code would you enter to place the caption "Product Catalog" below a table? Where must this code be placed in relation to the <TABLE> and </TABLE> tags?

You've completed your work with the initial structure of the products table. Overall, Nicole is pleased with your progress, but she would like you to make some improvements in the table's appearance. In the next session, you'll learn how to control the appearance and placement of your table and the text in it.

SESSION

4.2

In this session you will learn how to create table and cell borders and how to control the width of each. You'll learn how to specify the space between table text and the surrounding table. You'll also work with the placement and size of the table on your Web page. Finally, you'll learn how to specify a table background color.

Modifying the Appearance of a Table

After viewing the products table in the browser, Nicole notes that the text is displayed with properly aligned columns, but that the format of the table could be improved. Nicole asks you to enhance the table's appearance with borders and color. She also wants you to control the placement of the table on the page as well as the table size. HTML provides tags and properties to do all of these things.

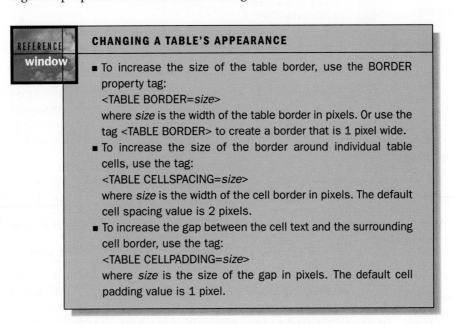

REFERENCE window

CHANGING A TABLE'S APPEARANCE

- To increase the size of the table border, use the BORDER property tag:
  <TABLE BORDER=*size*>
  where *size* is the width of the table border in pixels. Or use the tag <TABLE BORDER> to create a border that is 1 pixel wide.
- To increase the size of the border around individual table cells, use the tag:
  <TABLE CELLSPACING=*size*>
  where *size* is the width of the cell border in pixels. The default cell spacing value is 2 pixels.
- To increase the gap between the cell text and the surrounding cell border, use the tag:
  <TABLE CELLPADDING=*size*>
  where *size* is the size of the gap in pixels. The default cell padding value is 1 pixel.

You'll begin enhancing the products table by adding a table border.

Adding a Table Border

By default, your browser displays tables without table borders. You can create a table border with the BORDER property. The syntax for creating a table border is:

    <TABLE BORDER=*size*>

where *size* is the width of the border in pixels. The size value is optional; if you don't specify a size, but simply enter BORDER, the browser creates a border 1 pixel wide around the table. Figure 4-15 shows the effect of varying the border size on a table's appearance.

Figure 4-15 ◀
Tables with different values for the BORDER property

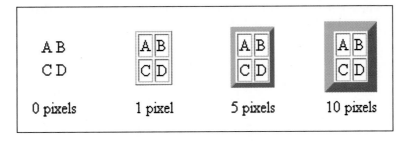

Nicole wants a good-sized border around the products table, so you'll format the table with a 10-pixel-wide border.

To insert a table border:

1. If you took a break after the previous session, start your text editor and open the MAAtable.htm file.

2. Go to the <TABLE> tag and within the tag, type **BORDER=10**. See Figure 4-16.

Figure 4-16 ◀
Adding a
10-pixel border
to the products
table

BORDER property ─

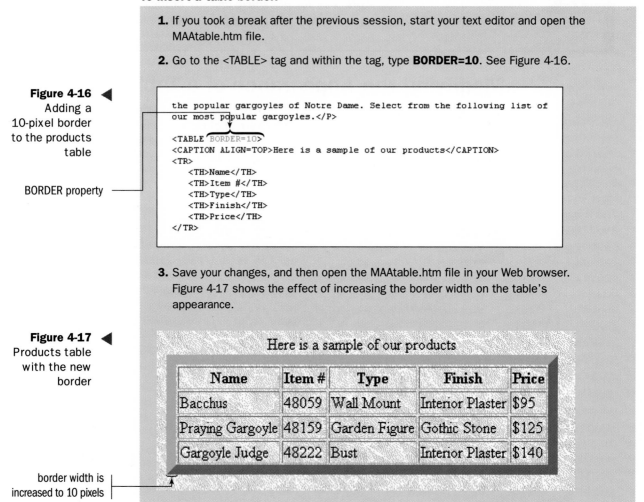

```
the popular gargoyles of Notre Dame. Select from the following list of
our most popular gargoyles.</P>

<TABLE BORDER=10>
<CAPTION ALIGN=TOP>Here is a sample of our products</CAPTION>
<TR>
    <TH>Name</TH>
    <TH>Item #</TH>
    <TH>Type</TH>
    <TH>Finish</TH>
    <TH>Price</TH>
</TR>
```

3. Save your changes, and then open the MAAtable.htm file in your Web browser. Figure 4-17 shows the effect of increasing the border width on the table's appearance.

Figure 4-17 ◀
Products table
with the new
border

Here is a sample of our products

Name	Item #	Type	Finish	Price
Bacchus	48059	Wall Mount	Interior Plaster	$95
Praying Gargoyle	48159	Garden Figure	Gothic Stone	$125
Gargoyle Judge	48222	Bust	Interior Plaster	$140

border width is
increased to 10 pixels

You've modified the outside border of the table, but Nicole would also like you to change the width of the *inside* border, between individual table cells. She feels that the table would look better if the interior borders were less prominent. This is done using the CELLSPACING property.

Controlling Cell Spacing

The CELLSPACING property controls the amount of space inserted between table cells. The syntax for specifying the cell spacing is:

```
<TABLE CELLSPACING=size>
```

where *size* is the width of the interior borders in pixels. The default cell spacing is 2 pixels. Figure 4-18 shows how different cell spacing values affect a table's appearance.

Figure 4-18 ◀
Tables with
different values
for the
CELLSPACING
property

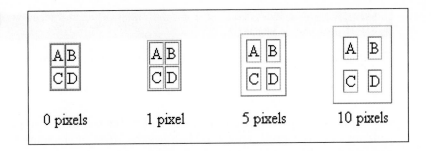

Nicole has decided that she wants the width of the borders between individual table cells to be as small as possible, so you'll decrease the width to 0 pixels. This will not remove the border between the cells (as long as you have a border around the entire table, you will always have a line separating individual table cells), but it will decrease the interior border width to a minimal size. This is because the interior border includes a drop shadow. Even if the cell spacing is set to 0, the drop shadow remains to give the effect of an interior border.

To change the cell spacing:

1. Return to the MAAtable.htm file in your text editor.

2. Go to the <TABLE> tag and type **CELLSPACING=0** within the tag, as shown in Figure 4-19.

Figure 4-19 ◀
Changing the
CELLSPACING
property to
0 pixels

CELLSPACING
property

```
<TABLE BORDER=10 CELLSPACING=0>
<CAPTION ALIGN=TOP>Here is a sample of our products</CAPTION>
<TR>
      <TH>Name</TH>
      <TH>Item #</TH>
      <TH>Type</TH>
      <TH>Finish</TH>
      <TH>Price</TH>
</TR>
```

3. Save your changes, and then reload the MAAtable.htm file in your Web browser. The new cell spacing is shown in Figure 4-20. Note that the line separating the cells has been slightly reduced, but has not totally disappeared (compare Figure 4-17 with Figure 4-20).

Figure 4-20 ◀
Products table
with decreased
cell spacing

interior borders are
now thinner

Here is a sample of our products

Name	Item #	Type	Finish	Price
Bacchus	48059	Wall Mount	Interior Plaster	$95
Praying Gargoyle	48159	Garden Figure	Gothic Stone	$125
Gargoyle Judge	48222	Bust	Interior Plaster	$140

After viewing the modified table, Nicole points out that it now appears crowded. She would like you to increase the space between the table text and the surrounding cell borders. You can do this by increasing the amount of cell padding in the table.

Controlling Cell Padding

To increase the space between the table text and the cell borders, you use the CELL-PADDING property. The syntax for this property is:

```
<TABLE CELLPADDING=size>
```

where *size* is the distance from the table text to the cell border in pixels. The default cell padding value is 1 pixel. Figure 4-21 shows the effect of changing the cell padding value on a sample table.

Figure 4-21 ◀
Tables with different values for the CELLPADDING property

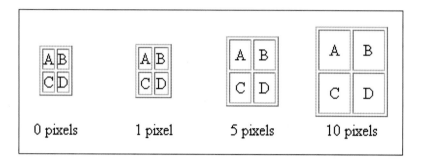

0 pixels   1 pixel   5 pixels   10 pixels

You might confuse the terms cell spacing and cell padding. Just remember that cell spacing refers to the space *between* the cells, and cell padding refers to the space *within* the table cells. You need to increase the amount of space within your table cells because the default 1-pixel gap is too small and causes the cell borders to crowd the cell text. You'll increase the cell padding to 4 pixels.

To increase the amount of cell padding:

1. Return to the MAAtable.htm file in your text editor.

2. Go to the <TABLE> tag and type **CELLPADDING=4** within the tag, as shown in Figure 4-22.

Figure 4-22 ◀
Increasing the CELLPADDING property to 4 pixels

CELLPADDING property

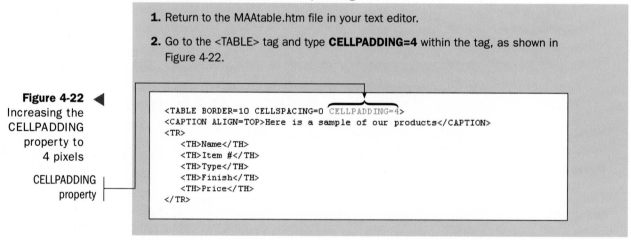

```
<TABLE BORDER=10 CELLSPACING=0 CELLPADDING=4>
<CAPTION ALIGN=TOP>Here is a sample of our products</CAPTION>
<TR>
    <TH>Name</TH>
    <TH>Item #</TH>
    <TH>Type</TH>
    <TH>Finish</TH>
    <TH>Price</TH>
</TR>
```

3. Save your changes, and then reload the MAAtable.htm file in your Web browser. Figure 4-23 shows the table with the increased amount of cell padding.

Figure 4-23 ◀
Products table with increased cell padding

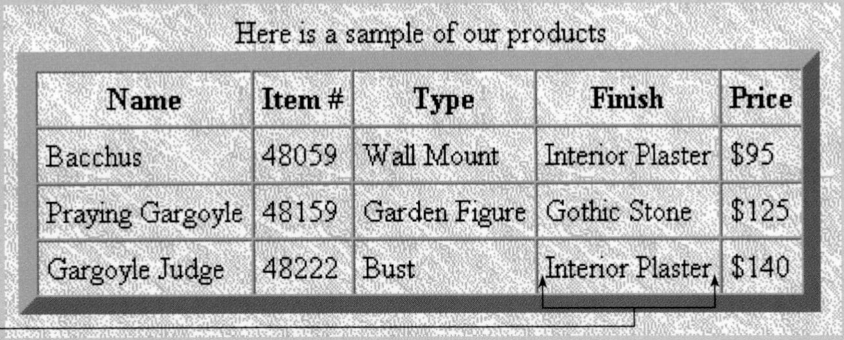

Here is a sample of our products

Name	Item #	Type	Finish	Price
Bacchus	48059	Wall Mount	Interior Plaster	$95
Praying Gargoyle	48159	Garden Figure	Gothic Stone	$125
Gargoyle Judge	48222	Bust	Interior Plaster	$140

cells now include more space around the text

By increasing the cell padding, you added needed space to the table. Next you'll work with the alignment of the table on the page and the text within the table.

Controlling Table and Text Alignment

By default, the browser places a table on the page's left margin, with surrounding text placed either above or below the table. You can change this placement by using the ALIGN property. The syntax for this property is:

```
<TABLE ALIGN=alignment>
```

where *alignment* equals either left or right. The ALIGN property is similar to the ALIGN property used with the <IMG> tag, except that images have more alignment options. As with inline images, using left or right alignment places the table on the page's margin and wraps surrounding text to the side, as illustrated in Figure 4-24.

Figure 4-24 ◀
Tables with different ALIGN values

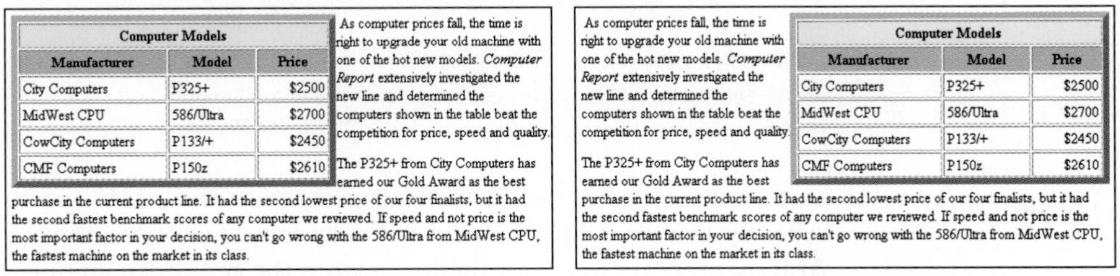

ALIGN=LEFT   ALIGN=RIGHT

The ALIGN property is a recent addition to HTML and is available only with Netscape Navigator, Internet Explorer, or browsers that support HTML 3.2. Earlier browsers will ignore the ALIGN property and leave the table on the left margin without wrapping text around it.

ALIGNING A TABLE ON THE PAGE

- To align the table with the left page margin, wrapping text to the right of the table, enter:
  <TABLE ALIGN=LEFT>
- To align the table with the right page margin, wrapping text to the left, enter:
  <TABLE ALIGN=RIGHT>
- To center the table on the page, enclose the <TABLE> tags within <CENTER> tags as follows:
  <CENTER>
    <TABLE>
  ....
    </TABLE>
  </CENTER>

Another possible value for the ALIGN property is CENTER, which centers the table on the page. However, this option is not supported by all browsers. To ensure that your table is centered, you should instead enclose the entire table structure within <CENTER> tags. The <CENTER> tag can be used to center any text, table, or graphic on the page.

Nicole wants the products table to be centered, to better balance the layout of the page. You'll use the <CENTER> tag to accomplish this.

To center the products table:

1. Return to the MAAtable.htm file in your text editor.

2. Insert a blank line *above* the <TABLE> tag.

3. Type **<CENTER>** in the new line.

4. Insert a blank line *below* the </TABLE> tag, and then type **</CENTER>**.

5. Save your changes, and then reload the file in your Web browser. The products table should now be centered on the page.

You can also use the ALIGN property with the <TD> tag to align text within table cells. By default, text is aligned with the left edge of the table cell, but you can use the ALIGN property to center the text within the cell or to align it with the cell's right edge. Another property, VALIGN, allows you to control the vertical placement of text within the table cell. By default, text is placed at the top of the cell, but with the VALIGN property you can align text with the top, middle, or bottom of the cell. Figure 4-25 shows how the combination of the ALIGN and VALIGN properties affects the placement of text within a table cell.

Figure 4-25 ◄
Values of the ALIGN and VALIGN properties

ALIGN=LEFT VALIGN=TOP	ALIGN=LEFT VALIGN=MIDDLE	ALIGN=LEFT VALIGN=BOTTOM
ALIGN=CENTER VALIGN=TOP	ALIGN=CENTER VALIGN=MIDDLE	ALIGN=CENTER VALIGN=BOTTOM
ALIGN=RIGHT VALIGN=TOP	ALIGN=RIGHT VALIGN=MIDDLE	ALIGN=RIGHT VALIGN=BOTTOM

Looking over the table, Nicole decides that the values in the Price column should be right-aligned so that the numbers align properly. Because of the way HTML works with table columns, if you want to align the text for a single column, you must apply the ALIGN property to every cell within that column.

To right-align the Price column values:

1. Return to the MAAtable.htm file in your text editor.

2. For each <TD> tag in the Price column, insert the text **ALIGN=RIGHT**. Figure 4-26 shows the revised HTML code in your file.

Figure 4-26 ◄
Right-aligning
the values in
the Price
column

ALIGN property

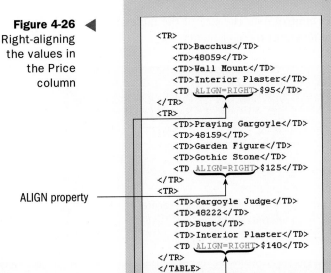

```
<TR>
      <TD>Bacchus</TD>
      <TD>48059</TD>
      <TD>Wall Mount</TD>
      <TD>Interior Plaster</TD>
      <TD ALIGN=RIGHT>$95</TD>
</TR>
<TR>
      <TD>Praying Gargoyle</TD>
      <TD>48159</TD>
      <TD>Garden Figure</TD>
      <TD>Gothic Stone</TD>
      <TD ALIGN=RIGHT>$125</TD>
</TR>
<TR>
      <TD>Gargoyle Judge</TD>
      <TD>48222</TD>
      <TD>Bust</TD>
      <TD>Interior Plaster</TD>
      <TD ALIGN=RIGHT>$140</TD>
</TR>
</TABLE>
```

3. Save your changes, and then reload the page in your Web browser. The prices are now right-aligned. See Figure 4-27.

Figure 4-27 ◄
Right-aligned
prices in the
products table

prices are aligned
with the right edge of

Here is a sample of our products

Name	Item #	Type	Finish	Price
Bacchus	48059	Wall Mount	Interior Plaster	$95
Praying Gargoyle	48159	Garden Figure	Gothic Stone	$125
Gargoyle Judge	48222	Bust	Interior Plaster	$140

You can also use the ALIGN and VALIGN properties with the <TR> tag if you want to align all the text within a single row in the same way. Your next task will be to work with the size of your table and table cells.

Working with Table and Cell Size

The size of a table is determined by the text it contains. By default, HTML places text on a single line. If you insert additional text in a cell, the width of the column and the table will increase up to the page edge, still keeping the text confined to a single line (unless you've inserted a break, paragraph, or header tag within the cell). Once the page edge is reached, the browser will reduce the size of the remaining columns to keep the text to a single line. The browser will wrap the text to a second line within the cell only when it can no longer increase the size of the column and table or decrease the size of the remaining columns. As more text is added, the height of the table automatically expands to accommodate the additional text.

If you want to have greater control over the size of the table and table cells, you can explicitly define the width and height of these elements.

CHOOSING TABLE AND CELL SIZE

- Do not specify a table size beyond about 610 pixels (roughly), or else the table will extend beyond the display area of most monitors set at resolutions of 640 x 480.
- Specify a cell width (either absolute or relative) for all of your table cells, so that you can be sure that the table will be rendered accurately in the browser.
- Test the appearance of your table under several different monitor resolutions, from 640 x 480 on up.

Defining the Table Size

The syntax for specifying the table size is:

```
<TABLE WIDTH=size HEIGHT=size>
```

Here *size* is the width and height of the table either in pixels or as a percentage of the display area. If you want your table to fill the entire width of the display area, regardless of the resolution of the user's monitor, you would set the WIDTH property to 100%. Note that the percent value should be placed within double quotation marks (use WIDTH="100%" *not* WIDTH=100%). Similarly, to create a table whose height is equal to the height of the display area, enter the property HEIGHT="100%".

On the other hand, you must specify the size of a table exactly, so that its absolute size remains constant, regardless of the browser used. If you use this approach, remember that some monitors will display your page at a resolution of 640 by 480 pixels. If it's important that the table not exceed the browser's display area, you should specify a table width of less than 610 pixels (roughly) to allow space for other window elements such as scroll bars.

SPECIFYING THE TABLE SIZE

- To create a table of a specific size, enter the following tag:
  `<TABLE WIDTH=size HEIGHT=size>`
  where *size* is the table's height or width either in pixels or as a percentage of the browser's display area. Percentages must be enclosed in quotation marks (for example, WIDTH="70%").

You'll set the width of the products table to 550 pixels. This will ensure that the table will not extend beyond the display area, but will also provide more room in the table cells if you want to insert additional text. You don't need to specify the height of the table, because the table's height will expand as additional products are added.

To increase the width of the products table:

1. Return to the MAAtable.htm file in your text editor and move to the <TABLE> tag.

2. Within the <TABLE> tag, type **WIDTH=550**, as shown in Figure 4-28.

Figure 4-28 ◄
Increasing the width of the products table to 550 pixels

WIDTH property ─

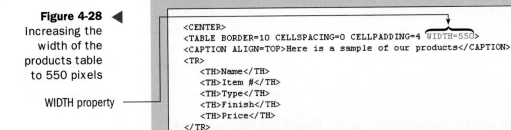

```
<CENTER>
<TABLE BORDER=10 CELLSPACING=0 CELLPADDING=4 WIDTH=550>
<CAPTION ALIGN=TOP>Here is a sample of our products</CAPTION>
<TR>
    <TH>Name</TH>
    <TH>Item #</TH>
    <TH>Type</TH>
    <TH>Finish</TH>
    <TH>Price</TH>
</TR>
```

3. Save your changes, and then reload the file in your Web browser. Figure 4-29 shows the revised page with the table width increased to 550 pixels.

Figure 4-29 ◄
Products table with its width increased

The Gargoyle Collection

Throughout Europe, countless gargoyles peer down from the towers and parapets of medieval cathedrals. In honor of these fascinating creations Middle Age Arts presents an exclusive line of gargoyle replicas. Choose representations from the most famous cathedrals in the world, including the popular gargoyles of Notre Dame. Select from the following list of our most popular gargoyles.

Here is a sample of our products

Name	Item #	Type	Finish	Price
Bacchus	48059	Wall Mount	Interior Plaster	$95
Praying Gargoyle	48159	Garden Figure	Gothic Stone	$125
Gargoyle Judge	48222	Bust	Interior Plaster	$140

table width increased to 550 pixels

Now that you've set the width of the table, you need to set the width of individual cells.

Defining Cell and Column Sizes

The <TH> and <TD> tags support the WIDTH property as well. To set the size of an individual cell, you enter the HTML code:

```
<TD WIDTH=size>
```

where *size* once again can be expressed either in pixels or as a percentage of the table width. For example, a width value of 30% displays a cell that is 30% of the total width of the table (whatever that might be). To create a cell that is 35 pixels wide, you would enter WIDTH=35 within the <TD> tag. Whether you enter the pixel value or the percentage depends on whether you're trying to create a table that will fill a specific space or a relative space.

Specifying a width for an individual cell does not guarantee that the cell will take that width when displayed in the browser. The problem is that the cell is part of a column containing other cells. If one of those other cells is set to a different width or expands because of the text entered into it, the widths of all cells in the column change accordingly. Setting a width for one cell guarantees only that the cell width will not be *less* than that value. If you want to ensure that the cells do not change in size, neither increasing nor decreasing from the value you set, you must set the WIDTH property of *all* the cells in the column to the same value.

Internet Explorer also supports the HEIGHT property for individual cells. Like the WIDTH property, the HEIGHT property can be expressed either in pixels or as a percentage of the height of the table. If you include more text than can be displayed within that height value, the browser will expand to display the additional text.

Nicole decides that the widths of both the Item # and Price columns can be reduced. Reducing these columns will make more space available to the remaining three columns, in which she expects that additional text might be entered. A width of 60 pixels for the Item # column and 50 pixels for the Price column should work well for the products table.

To set the column widths for the Item # and Price columns:

1. Return to the MAAtable.htm file in your text editor.

2. For the <TH> and <TD> tags in the Item # column, enter the property **WIDTH=60**.

3. For the <TH> and <TD> tags in the Price column, enter the property **WIDTH=50**.

Figure 4-30 shows the revised HTML code in your file. Check your code carefully because it's easy to place the properties in the wrong columns.

Figure 4-30 ◀
Increasing the width of the Item # and Price columns

```
<TR>
    <TH> Name </TH>
    <TH WIDTH=60> Item # </TH>
    <TH> Type </TH>
    <TH> Finish </TH>
    <TH WIDTH=50> Price </TH>
</TR>
<TR>
    <TD>Bacchus</TD>
    <TD WIDTH=60>48059</TD>
    <TD>Wall Mount</TD>
    <TD>Interior Plaster</TD>
    <TD ALIGN=RIGHT WIDTH=50>$95</TD>
</TR>
<TR>
    <TD>Praying Gargoyle</TD>
    <TD WIDTH=60>48159</TD>
    <TD>Garden Figure</TD>
    <TD>Gothic Stone</TD>
    <TD ALIGN=RIGHT WIDTH=50>$125</TD>
</TR>
<TR>
    <TD>Gargoyle Judge</TD>
    <TD WIDTH=60>48222</TD>
    <TD>Bust</TD>
    <TD>Interior Plaster</TD>
    <TD ALIGN=RIGHT WIDTH=50>$140</TD>
</TR>
```

WIDTH property ⎯⎯⎯⎯⎯⎯⎯

4. Save your changes, and then reload the page in your Web browser to verify that the column widths for the Item # and Price columns have been decreased.

You've completed your work with the layout, and now Nicole would like you to turn your attention to the table color. By default, the table background color matches the page background color, but some browsers allow you to change that.

Modifying the Table Background

One of the extensions supported by both Internet Explorer and Netscape Navigator is the ability to define the background color or image for a table. To change the background color, insert the BGCOLOR property in the <TABLE>, <TR>, <TH>, and/or <TD> tags. You can use either the color name or the RGB color value. Your color choices might not show up on other browsers, so you should make sure that any design decisions you make work with the background color either on or off.

Setting color for the table follows a hierarchy. Using the BGCOLOR property for the <TABLE> tag sets the background color for all cells in the table. You can override this color choice for a single row by using the BGCOLOR property in the <TR> tag. You can also override the table or row color choices for a single cell by inserting the BGCOLOR property in a <TD> or <TH> tag. To set the background color for a column, you must define the background color for each cell in that column.

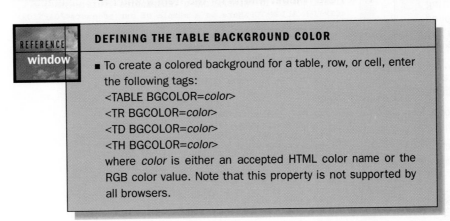

REFERENCE window

DEFINING THE TABLE BACKGROUND COLOR

■ To create a colored background for a table, row, or cell, enter the following tags:
<TABLE BGCOLOR=*color*>
<TR BGCOLOR=*color*>
<TD BGCOLOR=*color*>
<TH BGCOLOR=*color*>
where *color* is either an accepted HTML color name or the RGB color value. Note that this property is not supported by all browsers.

After considering many different colors, Nicole decides that she would like to have the background color of the header row set to green, the rows of the table set to white, and the background of the names of the products set to yellow. She asks you to make these changes now. You'll start by setting the table background color.

To define the table background color:

1. Return to the MAAtable.htm file in your text editor and go to the <TABLE> tag.

2. Type **BGCOLOR=WHITE** within the <TABLE> tag.

Now that you've set the background color of each cell to white, you'll override this option for the header row, setting the background for cells in that row to a shade of green. The RGB color value is (51,204,102), which translates to 33CC66.

To define the background color for the header row:

1. Go to the first <TR> tag in the products table (the row containing the <TH> tags).

2. Type **BGCOLOR="#33CC66"** within the <TR> tag.

Finally you'll change the background color of the three product names to yellow.

To define the background color for the cells in the first column:

1. Go to the <TD> tag for the Bacchus cell.

2. Type **BGCOLOR=YELLOW** within the <TD> tag.

3. Insert the BGCOLOR=YELLOW property within the remaining two cells for the first column (the Praying Gargoyle cell and the Gargoyle Judge cell). Figure 4-31 shows the revised HTML code for your page.

Figure 4-31
Setting background colors for the table, the header row, and individual table cells

background color for the table

background color for the header row

background color for an individual table cell

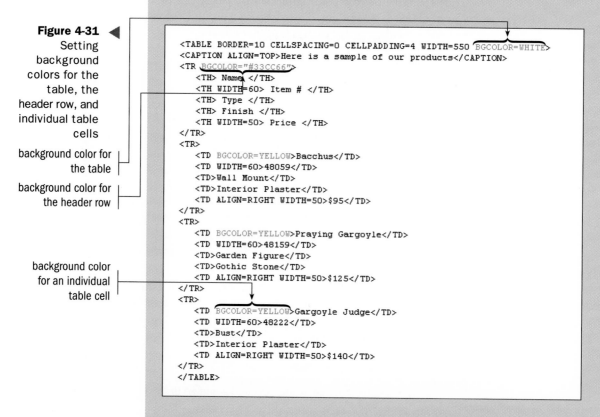

```
<TABLE BORDER=10 CELLSPACING=0 CELLPADDING=4 WIDTH=550 BGCOLOR=WHITE>
<CAPTION ALIGN=TOP>Here is a sample of our products</CAPTION>
<TR BGCOLOR="#33CC66">
    <TH> Name </TH>
    <TH WIDTH=60> Item # </TH>
    <TH> Type </TH>
    <TH> Finish </TH>
    <TH WIDTH=50> Price </TH>
</TR>
<TR>
    <TD BGCOLOR=YELLOW>Bacchus</TD>
    <TD WIDTH=60>48059</TD>
    <TD>Wall Mount</TD>
    <TD>Interior Plaster</TD>
    <TD ALIGN=RIGHT WIDTH=50>$95</TD>
</TR>
<TR>
    <TD BGCOLOR=YELLOW>Praying Gargoyle</TD>
    <TD WIDTH=60>48159</TD>
    <TD>Garden Figure</TD>
    <TD>Gothic Stone</TD>
    <TD ALIGN=RIGHT WIDTH=50>$125</TD>
</TR>
<TR>
    <TD BGCOLOR=YELLOW>Gargoyle Judge</TD>
    <TD WIDTH=60>48222</TD>
    <TD>Bust</TD>
    <TD>Interior Plaster</TD>
    <TD ALIGN=RIGHT WIDTH=50>$140</TD>
</TR>
</TABLE>
```

4. Save your changes, and then reload the file in your Web browser. Figure 4-32 shows the revised table with the new color scheme.

Figure 4-32
Products table with the new background colors

Here is a sample of our products				
Name	**Item #**	**Type**	**Finish**	**Price**
Bacchus	48059	Wall Mount	Interior Plaster	$95
Praying Gargoyle	48159	Garden Figure	Gothic Stone	$125
Gargoyle Judge	48222	Bust	Interior Plaster	$140

TROUBLE? If your page looks different from the one shown in Figure 4-32, it could be because of your browser. The Internet Explorer browser applies the table background color to the caption. The Netscape Navigator browser does not. Also the Netscape Navigator browser might align the table text differently.

Spanning Rows and Columns

Nicole has reviewed your table and would like to make a few more changes. She notes that the Gargoyle Judge item comes in two finishes, interior plaster and gothic stone. The gothic stone version has item number 48223, and Nicole wants this information added to the table. You can add the information by inserting a new row in the table, but that would leave you with two rows with the same item name. Is there a way that you can use the cell containing the item name in both rows? Yes, with a spanning cell.

A **spanning cell** is a cell that occupies more than one row or column in a table. Figure 4-33 shows a table of opinion poll data in which some of the cells span several rows and/or columns.

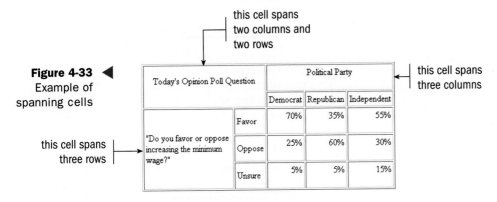

Figure 4-33 ◀
Example of spanning cells

this cell spans two columns and two rows

this cell spans three columns

this cell spans three rows

Nicole wants to include similar spanning cells in the products table. She sketches how she expects the table to appear with the new Gargoyle Judge entry (Figure 4-34). She has indicated two new spanning cells: the Gargoyle Judge entry will span two rows, and the Type and Finish columns will be combined into a single cell spanning two columns.

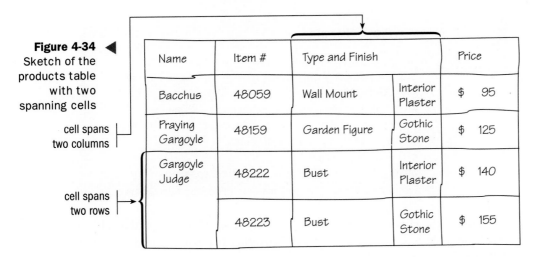

Figure 4-34 ◀
Sketch of the products table with two spanning cells

cell spans two columns

cell spans two rows

You can create spanning cells in HTML using the ROWSPAN and COLSPAN properties in a <TD> or <TH> tag. The syntax for the <TD> tag is:

```
<TD ROWSPAN=value COLSPAN=value> Cell Text </TD>
```

where *value* is the number of rows or columns that the cell will span within the table. Spanning is always downwards and to the right of the cell containing the ROWSPAN and COLSPAN properties. For example, to create a cell that spans two columns in the table, you would enter a <TD COLSPAN=2> tag. For a cell that spans two rows, the tag is <TD ROWSPAN=2>, and to span two rows and two columns, the tag is <TD ROWSPAN=2 COLSPAN=2>.

The important thing to remember when you have a cell that spans several rows or columns is that you must adjust the number of cell tags used in the table row. If a row has five columns, but one of the cells in the row spans three columns, you would only need to have three <TD> tags: two <TD> tags for the cells that occupy a single column, and the third for the <TD> spanning three rows.

When a cell spans several rows, the rows below the spanning cell must also be adjusted. Consider a table with three rows and four columns. The first cell in the first row is a spanning cell that spans three rows. You would need four <TD> tags for the first row, but only three <TD> tags for rows two and three. This is because the spanning cell from row one occupies the cells that would normally appear in rows two and three (Figure 4-35).

Figure 4-35 ◀
Table structure
with a
row-spanning
cell

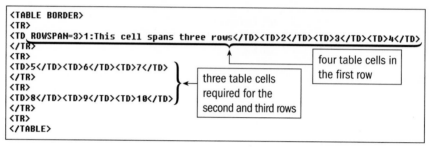

HTML code

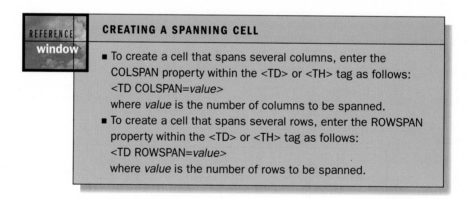

resulting table

REFERENCE
window

CREATING A SPANNING CELL

- To create a cell that spans several columns, enter the COLSPAN property within the <TD> or <TH> tag as follows:
  <TD COLSPAN=*value*>
  where *value* is the number of columns to be spanned.
- To create a cell that spans several rows, enter the ROWSPAN property within the <TD> or <TH> tag as follows:
  <TD ROWSPAN=*value*>
  where *value* is the number of rows to be spanned.

To make the changes Nicole requested, you must first change the cell containing the text "Gargoyle Judge" to a spanning cell covering two rows, and then you need to add a new row to the bottom of the table.

To create a cell that spans two rows:

1. Return to the MAAtable.htm file in your text editor and locate the <TD> tag for the Gargoyle Judge cell in the last row of the table.

2. Type **ROWSPAN=2** within the <TD> tag.

3. Go to the </TR> tag at the end of the row, and then press the **Enter** key to create a new blank line below it.

4. Enter the following text, starting at the new line you just inserted:

<TR>
   <TD WIDTH=60>48223</TD>
   <TD>Bust</TD>
   <TD>Gothic Stone</TD>
   <TD ALIGN=RIGHT WIDTH=50>$155</TD>
</TR>

Note that this new row has four cell tags, and not five like the other rows in the table, because one of the cell tags is being replaced by the spanning cell you created in the previous row. Figure 4-36 shows the revised HTML code.

Figure 4-36 ◄
Creating a
row-spanning
cell in the
products table

ROWSPAN property ———

new table row ———

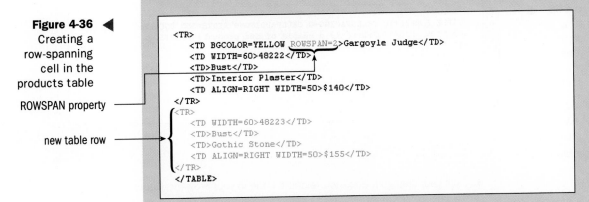

```
<TR>
   <TD BGCOLOR=YELLOW ROWSPAN=2>Gargoyle Judge</TD>
   <TD WIDTH=60>48222</TD>
   <TD>Bust</TD>
   <TD>Interior Plaster</TD>
   <TD ALIGN=RIGHT WIDTH=50>$140</TD>
</TR>
<TR>
   <TD WIDTH=60>48223</TD>
   <TD>Bust</TD>
   <TD>Gothic Stone</TD>
   <TD ALIGN=RIGHT WIDTH=50>$155</TD>
</TR>
</TABLE>
```

5. Save your changes, and then reload the file in your Web browser. The Gargoyle Judge cell now spans two rows in the first column. See Figure 4-37.

Figure 4-37 ◄
Row-spanning
cell in the
products table

cell spans two rows ———

Name	Item #	Type	Finish	Price
colspan: Here is a sample of our products					
Bacchus	48059	Wall Mount	Interior Plaster	$95
Praying Gargoyle	48159	Garden Figure	Gothic Stone	$125
Gargoyle Judge	48222	Bust	Interior Plaster	$140
	48223	Bust	Gothic Stone	$155

The text in the spanning cell is centered vertically, but it would look better if it were placed at the top of the cell. You can do this using the VALIGN property mentioned earlier.

To align the text with the top of the spanning cell:

1. Return to the MAAtable.htm file in your text editor.

2. Within the <TD> tag for the spanning cell you just created, type **VALIGN=TOP**.

Your next task is to merge the Type and Finish header cells into one cell. To do this, you can create a spanning cell to span across the Type and Finish columns.

To span a cell across the two columns:

1. Go to the <TH> tag in the first row of the table for the word "Type."

2. Within the <TH> tag, type **COLSPAN=2**.

3. Change the table header "Type" to **Type and Finish**.

Because this cell now spans two columns, you have to remove the Finish cell from the header row.

4. Delete the <TH> tags and enclosed text for the Finish table header. Figure 4-38 shows the revised HTML code.

Figure 4-38 ◀
Creating a column-spanning cell in the products table

the old Finish table header has been removed

column-spanning cell

```
<TABLE BORDER=10 CELLSPACING=0 CELLPADDING=4 WIDTH=550 BGCOLOR=WHITE>
<CAPTION ALIGN=TOP>Here is a sample of our products</CAPTION>
<TR BGCOLOR="#33CC66">
    <TH> Name </TH>
    <TH WIDTH=60> Item # </TH>
    <TH COLSPAN=2> Type and Finish </TH>
    <TH WIDTH=50> Price </TH>
</TR>
```

5. Save your changes, and then reload the file in your browser. Figure 4-39 shows the final layout of the gargoyle products table.

Figure 4-39 ◀
Final version of the gargoyle products table

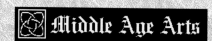

Middle Age Arts

The Gargoyle Collection

Throughout Europe, countless gargoyles peer down from the towers and parapets of medieval cathedrals. In honor of these fascinating creations Middle Age Arts presents an exclusive line of gargoyle replicas. Choose representations from the most famous cathedrals in the world, including the popular gargoyles of Notre Dame. Select from the following list of our most popular gargoyles.

Here is a sample of our products

Name	Item #	Type and Finish		Price
Bacchus	48059	Wall Mount	Interior Plaster	$95
Praying Gargoyle	48159	Garden Figure	Gothic Stone	$125
Gargoyle Judge	48222	Bust	Interior Plaster	$140
	48223	Bust	Gothic Stone	$155

Quick Check

1. What HTML code would you enter to create a table that has a 5-pixel-wide border with a 3-pixel border between table cells and 4 pixels between the cell text and the surrounding cell border?

2. What HTML code would you enter to align text with the top of a table header cell?

3. What HTML code would you enter to center *all* of the text within a given row?

4. What are the two ways of expressing table width? What are the advantages and disadvantages of each?

5. What HTML code would you enter to create a table that fills up half the width of the browser's display area, regardless of the resolution of the user's monitor?

6. What HTML code would you enter to set the width of a cell to 60 pixels? Will this keep the cell from exceeding 60 pixels in width? Will this keep the cell from being less than 60 pixels wide? How would you guarantee that the cell width will be exactly 60 pixels?

7. What HTML code would you enter to set the background color of your table to yellow? What are the limitations of this code?

8. What HTML code would you enter to create a cell that spans three rows and two columns?

You've completed your work on the appearance of the products table. You've learned how to control table size, alignment, border style, and color. You've also seen how to create cells that span several rows or columns in your table. In the next session you'll learn how to use tables to enhance the layout of an entire Web page.

SESSION

4.3

In this session you will work with tables to create a newspaper-style layout for a Web page. You'll create nested tables to enhance the page's design. Finally, you'll learn about some extensions supported by Internet Explorer that you can use on your tables.

Creating a Page Layout with Tables

In the first two sessions you've used the <TABLE> tag to create a table of products. In practice, however, the table features of HTML are most often used to control the layout of the page. If you want to design a page that displays text in newspaper-style columns, or separates the page into different topical areas, you'll find tables a handy tool. One of the most useful features of tables is that within each table cell you can use any of the HTML layout tags you've learned so far. For example, you can insert an <H1> header within a cell, or you can insert an ordered list of items. You can even nest one table inside another.

Nicole is satisfied with your prototype page of Middle Age Arts products. She now wants you to create a home page for the Gargoyle Collection product line. The page will contain a list of links to other Middle Age Arts pages, a message from the company president, a few notes about the uses of gargoyles, and a profile of one of Middle Age Arts' artists.

Nicole sketches a layout for the home page (Figure 4-40).

Figure 4-40 ◀
Nicole's sketch
of the Gargoyle
Collection
Home Page

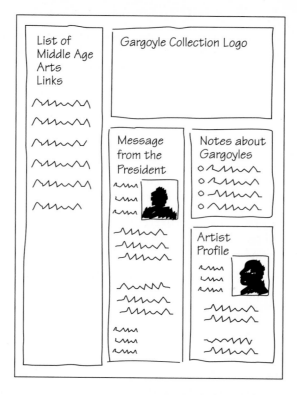

To create the layout specified in Nicole's sketch, you will create two tables, one nested inside the other. The first table, shown in Figure 4-41, consists of one row with two columns. The first column will contain the list of hypertext links. The second column will contain the nested table along with the rest of the page material. You'll create this outer table first.

Figure 4-41 ◀
Outer table of
the Gargoyle
Collection
Home Page

1 row x 2 columns —

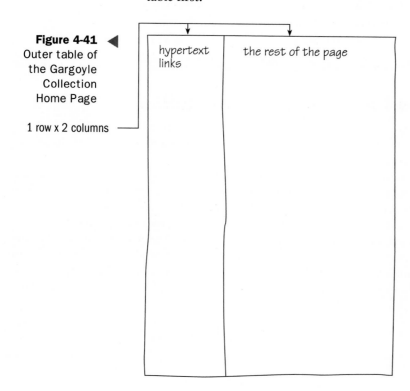

Designing the First Half of the Page

When designing a page that contains tables and other elements within tables, it's best to begin with the outer table and work inward. In the case of the Gargoyle Collection Home Page, you'll start by creating the outer table, which has one row and two columns. Because you want to control the layout exactly, you'll specify a width of 610 pixels for the table. This will preserve the layout of the various page elements and allow users with monitor resolutions of 640 × 480 to view the page correctly. You'll set the width of the first column to 165 pixels and the width of the second column to 445 pixels. As you design Web pages, you'll decide on column widths like these through trial and error, and whatever "looks right." In this case, you've been given the values beforehand.

The HTML code for pages like the one you're about to create can be long and complicated. One aid for you and for others who will be viewing the source code of your page is to include comments that describe the different sections of the page. The text entered into comments will not appear on the Web page. The format for a comment tag is:

```
<! comment text >
```

Any text appearing within the tag after the exclamation point is ignored by the browser.

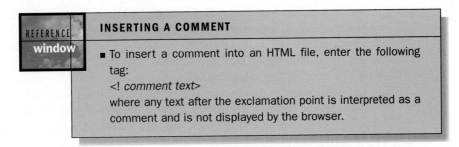

REFERENCE
window

INSERTING A COMMENT

- To insert a comment into an HTML file, enter the following tag:

  `<! comment text>`

  where any text after the exclamation point is interpreted as a comment and is not displayed by the browser.

The initial file that you'll use for the Gargoyle Collection Home Page has been created for you. The file, named GHome.htm, contains no text but does have a page title and a background image consisting of a single maroon-colored stripe. Now you need to open the file and create the outer table structure. You'll include comments along with the <TABLE> tags to help you document the different elements of the page layout.

To create the outer table and comments:

1. If you took a break after the previous session, start your text editor.

2. Open the file **GHome.htm** in the Tutorial.04 folder of your Student Disk.

3. Save the file as **Gargoyle.htm**.

4. Between the <BODY> tags, enter the following:

```
<TABLE WIDTH=610 CELLPADDING=0 CELLSPACING=0>
<TR>
    <!- -List of Hypertext Links- ->
    <TD WIDTH=165 VALIGN=TOP>
    </TD>
    <!- -Articles about the Gargoyle Collection- ->
    <TD WIDTH=445 VALIGN=TOP>
    </TD>
</TR>
</TABLE>
```

The Gargoyle.htm file should look like Figure 4-42.

Figure 4-42 ◀
Tags for the
outer table and
comments
in the
Gargoyle.htm
file

comment tags ⟶

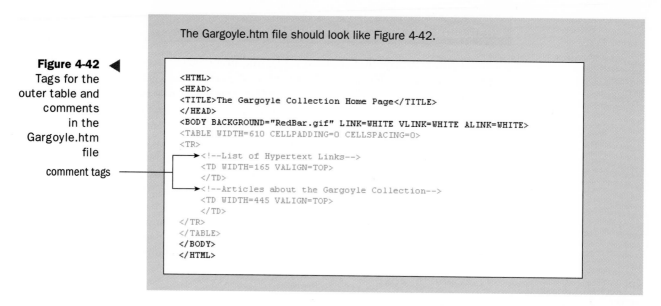

```
<HTML>
<HEAD>
<TITLE>The Gargoyle Collection Home Page</TITLE>
</HEAD>
<BODY BACKGROUND="RedBar.gif" LINK=WHITE VLINK=WHITE ALINK=WHITE>
<TABLE WIDTH=610 CELLPADDING=0 CELLSPACING=0>
<TR>
    <!--List of Hypertext Links-->
    <TD WIDTH=165 VALIGN=TOP>
    </TD>
    <!--Articles about the Gargoyle Collection-->
    <TD WIDTH=445 VALIGN=TOP>
    </TD>
</TR>
</TABLE>
</BODY>
</HTML>
```

Note that in both cells of this outer table, you've set the vertical alignment to top, rather than using the default value of middle. This is because the cells in this table will act as newspaper columns, with text flowing from the cell top down. You'll follow this practice with other table cells on the page. You've also set the cell padding and cell spacing values to 0. This allows any text entered into those cells to use the full cell width. You won't be creating any table borders in this layout.

Leaving aside the contents of the second cell of the outer table until later, you'll concentrate on the first cell, which will contain the list of Middle Age Arts hypertext links. A page has already been created with this information, shown in Figure 4-43.

Figure 4-43 ◀
Page with the
list of
hypertext links

hypertext links ⟶

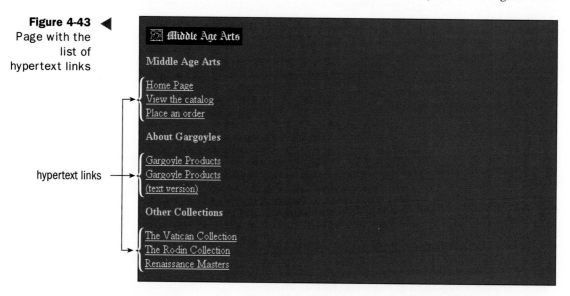

To create the contents for the table's first column, you'll copy the information contained in the document shown in Figure 4-43 and paste it between the table cell tags. (If you don't know how to copy and paste with your text editor, ask your instructor or technical support person for assistance.)

To insert the first column's contents:

1. Insert a blank line between the first set of <TD> and </TD> tags in the Gargoyle.htm file.

2. Open the file **Links.htm** from the Tutorial.04 folder of your Student Disk.

   TROUBLE? You might have to close your text editor if your operating system does not permit you to have multiple copies of the editor running at the same time. If so, save the changes to the Gargoyle.htm file before opening Links.htm.

3. Copy the HTML code within the <BODY> tags of the Links.htm file, but do *not* include the <BODY> tags themselves. Note that all the code you need to copy is indented in the file.

4. Return to the Gargoyle.htm file in your text editor.

5. Paste the HTML code you copied from Links.htm in the blank space you created between the first set of <TD> and </TD> tags. See Figure 4-44.

Figure 4-44 ◀
HTML code for the list of hypertext links

```
<TR>
    <!--List of Hypertext Links-->
    <TD WIDTH=165 VALIGN=TOP>
        <IMG SRC="MAA2.gif" WIDTH=144 HEIGHT=25 ALT="Middle Age Arts">
        <H4><FONT COLOR=YELLOW>Middle Age Arts</FONT></H4>
        <FONT COLOR=WHITE>
        <A HREF="Index.htm">Home Page</A><BR>
        <A HREF="Catalog.htm">View the catalog</A><BR>
        <A HREF="Orders.htm">Place an order</A><BR>
        </FONT>
        <H4><FONT COLOR=YELLOW>About Gargoyles</FONT></H4>
        <FONT COLOR=WHITE>
        <A HREF="MAAtable.htm">Gargoyle Products</A><BR>
        <A HREF="MAAtext.htm">Gargoyle Products<BR>(text version)</A><BR>
        </FONT>
        <H4><FONT COLOR=YELLOW>Other Collections</FONT></H4>
        <FONT COLOR=WHITE>
        <A HREF="Vatican.htm">The Vatican Collection</A><BR>
        <A HREF="Rodin.htm">The Rodin Collection</A><BR>
        <A HREF="Masters.htm">Renaissance Masters</A><BR>
        </FONT>
    </TD>
```

6. Save your changes, and then open the Gargoyle.htm file in your Web browser. Figure 4-45 shows the current state of the Gargoyle Collection Home Page.

Figure 4-45 ◀
Initial Gargoyle Collection Home Page

TROUBLE? Note that not all of the links on this page point to existing files.

Notice that the contents of the original Links.htm file are contained within the boundaries of the first column of the outer table. You've completed the first half of the page. Now you'll turn your attention to the second half.

Designing the Second Half of the Page

The material in the second column will be organized inside another table. This inner, or nested, table has three rows and three columns, as shown in Figure 4-46. The first row contains a single cell with the Gargoyle Collection logo spanning the three columns. The first cell in the second row contains the president's message spanning the second and third rows of the table. The second cell in that row will act as a **gutter**, which is a blank space separating the material between columns (in this case, between the first and third columns). The gutter will also span the second and third rows. Finally, the third cell in the second row contains the notes about gargoyles, and the third cell in the last row contains the artist's profile.

Figure 4-46 ◀
Inner table of the Gargoyle Collection Home Page

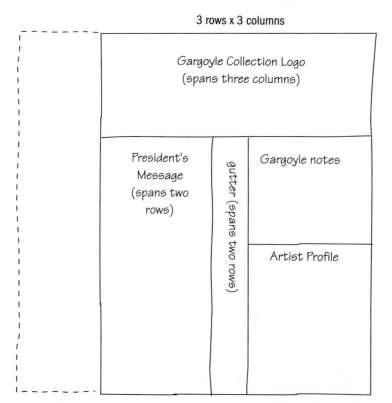

As with previous tables, you'll first enter the table structure and then enter the table text. Nested tables work in the same way as regular tables, except that they must be inserted within <TD> tags.

To create the nested table:

1. Return to the Gargoyle.htm file in your text editor.

2. Insert a blank line between the second set of <TD> and </TD> tags.

HTML

3. Enter the following text, indented three spaces in from the <TD> tag:

```
<TABLE WIDTH=445 CELLSPACING=0 CELLPADDING=0>
<TR>
   <!– The Gargoyle Collection Logo–>
   <TD COLSPAN=3 VALIGN=TOP ALIGN=CENTER>
   </TD>
</TR>
<TR>
   <!–A message from the company president–>
   <TD ROWSPAN=2 WIDTH=220 VALIGN=TOP>
   </TD>
   <!–The table gutter–>
   <TD ROWSPAN=2 WIDTH=5></TD>
   <!–Notes about gargoyles–>
   <TD WIDTH=220 VALIGN=TOP>
   </TD>
</TR>
<TR>
   <!–Profile of an artist–>
   <TD WIDTH=220 VALIGN=TOP>
   </TD>
</TR>
</TABLE>
```

Your file should appear as shown in Figure 4-47. Note that by indenting the text for the nested table three spaces, you have improved the readability of the HTML code without affecting the code itself.

Figure 4-47 ◀
HTML code for
the inner table

```
<!--Articles about the Gargoyle Collection-->
<TD WIDTH=445 VALIGN=TOP>
   <TABLE WIDTH=445 CELLSPACING=0 CELLPADDING=0>
   <TR>
      <!-- The Gargoyle Collection Logo-->
      <TD COLSPAN=3 VALIGN=TOP ALIGN=CENTER>
      </TD>
   </TR>
   <TR>
      <!--A message from the company president-->
      <TD ROWSPAN=2 WIDTH=220 VALIGN=TOP>
      </TD>
      <!--The table gutter-->
      <TD ROWSPAN=2 WIDTH=5></TD>
      <!--Notes about gargoyles-->
      <TD WIDTH=220 VALIGN=TOP>
      </TD>
   </TR>
   <TR>
      <!--Profile of an artist-->
      <TD WIDTH=220 VALIGN=TOP>
      </TD>
   </TR>
   </TABLE>
</TD>
```

Before proceeding, you should study the HTML code you just entered and compare it to Figure 4-46. Make sure that you understand the purpose of each tag in the nested table.

The first item you'll enter in the nested table is an inline image, GLogo.jpg, which you'll place in the table's first row.

To insert the Gargoyle Collection logo:

1. Insert a blank line below the first <TD> tag in the nested table.

2. Type the following in the blank line, indented three spaces in from the <TD> tag, to make the code more readable:

<IMG SRC="GLogo.jpg" WIDTH=440 HEIGHT=220>

Figure 4-48 shows the revised HTML code.

Figure 4-48 ◀
Inserting the
Gargoyle
Collection logo

```
<TD WIDTH=445 VALIGN=TOP>
   <TABLE WIDTH=445 CELLSPACING=0 CELLPADDING=0>
   <TR>
     <!-- The Gargoyle Collection Logo-->
     <TD COLSPAN=3 VALIGN=TOP ALIGN=CENTER>
        <IMG SRC="GLogo.jpg" WIDTH=440 HEIGHT=220>
     </TD>
   </TR>
```

With the logo in place, you'll insert the message from the company president next. The message has already been saved for you in the file Oneil.htm. This page is shown in Figure 4-49.

Figure 4-49 ◀
Message from
the company
president

From the President

This month Middle Age Arts introduces the Gargoyle Collection. I'm really excited about this new set of classical figures.

The collection contains faithful reproductions of gargoyles from some of the famous cathedrals of Europe, including Notre Dame, Rheims and Warwick Castle. All reproductions are done to exacting and loving detail.

The collection also contains original works by noted artists such as Susan Bedford and Antonio Salvari. Our expert artisans have produced some wonderful and whimsical works, perfectly suited for home or garden use.

Don't delay, order your gargoyle today.

Irene O'Neil
President,
Middle Age Arts

As you did with the list of hypertext links, you'll copy and paste the contents of the page body into a table cell. The pasted text needs to be placed in the first column of the second row of the nested table.

To insert the message from the company president:

1. Insert a blank line below the first <TD> tag in the second row of the nested table.

2. Open the file **Oneil.htm** from the Tutorial.04 folder of your Student Disk.

3. Copy the HTML code between, but not including, the <BODY> tags. All of the code you need to copy is already indented.

4. Return to the Gargoyle.htm file in your text editor.

5. Paste the HTML code you copied from Oneil.htm in the blank line you created in Step 1. See Figure 4-50.

Figure 4-50 ◄
HTML code for
the president's
message

table cell from the
second row,
first column of
the nested table

```
<TR>
    <!--A message from the company president-->
    <TD ROWSPAN=2 WIDTH=220 VALIGN=TOP>
        <H4 ALIGN=CENTER><FONT COLOR=GREEN>From the President</FONT></H4>
        <IMG SRC="Oneil.jpg" ALIGN=RIGHT WIDTH=86 HEIGHT=111>
        <P>This month Middle Age Arts introduces the Gargoyle
        Collection. I'm really excited about this new set of classical
        figures.</P>
        <P>The collection contains faithful reproductions of gargoyles
        from some of the famous cathedrals of Europe, including Notre
        Dame, Rheims and Warwick Castle. All reproductions are done to
        exacting and loving detail.</P>
        <P>The collection also contains original works by noted artists
        such as Susan Bedford and Antonio Salvari. Our expert artisans
        have produced some wonderful and whimsical works, perfectly
        suited for home or garden use.</P>
        <P>Don't delay, order your gargoyle today.</P>
        <I>Irene O'Neil</I><BR>
        <B>President,<BR>
        Middle Age Arts</B>
    </TD>
```

6. Save your changes, and then reload the file in your browser. The page now displays the column from the company president, as well as the Gargoyle Collection logo. See Figure 4-51.

Figure 4-51 ◀
Logo and president's message as they appear on the page

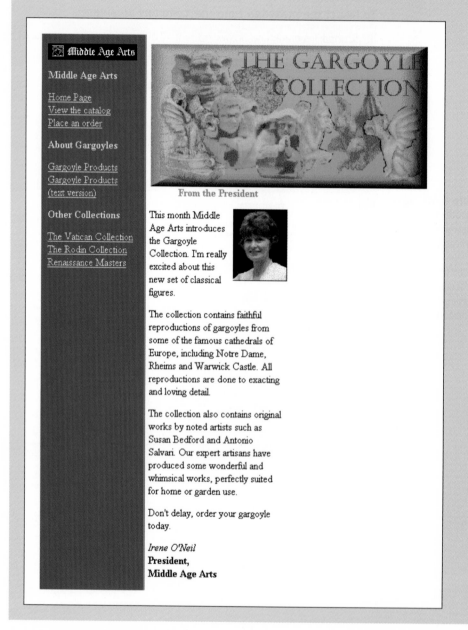

The next cell in the nested table creates a space (gutter) between the first and third columns. You do not have to enter any text into this cell, but you should leave a blank space between the <TD> and </TD> tags. The blank space ensures that the cell occupies the 5-pixel width set aside for it. Without anything in the table cell, some browsers will not display the cell, even if you have specified a width for it.

To insert a blank space into the gutter:

1. Return to the Gargoyle.htm file in your text editor.

2. Go to the <TD> tag after the table gutter comment tag.

3. Insert a blank space between the <TD> and </TD> tags.

The blank space you inserted will help ensure that the column retains its 5-pixel width. The next cell in the table will include a whimsical list describing the "uses" of gargoyle products. The contents of the list have been saved in the GNotes.htm file, shown in Figure 4-52.

Figure 4-52 ◀
List of gargoyle "uses"

> **What do I do with a gargoyle?**
>
> Don't think you need a gargoyle? Think again. Gargoyles are useful as:
>
> - Bird baths
> - Wind chimes
> - Pen holders
> - Paperweights
> - Bookends

Note that the background of this page is yellow. This is a feature you'll want to keep when you transfer the contents of this page into the table cell. You'll accomplish this using the BGCOLOR property of the cell.

To insert the gargoyle notes:

1. Make sure the Gargoyle.htm file is displayed in your text editor.

2. Insert a blank line below the <TD> tag located in the second row of the nested table.

3. Open the file **GNotes.htm** from the Tutorial.04 folder of your Student Disk.

4. Copy the HTML code between the <BODY> tags. Once again, do *not* include the <BODY> tags themselves.

5. Return to the Gargoyle.htm file.

6. Paste the HTML code in the blank line you created in Step 1.

   Next, you'll change the color of the cell background to yellow.

7. Type **BGCOLOR=YELLOW** within the <TD> tag for the cell. The revised code is shown in Figure 4-53.

Figure 4-53 ◀
HTML code for the list of gargoyle uses

table cell from the second row, third column of the nested table

table cell background color changed to yellow

```
<!--The table gutter-->
<TD ROWSPAN=2 WIDTH=5> </TD>
<!--Notes about gargoyles-->
<TD WIDTH=220 VALIGN=TOP BGCOLOR=YELLOW>
   <FONT COLOR="#800000">
   <H4 ALIGN=CENTER>What do I do with a gargoyle?</H4>
   Don't think you need a gargoyle? Think again. Gargoyles are
   useful as:
   <UL>
      <LI>Bird baths
      <LI>Wind chimes
      <LI>Pen holders
      <LI>Paperweights
      <LI>Bookends
   </UL>
   </FONT>
</TD>
</TR>
```

8. Save your changes, and then reload the file in your browser. The revised Gargoyle Collection page is shown in Figure 4-54.

Figure 4-54 ◀
Gargoyle notes on the Web page

TROUBLE? The space between the columns might look different in your browser from what is shown in Figure 4-54. Different browsers handle column spaces and gutters in slightly different ways.

The last component of the page is the profile of the artist, Michael Cassini. The contents of this profile can be found in the Cassini.htm file, shown in Figure 4-55.

Figure 4-55 ◄
Artist profile
page

Profile of the Artist

This month's artist is Michael Cassini. Michael has been a professional sculptor for ten years. He has won numerous awards, including the prestigious *Reichsman Cup* and an Award of Merit at the 1997 Tuscany Arts Competition.

Michael specializes in recreations of gargoyles from European cathedrals. You'll usually find Michael staring intently at the church walls in northern France. His work is represented by the *Turin Gargoyle*, a great entry to our Gargoyle Collection.

You need to place the text for the profile in the last cell in the third row. Remember that the first two cells of the third row have been already filled in, being merely extensions of the spanning cells created in the table's second row.

To insert the profile of Michael Cassini:

1. Return to the Gargoyle.htm file in your text editor.

2. Insert a blank line below the final <TD> tag, located in the third row of the nested table.

3. Open the file **Cassini.htm** from the Tutorial.04 folder of your Student Disk. Again, the HTML code is already indented.

4. Copy the HTML code between the <BODY> tags.

5. Return to the Gargoyle.htm file.

6. Paste the HTML code in the blank line you created earlier. See Figure 4-56.

Figure 4-56 ◄
HTML code
for the artist
profile

table cell from the
third row,
third column of
the nested table

```
<TR>
  <!--Profile of an artist-->
  <TD WIDTH=220 VALIGN=TOP>
    <H4 ALIGN=CENTER><FONT COLOR=GREEN>Profile of the Artist</FONT></H4>
    <IMG SRC="Cassini.jpg" ALIGN=RIGHT WIDTH=64 HEIGHT=74>
    <P>This month's artist is Michael Cassini. Michael has been a
    professional sculptor for ten years. He has won numerous awards,
    including the prestigious <I>Reichsman Cup</I> and an Award of
    Merit at the 1997 Tuscany Arts Competition.</P>
    <P>Michael specializes in recreations of gargoyles from European
    cathedrals. You'll usually find Michael staring intently at the
    church walls in northern France. His work is represented by the
    <I>Turin Gargoyle</I>, a great entry to our Gargoyle
    Collection.</P>
  </TD>
</TR>
</TABLE>
```

7. Save your changes, and then reload the file in your browser. Figure 4-57 shows the final version of the page.

Figure 4-57 ◀

Final version of the Gargoyle Collection Home Page

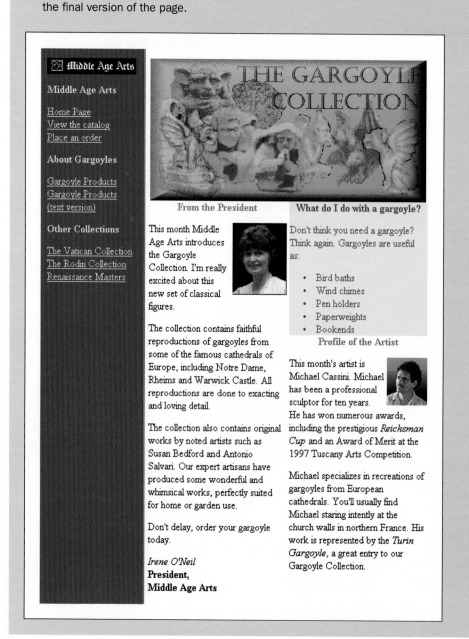

You've completed the design of the Gargoyle Collection Home Page. By using tables, you managed to create an interesting and attractive layout. This process illustrated several principles that you should keep in mind when creating such layouts in the future:

- Diagram the layout before you start writing the HTML code.

- Create the text for various columns and cells in separate files, which you'll insert later.

- Create the table structure for the outer table first, and then gradually work inward.

- Insert comment tags to identify the different sections of the page.

- Indent the various levels of nested tables, to make your code easier to follow.

- Test and review your code as you proceed, in order to catch errors early.

CREATING A PAGE LAYOUT WITH TABLES

- Create gutters and use cell padding to keep your columns from crowding each other.
- Add background colors to columns to provide visual interest and variety.
- Use the VALIGN=TOP property in cells containing articles, to ensure that the text flows from the top down.
- Use row spanning to vary the size and starting point of articles within your columns. Having all articles start and end within the same row creates a static layout that is difficult to read.
- Avoid having more than three columns of text, if possible. Inserting additional columns could make the column widths too narrow and make the text hard to read.

You show the final version of the page to Nicole. She's pleased that you were able to create a page to match her sketch. She'll look over the page you created and get back to you with any additional changes. As you wait for her feedback, you can learn a little more about tables and HTML tags.

Extensions to Tables

If you want to enhance the appearance of your tables, Internet Explorer supports several additional tags, not supported by all other browsers. These additional tags, or **extensions**, allow you to specify table border colors and control the appearance of cell boundaries. Although you won't apply them to any of the tables you've created so far, you might want to use them in tables you create in the future.

Specifying the Table Border Color

By default, a table's borders are displayed in two shades of gray, creating a three-dimensional effect. Both Internet Explorer and Netscape Navigator support an extension that allows you to choose the border color. The syntax of this extension is:

    <TABLE BORDERCOLOR=color>

where *color* is either the color name or color value. Figure 4-58 shows examples of tables using the BORDERCOLOR property.

Figure 4-58 ◄
Applying
Internet
Explorer's
BORDERCOLOR
property to
table borders

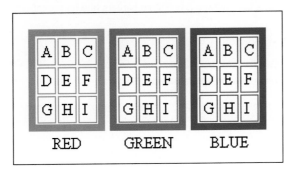

Note that this tag applies the color to the entire border, which eliminates the three-dimensional effect of the default color scheme. What if you want to keep the 3-D effect, but you want to use a different set of colors? Only Internet Explorer provides two additional properties—the BORDERCOLORLIGHT and BORDERCOLORDARK properties—which make this possible. The syntax for specifying the light and dark border colors is:

    <TABLE BORDERCOLORDARK=color BORDERCOLORLIGHT=color>

Figure 4-59 shows an example of the use of the BORDERCOLORDARK and BORDERCOLORLIGHT properties to create a 3-D border effect with shades of blue.

Figure 4-59 ◀
Applying the
BORDER-
COLORLIGHT
and BORDER-
COLORDARK
properties

BORDERCOLORLIGHT
= "#0099CC"

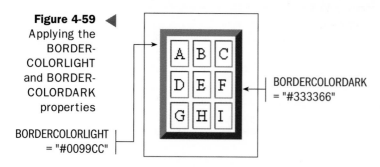

BORDERCOLORDARK
= "#333366"

When using these extensions, be sure to view your page in browsers other than Internet Explorer, to verify that the table still looks good even when the color extensions are not supported.

Creating Frames and Rules

Two additional properties introduced in HTML 4.0, which may not be supported by older browsers, are the FRAME and RULE properties. As you've seen, when borders are displayed, they surround the entire table on all four sides. The FRAME property allows you to control which sides of the table will have borders. The syntax for the FRAME property is:

`<TABLE FRAME=value>`

where *value* is either BOX (the default), ABOVE, BELOW, HSIDES, VSIDES, LHS, RHS, or VOID. Figure 4-60 describes each of these values.

Figure 4-60 ◀
Values of
Internet
Explorer's
FRAME
property

FRAME Value	Description
BOX	Draws borders around all four sides
ABOVE	Draws only the top border
BELOW	Draws only the bottom border
HSIDES	Draws both the top and bottom borders (the horizontal sides)
LHS	Draws only the left-hand side
RHS	Draws only the right-hand side
VSIDES	Draws both the left and right borders (the vertical sides)
VOID	Does not draw borders on any of the four sides

Figure 4-61 shows the effect of each of these values on the table grid.

Figure 4-61 ◄
Effect of
different
FRAME values

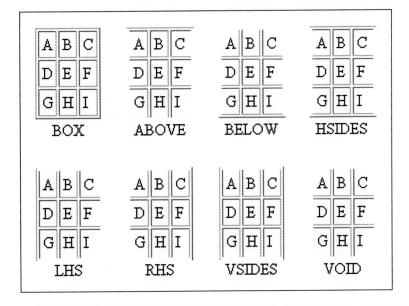

By default, borders are drawn around each cell in the table. The RULES property lets you control this by specifying how you want the table grid to be drawn. The syntax of the RULES property is:

```
<TABLE RULES=value>
```

where *value* is either ALL, ROWS, COLS, or NONE. The ALL value causes all cell borders to be drawn. The ROWS and COLS values cause borders to be drawn around only the table rows and columns, respectively. NONE suppresses the display of any cell borders. Figure 4-62 shows the effect of different RULES property values on a table's appearance.

Figure 4-62 ◄
Effect of
different
RULES values

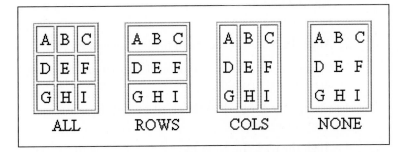

Once again, remember that when you use these Internet Explorer extensions, the effects you see will not be duplicated in other Web browsers, which will display tables with the usual grid layout. Therefore, you should always test under different Web browsers.

You've finished your work on the Web page and can now close your browser and text editor.

To close your work:

1. Close your Web browser.

2. Return to your text editor, and then close the Gargoyle.htm file.

Quick Check

1. What HTML code would you enter to create two 2 × 2 tables, one nested inside the upper-left cell of the other?

2. What HTML code inserts the comment "Nested table starts here"?

3. What code would you enter to change the border color of your table to yellow?

4. What code would you enter to use red for the light border color and blue for the dark border color?

5. What code would you enter to display only the top border of your table?

6. What code would you enter to create dividing lines around your table columns only?

7. What is the limitation of the code you created for Quick Checks 3 through 6?

You've completed your work with HTML tables. You've learned how to create text tables and graphical tables. You've seen how to control the appearance of your table and the text it contains, and you've seen how tables can help you create attractive page designs.

Tutorial Assignments

Nicole has finished reviewing the pages you created for her. She has made a few changes and has a few additional suggestions that she wants you to implement. These involve updating the text table you created to reflect the changes made to the graphical table, altering the appearance of the products table, and making some changes to the Gargoyle Collection Home Page.

To implement Nicole's suggestions:

1. In your text editor, open the MAA4.htm file in the TAssign folder of the Tutorial.04 folder on your Student Disk, and then save the file as Gtable.htm in the same folder.

2. Align the Name header with the left edge of its cell.

3. Increase the size of the table border to 10 pixels. Increase the size of the cell spacing to 3 pixels.

4. Change the Bust cell in the third row of the table body to a spanning cell that spans two rows.

5. Align the text "Bust" in the spanning cell with the cell's top edge.

6. Add the following new item to the bottom of the products table: Item Name—Spitting Gargoyle, Item #—49010, Type—Garden Figure, Finish—Gothic Stone, Price—$110.

7. Change the color of the header row to a greenish-blue. The color value (in hexadecimal) is 33FFFF. Save the changes to the Gtable.htm file.

8. Open the MAA3.htm file in the TAssign folder of the Tutorial.04 folder on your Student Disk, and then save the file as Gtext.htm in the same folder.

9. Add a fourth and fifth row to the text table body to match the items listed in the graphical table. Save your changes.

10. Open the GHome2.htm file in the TAssign folder of the Tutorial.04 folder on your Student Disk, and then save the file as Gcollect.htm in the same folder.

11. Add a fourth row at the bottom of the nested table. The row should have one cell that spans three columns.

12. Within the cell, insert the text "View a table of gargoyle products". Format the text as a hypertext link to the Gtable.htm file.

13. Align the text in the cell with the top and center of the cell.

14. Change the background color of the table cell to the hexidecimal value #800000. Save your changes.

15. Print both the page and the HTML code for the Gtext.htm, Gtable.htm, and GCollect.htm files.

16. Close your Web browser and your text editor.

Case Problems

1. Creating a Calendar of Activities at Avalon Books You've been asked to create a Web page that displays a calendar of activities at the Avalon Books bookstore for the month of May, 1999. Updating the calendar is a monthly activity, so a page has already been created containing a graphical table of the days of the month. Your job will be to update this table with the May activities. You will also add a caption and title to the table and format it.

The calendar should include the following activities:

- Every Monday: Noon storytime with Susan Sheridan
- Every Friday: Noon storytime with Doug Evans
- May 1st: Young authors' workshop from 1 to 4 p.m.
- May 5th: Ecology workshop with Nancy Fries from 9 to 11 a.m.
- May 15th: Ms. Frizzle teaches about science from 2 to 3 p.m.
- May 19th: Origami with Rita Davis from 2 to 3 p.m.
- May 22nd: Making a model of the solar system from 2 to 3 p.m.
- May 29th: Spenser Brown's Clown Show from 1 to 2 p.m.

To create the Avalon Books calendar:

1. In your text editor, open the Avalon.htm file in the Cases folder of the Tutorial.04 folder on your Student Disk, and then save the file as May_List.htm in the same folder.

2. Set the table width to use 100% of the display area.

3. Modify each cell in the table, changing the cell for Sundays to 16% of the table width, and make the width of each of the remaining days 14% of the table width. Align the text in each cell with the top of the cell border.

4. At the beginning of the table, insert a new row that spans the seven table columns. Set the width of this cell to 100% of the width of the table.

5. Within the spanning cell, insert the text "Children's Events in May, 1999". Center this text within the spanning cell and format it as an <H3> header.

6. Insert the days of the week in the cells of the table header row, starting with Sunday.

7. Enter the activities listed earlier. Note that some of the activities are repeated throughout the month.

8. Insert the table caption "For more information call Debbie at 555-4892" aligned with the bottom of the table.

9. Increase the width of the table border to 5 pixels.

10. Save your changes, and then view the page in your Web browser. If your monitor allows it, view the table at different screen resolutions (you might need to ask your instructor how to modify your monitor's resolution). How does the appearance of the table change under different resolutions?

11. Print the HTML code for the calendar page. Print the page itself; if you change your monitor resolution, print the page at the 640 × 480 and 800 × 600 screen resolutions.

12. Close your Web browser and your text editor.

2. Creating a Television Schedule at WMTZ You're in charge of creating Web pages for WMTZ in Atlanta. One of these pages contains the weekly prime-time television schedule from 7:00 p.m to 10 p.m. You'll create this schedule with a table broken down in half-hour installments. Because some programs in the schedule last longer than 30 minutes, you will have to include spanning cells to cover those time periods. Figure 4-63 shows the completed table.

Figure 4-63 ◀

Day	7:00	7:30	8:00	8:30	9:00	9:30
Mon.	The Nanny	Fred's Place	Old Friends	Cybill	Emergency Center	
Tue.	Babylon 5		Tonite!	911 Stories	Mission Impossible	
Wed.	Special: The Budget Crisis		Perfume		48 Hours	
Thu.	Mel's Diner	Alien World	Movie: Wayne's World III			
Fri.	Movie Special: Schindler's List					
Sat.	Dr. Quinn		Murder for Hire		New York Streets	
Sun.	Hey Dogs!	Wild Life	Movie: The Lost World			

To create the television schedule table:

1. In your text editor, open the WMTZ.htm file in the Cases folder of the Tutorial.04 folder on your Student Disk, and then save the file as TVList.htm in the same folder.

2. Create a table that has seven columns and eight rows, one of the rows consisting of table headers.

3. Set the table border width to 5 pixels, the cell spacing to 3 pixels, and the cell padding to 5 pixels.

4. Using the Internet Explorer extensions, change the color of the dark part of the table border to the color value 0000FF and the color of the light part of the table border to CCCCFF.

5. Set the width of each cell in the first column to 50 pixels.

6. Set the width of the table header cells (aside from the first column) to 90 pixels.

7. Enter the table text. Create spanning cells as indicated in Figure 4-63.

8. For each half-hour program, set the cell width to 90 pixels; set the cell width of hour programs to 180 pixels, of two-hour programs to 360 pixels, and of three-hour programs to 540 pixels.

9. Set the background color of the first row and first column of the table to yellow.

10. Center the table on the page.

11. Save your changes to the file.

12. View the page. What would be the difference between the way the page appears in the Netscape Navigator browser and the Internet Explorer browser?

13. Print a copy of your HTML code and the finished Web page.

14. Close your Web browser and your text editor.

3. Creating the Dunston Retreat Center Home Page   The Dunston Retreat Center, located in northern Wisconsin, offers weekends of quiet and solitude for all who visit. The center, started by a group of Trappist monks, has grown in popularity over the last few years as more people have become aware of its services. The director of the center, Benjamin Adams, wants to advertise the center on the Internet and has asked you to create a home page. The page will include a welcoming message from Benjamin Adams, a list of upcoming events, a letter from one of the center's guests, and a description of the current week's events. The home page you'll create is shown in Figure 4-64.

Figure 4-64 ◄

Welcome

Welcome to the Dunston Retreat Center. Whether you are planning to attend one of our many conferences or embarking on a private retreat, we're sure that you will enjoy your stay.

Located in the northern woods of Wisconsin, the Dunston Retreat Center provides comfortable and attractive accommodations while you enjoy the rustic setting available just outside your door. The Retreat Center has 32 beds, large meeting rooms, a chapel, and kitchen facilities. If you want to get out, there are ample opportunities for hiking, canoeing and horseback riding in the surrounding area.

Throughout the year the center staff conducts retreats to accommodate the needs of various groups. We offer retreats for men, for women, and for couples. Please call about special needs retreats.

If you prefer, an individually directed retreat is possible. The retreat includes a time of daily sharing and guidance by a retreat director to supplement your private time of solitude and meditation.

At the Dunston Retreat Center we make everything as easy as possible, providing meals, towels, bedding - everything you need. Just bring yourself.

Benjamin Adams
Director,
Dunston Retreat Center

Next week at the Dunston Retreat Center

The annual meeting of the Midwest Marriage Encounter occurs at the Dunston Retreat Center, June 11-13. Registration is $50 and includes room and board. A boating trip on Lake Superior is planned for Saturday night ($10 fee).

Contact Maury Taylor at 555-2381 for reservation information.

Upcoming Events

June 11-13 Marriage Encounter

June 18-20 Recovering Alcoholics

June 25-27 Spirituality Workshop

July 2-4 Lutheran Brotherhood

July 9-11 Recovering Alcoholics

July 16-18 Duluth Fellowship

July 23-25 Special Needs Children

August 6-8 St. James Men's Group

August 13-15 St. James Women's Group

August 20-22 Recovering Alcoholics

August 27-29 Knights of Columbus

A letter from one of our guests

I'm writing to tell you how much I enjoyed my retreat at Dunston. I came to your center haggard and worn out from a long illness and job difficulties. I left totally refreshed. I especially want to thank Father Thomas Holloway for his support.

I've enthusiastically told all of my friends about the wonderful place you have. Some of us are hoping to organize a group retreat. Rest assured that you'll see me again. Going to Dunston will become a yearly event for me.

Sincerely,

Doris Patterson

To create this home page, you'll use tables and nested tables to organize the page design elements.

To create the Dunston Retreat Center Home Page:

1. In your text editor, open the DRCtext.htm file in the Cases folder of the Tutorial.04 folder on your Student Disk, and then save the file as Dunston.htm in the same folder.

2. Create a table that has three columns and one row. The width of the first column should be 200 pixels, the second column 5 pixels, and the third column 395 pixels.

3. Above the first column, insert the comment "Welcoming Message"; above the second column, insert the comment "Gutter"; and, above the third column, insert the comment "Nested Table."

4. Specify that any text within the three cells should be vertically aligned with the top of the cell.

5. Insert the contents (but not the <BODY> tags or information within the <HEAD> tags) of the Welcome.htm file (from the Cases folder) into the first column of the table. Format the background of this cell using the same background color found in the Welcome.htm file.

6. Within the third cell, insert a nested table with the following dimensions: four rows by three columns. Both the first and second rows of the table should contain a single cell that spans three columns. The third row of the table should have a single nonspanning cell with a width of 210 pixels, followed by a cell that spans two rows and is 5 pixels wide, and then a third cell that is 180 pixels wide and also spans two rows. The fourth row of the table should contain a single cell 210 pixels in width—making a total of six cells in the table.

7. Insert comments into the nested table. Label the first cell "Dunston Logo," the second cell "Dunston Photo," the third cell "Midwest Marriage Encounter," the fourth cell "Nested Table Gutter," the fifth cell "Letter," and the sixth cell "List of upcoming events."

8. Vertically align the contents of the nested table cells with the cell top.

9. Insert the inline image DLogo.gif (from the Cases folder) into the first cell of the nested table. Specify that the dimensions of the image should be 390 pixels wide by 75 pixels high.

10. Insert the inline image Dunston.jpg (from the Cases folder) into the second cell of the nested table. Enter a dimension of 390 pixels by 170 pixels for the image's width and height.

11. Insert the body contents of the Nextweek.htm file (from the Cases folder) into the third cell of the nested table.

12. Insert a blank space into the fourth cell of the table.

13. Insert the body contents of the Letter.htm file (from the Cases folder) into the fifth cell of the table.

14. Insert the body contents of the Upcoming.htm file (from the Cases folder) into the sixth cell of the table.

15. Save your changes to the Dunston.htm file.

16. Print the HTML code and the resulting Web page.

17. Close your Web browser and your text editor.

EXPLORE

4. Creating the TravelWeb E-Zine Magazines on the Web, sometimes called e-zines, provide useful material to subscribers online. You have joined the staff of an e-zine called *TravelWeb*, which publishes travel information and tips. You've been asked to work on the layout for the e-zine's front page. You've been given files that you should use in creating the page. Figure 4-65 lists and describes these files.

Figure 4-65 ◀

File	Description
LuxAir.htm	Article about LuxAir reducing airfares to Europe
Photo.htm	Article about the Photo of the Week
PPoint.jpg	Image file of the Photo of the Week (320 × 228)
PPoint2.jpg	Small version of the Photo of the Week image (180 × 128)
Toronto.htm	Article about traveling to Toronto
TWLinks.htm	Links to other TravelWeb pages (list version)
TWLinks2.htm	Links to other TravelWeb pages (table version)
TWLogo.gif	Image file of the TravelWeb logo (425 × 105)
Yosemite.htm	Article about limiting access to Yosemite National Park
Yosemite.jpg	Image file of Yosemite National Park (112 × 158)

To create the TravelWeb e-zine front page:

1. Use the files listed in Figure 4-65 to create a newspaper-style page. All of these files are stored in the Cases folder of the Tutorial.04 folder on your Student Disk. The page should include several columns, but the number, size, and layout of the columns are up to you.

2. Use all of the files on the page, with the following exceptions: use only one of the two files TWLinks.htm and TWLinks2.htm, and use only one of the two image files PPoint.jpg and PPoint2.jpg. (*Note:* Not all of the links on this page point to existing files.)

3. Use background colors and spot color to give your page an attractive and interesting appearance.

4. Include comment tags to describe the different parts of your page layout.

5. Save your page as TW.htm in the Cases folder of the Tutorial.04 folder on your Student Disk.

6. Print a copy of the page and the HTML code.

7. Close your Web browser and your text editor.

Using Frames in a Web Page

Creating a Framed Presentation Containing Multiple Pages

CASE

Advertising for The Colorado Experience

One of the most popular climbing schools and backcountry touring agencies in Colorado is The Colorado Experience. Located in Vale Park, outside of Rocky Mountain National Park, The Colorado Experience specializes in teaching beginning and advanced climbing techniques. The school also sponsors several tours, leading individuals to some of the most exciting, challenging, and picturesque climbs in the Vale Park area. The school has been in existence for 15 years and, in that time, it has helped thousands of people experience the mountains in ways they never thought possible.

The Colorado Experience has stiff competition in the area from other climbing schools and touring groups. The owner, Debbie Chen, is always looking for ways to improve the visibility of the school. Early on, she decided to use the Internet and the World Wide Web as a means of advertising the school's services. She has already created an extensive number of Web pages to highlight the company's offerings.

Debbie has seen other Web pages that use frames, which are windows that allow the browser to display several HTML files within its display window. She feels that this would be a good way of showcasing the Web pages she has already created within an easy-to-use page design. She asks you to help her modify the company's Web presentation to take advantage of frames.

SESSION

5.1

In this session you will create a page that contains frames. You will learn about the HTML tags that control the placement and appearance of frames. You'll also learn how to specify a source document for each frame, and how to nest one set of frames inside another.

Introducing Frames

When Web presentations contain several pages, each page is usually dedicated to a particular subject or set of topics. One page might contain a list of hypertext links; another page might display contact information for the company or school; and another page might describe the company's history and philosophy. As more pages are created, you might start wishing that there were some way in which the user could view information from two or more pages simultaneously. One solution would be to repeat the information on several pages, but such a solution presents problems as well. For example, it would require a great deal of time and effort to type (or copy and paste) the same information over and over again. Also, if you had to change the information on one page, you would need to ensure that you changed the same information on all other pages in the presentation.

Such considerations led Netscape to create the <FRAME> tag. **Frames** are windows appearing within the browser's display area, each capable of displaying the contents of a different HTML file. An example of a page with frames is shown in Figure 5-1. In this example, a page consisting of hypertext links appears in a frame on the left, while the Products Home Page appears in a frame on the right.

Figure 5-1 ◀
Example of
a frame

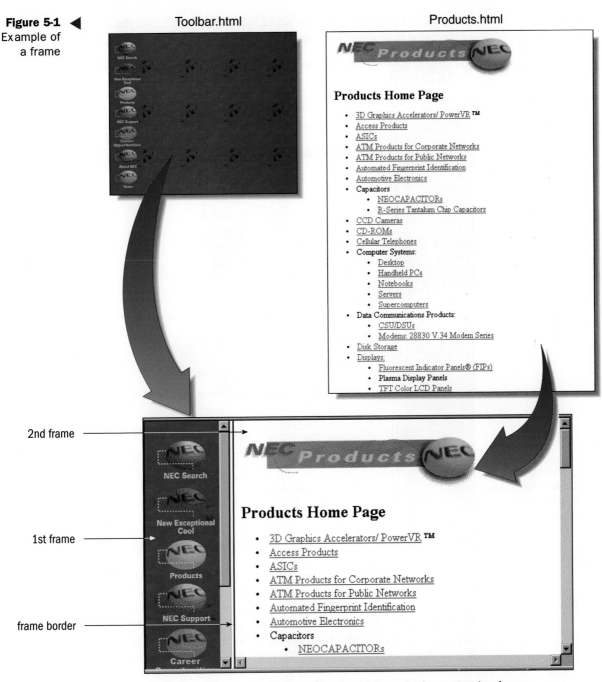

Both files are joined into a single page using frames

Frames can be set up to be permanent, allowing users to move through the contents of the Web presentation while always being able to see an overall table of contents.

Figure 5-2 illustrates how the list of hyperlinks remains on the screen while the contents of the home page change, depending on which hyperlink is clicked.

Figure 5-2 ◄
Activating a
hyperlink with
frames

When the user clicks
the Support
hyperlink ...

... the frame
containing the
document page is
updated, but the list
of hyperlinks remains
unchanged.

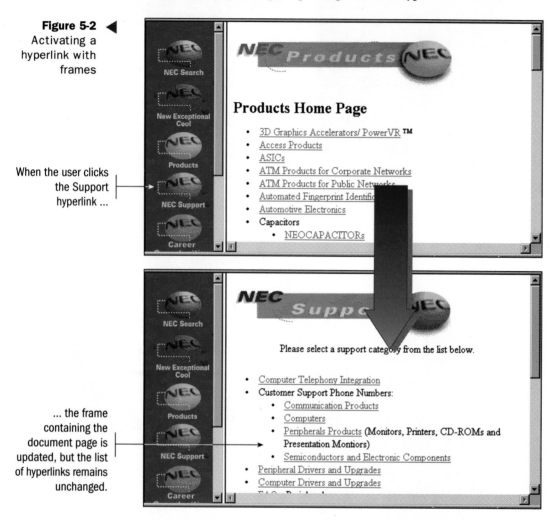

One downside to using frames is that you are causing the browser to load multiple HTML files rather than a single one, which could result in a longer delay for users. Also, not all browsers are able to display a framed page. Some earlier versions of Netscape Navigator and other non-Netscape browsers do not support frames. With the increasing popularity of frames, this is less of an issue, but you should still try to create both framed and nonframed versions of your Web presentations to accommodate all users and browsers.

Planning Your Frames

Before you start creating your frames, you should first plan their appearance and use. There are several issues to consider:

- What information will be displayed in each of the frames?

- How do you want the frames placed on the Web page? What is the size of each frame?

- Which frames will be **static**—that is, always showing the same content?

- Which frames will change in response to hyperlinks being clicked?

- What Web pages will users see first when they access the site?

- Do you want to allow users to resize the frames and change the layout of the page?

As you proceed in designing the Web page for The Colorado Experience, you'll consider each of these questions. Debbie has already thought about what information should be displayed on some of the pages in The Colorado Experience's Web site. Figure 5-3 lists the files for these pages.

Figure 5-3 ◀
Some of the files at The Colorado Experience's Web site

Topic	Filename	Content
Biographies	Staff.htm	Links to biographical pages of The Colorado Experience staff
Home page	TCE.htm	The Colorado Experience Home Page
Lessons	Lessons.htm	Climbing lessons offered by The Colorado Experience
Logo	Head.htm	A page containing the company logo
Philosophy	Philosph.htm	Statement of The Colorado Experience's business philosophy
Table of contents	Links.htm	Links to The Colorado Experience Web pages
Tours	Diamond.htm	Description of the Diamond climbing tour
Tours	Eldorado.htm	Description of the Eldorado Canyon climbing tour
Tours	Grepon.htm	Description of the Petit Grepon climbing tour
Tours	Kieners.htm	Description of the Kiener's Route climbing tour
Tours	Lumpy.htm	Description of the Lumpy Ridge climbing tour
Tours	Nface.htm	Description of the North Face climbing tour

The files are organized into various topic areas such as pages devoted to tour descriptions, climbing lessons, and company philosophy. Two of the files, Links.htm and Staff.htm, do not cover topics but rather contain hyperlinks to other Colorado Experience Web pages. How should this kind of material be organized on the Web page, and what should the user see first?

Debbie has considered these questions and has sketched a layout detailing how she would like the frames organized on the company's Web page (Figure 5-4).

Figure 5-4 ◀
Layout for the
Colorado
Experience
Web page

logo frame,
never changes

table of contents
frame, expands to
show tour list

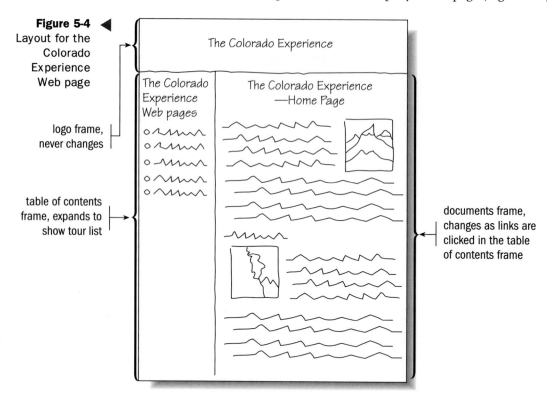

The Colorado Experience

The Colorado
Experience
Web pages

The Colorado Experience
—Home Page

documents frame,
changes as links are
clicked in the table
of contents frame

Debbie would like to have three frames in the presentation. The top frame will display the company logo and will always be visible to the user (that is, static). She has already created this information in the Head.htm file listed earlier in Figure 5-3. The frame on the left will display the table of contents page, Links.htm, with each item in the list acting as a hyperlink to a specific page. Finally, the frame on the right will display different Colorado Experience documents, depending on which hyperlink the user clicks in the table of contents frame. The Colorado Experience Home Page should be the first page that the user sees in this frame. This is a standard layout and a typical use for frames.

Your first task will be to insert the HTML code that creates the type of layout Debbie has in mind.

Creating a Frame Layout

Frame layout is defined using the <FRAMESET> tag. The general syntax for the <FRAMESET> tag in your HTML file is:

```
<HTML>
<HEAD>
<TITLE>Page Title</TITLE>
</HEAD>

<FRAMESET>
    Frame Definitions
</FRAMESET>
</HTML>
```

Notice that this code does not include the <BODY> tags. When you use the <FRAMESET> tag, you omit the <BODY> tag. Upon reflection, the reason for this should be clear: a page with frames displays the content of *other* pages. There is no page body to speak of. There is one situation in which you'll use the <BODY> tag in your page—when you are creating a page that can be displayed whether the browser supports frames or not. This situation is discussed later in the tutorial.

Specifying Frame Size and Orientation

The <FRAMESET> tag has two properties: ROWS and COLS. You use the ROWS property when you want to create frames that are laid out in rows, and you use the COLS property to lay the frames out in columns (Figure 5-5). You choose only one layout for a single <FRAMESET> tag, either rows or columns. You cannot use both properties at once.

Figure 5-5 ◀
Frames defined
in either rows
or columns

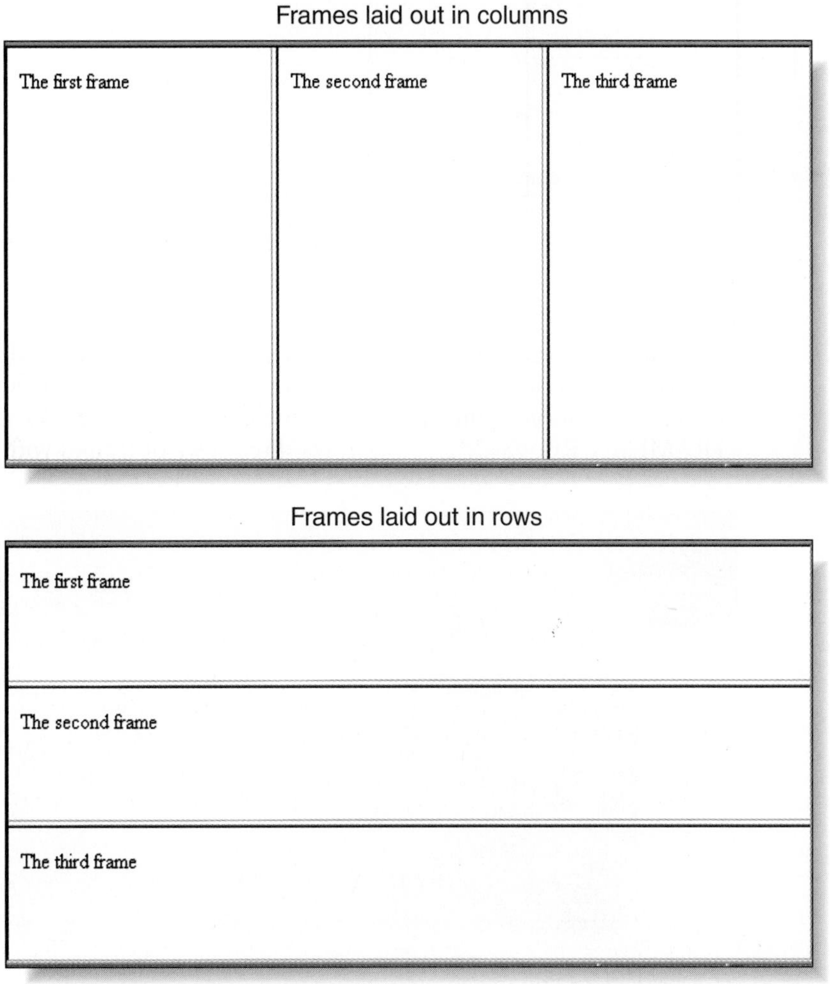

Frames laid out in columns

| The first frame | The second frame | The third frame |

Frames laid out in rows

The first frame

The second frame

The third frame

The syntax for specifying the row or column layout for the <FRAMESET> tag is:

```
<FRAMESET ROWS="row height, row height, row height, …">
```

or

```
<FRAMESET COLS="column width, column width, column width, …">
```

where *row height* is the height of each row, and *column width* is the width of each column. There is no limit to the number of rows or columns you can specify for a frameset.

Row and column sizes are specified in three ways: in pixels, as a percentage of the total size of the frameset, or by an asterisk (*). The asterisk tells the browser to allocate any unclaimed space in the frameset to the particular row or column. For example, the tag <FRAMESET ROWS="160,*"> creates two rows of frames. The first row has a height of 160 pixels, and the height of the second row is equal to whatever space remains in the display area. For a display area that is 400 pixels high, this would be 240 pixels.

You can use all three ways of specifying row or column size in a single <FRAMESET> tag. The tag <FRAMESET COLS="160,25%,*"> creates the series of columns shown in Figure 5-6. The first column is 160 pixels wide, the second column is 25% of the width of the display area, and the third column covers whatever space is left.

Figure 5-6 ◀
Frames with
different sizes

160 pixels wide

25% of the width of
the display area

whatever space is left

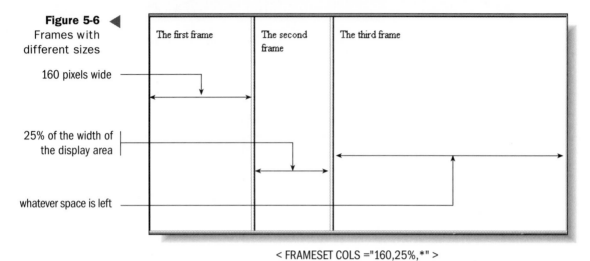

The first frame   The second frame   The third frame

< FRAMESET COLS ="160,25%,*" >

Invariably at least one of the rows or columns of your <FRAMESET> tag will be specified with an asterisk to guarantee that the frames fill up the screen regardless of the user's monitor resolution. You can also include multiple asterisks. For example, the tag <FRAMESET ROWS="*,*,*"> creates three rows of frames with equal heights.

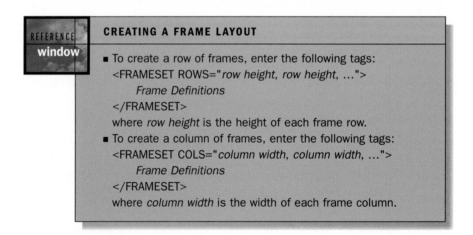

REFERENCE window

CREATING A FRAME LAYOUT

■ To create a row of frames, enter the following tags:
  <FRAMESET ROWS="*row height, row height, ...*">
      Frame Definitions
  </FRAMESET>
  where *row height* is the height of each frame row.
■ To create a column of frames, enter the following tags:
  <FRAMESET COLS="*column width, column width, ...*">
      Frame Definitions
  </FRAMESET>
  where *column width* is the width of each frame column.

An initial file for use in setting up the frames for the Colorado Experience Web page has been created for you and saved as COLtext.htm in the Tutorial.05 folder of your Student Disk. You'll open that file now and save it with a new name.

To open the COLtext.htm file and save it with a new name:

1. Start your text editor.

2. Open the file **COLtext.htm** from the Tutorial.05 folder on your Student Disk, and then save the file in the same folder as **Colorado.htm**.

The first set of frames you'll create for the Colorado Experience page will have two rows. The top row will be used for the company logo (saved in the Head.htm file), and the second row will be used for the rest of the page's content. A frame that is 60 pixels high should be tall enough to display the logo. The rest of the browser's display area will be taken up by the second row.

HTML

To create the first set of frames:

1. Create a new blank line directly below the </HEAD> tag in the Colorado.htm file.

2. Insert the following code:

```
<FRAMESET ROWS="60,*">
</FRAMESET>
```

This code specifies a height of 60 pixels for the top row and allocates the remaining space to the second row. Figure 5-7 shows the revised Colorado.htm file.

Figure 5-7 ◄
Creating two
rows of frames
in the
Colorado.htm
file

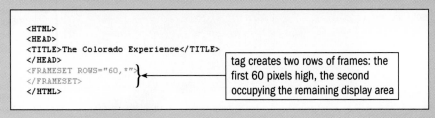

```
<HTML>
<HEAD>
<TITLE>The Colorado Experience</TITLE>
</HEAD>
<FRAMESET ROWS="60,*">
</FRAMESET>
</HTML>
```

tag creates two rows of frames: the first 60 pixels high, the second occupying the remaining display area

The initial frame layout is now defined. You'll be augmenting this layout later to include the third frame, following Debbie's design. For now, you need to specify the source for the two frame rows.

Specifying a Frame Source

The tag used to specify the page that will be inserted into a frame is the <FRAME> tag. The syntax for this tag is:

```
<FRAME SRC=document>
```

where *document* is the URL or filename of the page that you want to load. You must insert the <FRAME> tag between the <FRAMESET> and </FRAMESET> tags.

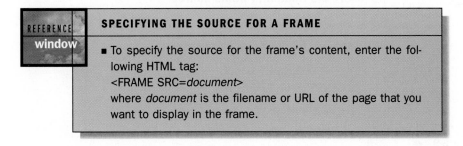

REFERENCE window

SPECIFYING THE SOURCE FOR A FRAME

■ To specify the source for the frame's content, enter the following HTML tag:
<FRAME SRC=document>
where *document* is the filename or URL of the page that you want to display in the frame.

The top frame displays the Head.htm file, which contains the company logo. Figure 5-8 previews the contents of this file and its placement on the page.

Figure 5-8 ◀
Head.htm file
containing the
Colorado
Experience
logo

transparent GIF

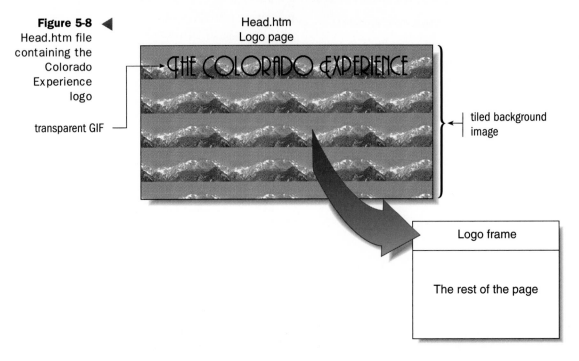

Head.htm
Logo page

tiled background
image

Logo frame

The rest of the page

Note that the logo consists of the company name, formatted as a transparent GIF and then placed on a tiled background of mountain images. Using a tiled background is a common technique for frames that display company logos. In this case, the advantage of this approach is that it guarantees that the mountain images will fill the frame under any monitor resolution.

To insert the Head.htm frame source:

1. Go to the end of the <FRAMESET> tag line, and then press the **Enter** key.

2. Type the following code (indent the code three spaces):

```
<!--- Company Logo --->
<FRAME SRC="Head.htm">
```

Figure 5-9 shows the inserted code.

Figure 5-9 ◀
Specifying the
source for the
first frame row

source file for the
frame in the first row

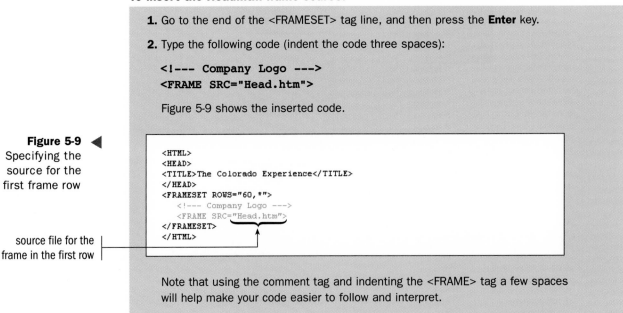

```
<HTML>
<HEAD>
<TITLE>The Colorado Experience</TITLE>
</HEAD>
<FRAMESET ROWS="60,*">
   <!--- Company Logo --->
   <FRAME SRC="Head.htm">
</FRAMESET>
</HTML>
```

Note that using the comment tag and indenting the <FRAME> tag a few spaces will help make your code easier to follow and interpret.

You've specified the source for the first row of the layout, but what about the second row? Looking back at Debbie's sketch in Figure 5-4, notice that this row will contain two additional frames. So rather than specify a source for the second row, you have to create another set of frames. To do this, you have to nest a second set of <FRAMESET> tags within the first.

Nesting <FRAMESET> Tags

Because a <FRAMESET> tag can include either a ROWS property or a COLS property, but not both, you have to nest <FRAMESET> tags if you want to create a grid of frames on your Web page. When you do this, the meaning of the ROWS or COLS property for the nested <FRAMESET> tag changes slightly. For example, a row height of 25% does not mean 25% of the display area, but rather 25% of the height of the frame into which that row has been inserted (or nested).

The second row of your current frame layout consists of two columns. The first column will display a table of contents, and the second column will display various Colorado Experience documents. You'll specify a width of 140 pixels for the first column, and whatever remains in the display area will be allotted to the second column.

To create the second set of frames:

1. Go to the end of the <FRAME> tag line that you just inserted, and then press the **Enter** key to create a blank line below it.

2. Type the following code (indent the text three spaces to make the code easier to follow):

```
<!--- Nested frames --->
<FRAMESET COLS="140,*">
</FRAMESET>
```

Your file should appear as shown in Figure 5-10.

Figure 5-10 ◀
Creating a
nested set of
frames in
the second
frame row

```
<HTML>
<HEAD>
<TITLE>The Colorado Experience</TITLE>
</HEAD>
<FRAMESET ROWS="60,*">
   <!--- Company Logo --->
   <FRAME SRC="Head.htm">
   <!--- Nested frames --->
   <FRAMESET COLS="140,*">
   </FRAMESET>
</FRAMESET>
</HTML>
```

two columns of
frames nested in the
second frame row

Next you'll specify the sources for the two frames in this row. The frame in the first column will display the contents of the Links.htm file. The Colorado Experience Home Page, stored in the TCE.htm file, will appear in the second frame. Figure 5-11 shows the content of these two pages and their placement on the Web page.

Figure 5-11 ◀
Links.htm and
TCE.htm pages

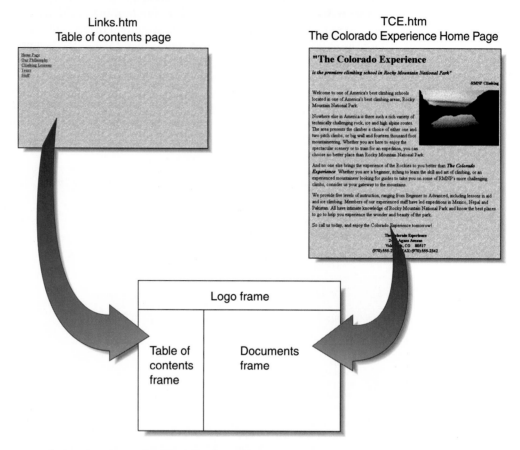

To insert the sources for the two frames:

1. Insert a blank line below the nested <FRAMESET> tag you just created.

2. Type the following code, indented six spaces:

```
<!--- List of Colorado Experience hyperlinks --->
<FRAME SRC="Links.htm">
<!--- Colorado Experience Web pages --->
<FRAME SRC="TCE.htm">
```

Figure 5-12 shows the code for the two new frames.

Figure 5-12 ◀
Sources for the
two frames in
the second row

table of
contents page

The Colorado
Experience
Home Page

```
<HTML>
<HEAD>
<TITLE>The Colorado Experience</TITLE>
</HEAD>
<FRAMESET ROWS="60,*">
   <!--- Company Logo --->
   <FRAME SRC="Head.htm">
   <!--- Nested frames --->
   <FRAMESET COLS="140,*">
      <!--- List of Colorado Experience hyperlinks --->
      <FRAME SRC="Links.htm">
      <!--- Colorado Experience Web pages --->
      <FRAME SRC="TCE.htm">
   </FRAMESET>
</FRAMESET>
</HTML>
```

3. Save your changes to the Colorado.htm file.

4. Open the file in your Web browser. Figure 5-13 shows the page's current appearance.

Figure 5-13
Colorado
Experience
Web page
with frames

text extends beyond
the frame border

logo

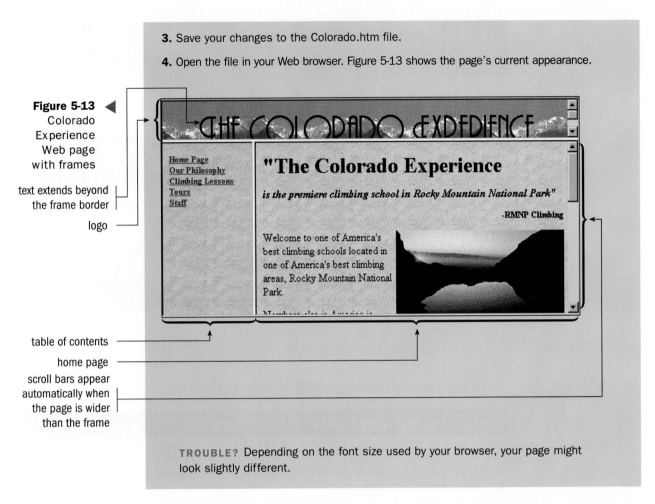

table of contents

home page

scroll bars appear
automatically when
the page is wider
than the frame

TROUBLE? Depending on the font size used by your browser, your page might look slightly different.

The page shows the three HTML files that Debbie wants on the page. However, the page's appearance needs some improvement. The company name is cut off in the logo frame, which also causes a scroll bar to appear. Scroll bars appear whenever the content of a page overflows the size of the frame. For example, scroll bars do not appear in the links frame, because the entire list of links is visible, but they do appear in the home page frame, because its contents are not completely visible. You can use the scroll bars to see the rest of the home page, but do not click any hypertext links yet. You will be working with hyperlinks and frames in the next session. For now, your task is to control how each frame appears on the page.

Controlling the Appearance of Frames

You can control three properties of a frame's appearance: the frame's scroll bars, the size of the margin between the source document and the frame border, and whether or not the user is allowed to change the frame's width or height.

REFERENCE window

CHANGING THE APPEARANCE OF FRAMES

- To control the appearance of a frame's scroll bars, use the SCROLLING property as follows:
  <FRAME SRC=*document* SCROLLING=*value*>
  where *value* can be either YES (to display scroll bars) or NO (to remove scroll bars). If you do not specify the SCROLLING property, scroll bars will appear only when the content of the frame source cannot fit within the frame's boundaries.
- To control the amount of space between the frame source and the frame boundary, enter the following tag:
  <FRAME SRC=*document* MARGINWIDTH=*value* MARGIN-HEIGHT=*value*>
  where *value* is expressed in pixels. The margin width is the space to the left and right of the frame source. The margin height is the space above and below the frame source. If you do not specify a margin height or width, the browser will assign dimensions based on the content of the frame source.
- To keep users from resizing frames, enter the tag:
  <FRAME SRC=*document* NORESIZE>

The first property you'll work with is the property for controlling scroll bars.

Controlling the Appearance of Scroll Bars

By default, scroll bars appear whenever the content of the source page cannot fit within the frame. You can override this setting using the SCROLLING property. The syntax for this property is:

```
<FRAME SRC=document SCROLLING=value>
```

where *value* can either be YES (to always display scroll bars) or NO (to never display scroll bars). If you don't specify a setting for the SCROLLING property, the browser will display scroll bars whenever it needs to.

Because the logo is not centered vertically within its frame and, therefore, is not entirely visible, scroll bars appear on the right side of the logo frame. Debbie feels that scroll bars are inappropriate for the logo frame, and wants to make sure that it never displays them. Therefore, you need to add the SCROLLING=NO property to the logo <FRAME> tag. However, Debbie does want scroll bars to appear for the other two frames, as needed, so you won't specify this property for their <FRAME> tags.

Note that when you are making changes to a framed Web page with Netscape Navigator, you will have to reopen the file to view the changes. If you simply click the Reload button, you will not see the results of your modifications. This is not the case with Internet Explorer 3.0 and above, in which you can view changes to the page by clicking the Refresh button.

ONLINE COMPANION

To remove the scroll bars from the logo frame:

1. Return to the Colorado.htm file in your text editor.

2. Within the <FRAME> tag for the logo frame, enter the property **SCROLLING=NO** as shown in Figure 5-14.

Figure 5-14
Removing the
scroll bars from
the logo frame

removes the
scroll bars

```
<FRAMESET ROWS="60,*">
    <!--- Company Logo --->
    <FRAME SRC="Head.htm" SCROLLING=NO>
    <!--- Nested frames --->
    <FRAMESET COLS="140,*">
        <!--- List of Colorado Experience hyperlinks --->
        <FRAME SRC="Links.htm">
        <!--- Colorado Experience Web pages --->
        <FRAME SRC="TCE.htm">
    </FRAMESET>
</FRAMESET>
```

3. Save your changes, and then view the file in your Web browser. You might have to reopen the Colorado.htm file to see the effects of your code changes.

Note that although the scroll bars for the logo frame have been removed, the logo itself is still not centered vertically within the frame. (You'll correct this problem next.)

When designing your Web pages, keep in mind that you should remove scroll bars from a frame only when you are convinced that all the contents of the frame source are displayed in the frame. To do this, you should view your page using several different monitor resolutions. A particular frame's contents might be displayed correctly in 800×600 resolution or higher, but this might not be the case with a resolution of 640×480. Few things are more irritating to users than to discover that some content is missing from a frame with no scroll bars available to display the missing content.

With that in mind, your next task is to solve the problem of the off-centered logo. To do so, you have to modify the internal margins of the frame.

Controlling Frame Margins

When your browser retrieves a Web page to display inside a frame, it automatically determines the amount of space between the page's content and the frame border. Sometimes the browser makes the margin between the border and the content too large. Generally you want the margin to be big enough to keep the source's text or images from running into the frame's borders; however, you do not want the margin to take up too much space, because you usually want to display as much of the source as possible.

The margin height for the logo frame is too large and has caused part of the logo's text to be pushed down beyond the frame's border. To fix this problem, you need to specify a smaller margin for the frame. This should cause the logo to move up in the frame and allow the entire text to be displayed.

The syntax for specifying the frame's margin is:

```
<FRAME SRC=document MARGINHEIGHT=value MARGINWIDTH=value>
```

Here, MARGINHEIGHT is the amount of space (in pixels) that appears above and below the content of the page in the frame, and MARGNWIDTH is the amount of space that appears to the page's left and right. You do not have to specify both the margin height and width; however, if you specify only one, the browser will assume that you want to use the same value for both. In general you will want to have margin sizes of 0 or 1 pixels for frames that display only an inline image (like the logo frame), and 5 to 10 pixels for frames that display text (such as the frame that is displaying the Colorado Experience Home Page). Setting margin values is a process of trial and error, as you try to determine what combination of margin sizes looks best.

To correct the problem with the logo frame, you'll decrease its margin size to 0 pixels. This setting should allow the complete logo to be displayed within the frame. Also, Debbie would like users to be able to view more of the home page without scrolling, so she asks you to decrease the margin height for the home page frame to 0 pixels. To keep the home page text from running into the frame borders, you'll also specify a margin width of 10 pixels for its frame. The links frame margin does not require any changes.

To set the margin sizes for the frames:

1. Return to the Colorado.htm file in your text editor.

2. Within the <FRAME> tag for the logo frame, enter the property **MARGINHEIGHT=0**.

3. Within the <FRAME> tag for the home page frame, enter the properties **MARGINHEIGHT=0 MARGINWIDTH=10**.

Figure 5-15 shows the revised HTML code in the Colorado.htm file.

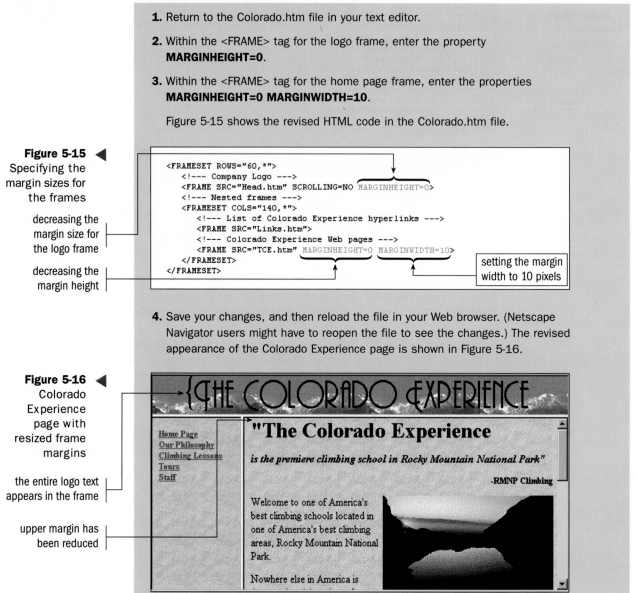

Figure 5-15
Specifying the margin sizes for the frames

decreasing the margin size for the logo frame

decreasing the margin height

```
<FRAMESET ROWS="60,*">
   <!--- Company Logo --->
   <FRAME SRC="Head.htm" SCROLLING=NO MARGINHEIGHT=0>
   <!--- Nested frames --->
   <FRAMESET COLS="140,*">
      <!--- List of Colorado Experience hyperlinks --->
      <FRAME SRC="Links.htm">
      <!--- Colorado Experience Web pages --->
      <FRAME SRC="TCE.htm" MARGINHEIGHT=0 MARGINWIDTH=10>
   </FRAMESET>
</FRAMESET>
```

setting the margin width to 10 pixels

4. Save your changes, and then reload the file in your Web browser. (Netscape Navigator users might have to reopen the file to see the changes.) The revised appearance of the Colorado Experience page is shown in Figure 5-16.

Figure 5-16
Colorado Experience page with resized frame margins

the entire logo text appears in the frame

upper margin has been reduced

Debbie is satisfied with the changes to the page's appearance. Your next task is to "lock in" the sizes and margins for each frame on the page, to prevent users from moving the borders.

Controlling Frame Resizing

By default, users can resize frame borders in the browser. Many Web authors prefer to make their frames static in size. To do this for the Colorado Experience page, you have to specify that the frame borders cannot be resized. The syntax for controlling frame resizing is:

```
<FRAME SRC=document NORESIZE>
```

The NORESIZE property takes no value—you simply include it within the <FRAME> tag to prevent users from modifying the size of your frames. You'll add this property now to all the frames in the Colorado.htm file.

To prevent the frames from being resized:

1. Return to your text editor and the Colorado.htm file.

2. Add the property **NORESIZE** within each of the three <FRAME> tags in the file.

3. Save your changes, and then reload the file in your Web browser. Verify that you cannot resize any of the frames.

Quick Check

1 What are frames, and why are they useful in displaying a Web presentation?

2 Why is the <BODY> tag unnecessary for pages that contain frames?

3 What HTML tag would you enter to create three rows of frames with the height of the first row set to 200 pixels, the height of the second row set to 50% of the display area, and the height of the third row set to the space that is left?

4 What HTML tag would you enter to use the Home.htm file as a source for a frame?

5 What HTML code would you enter to remove the scroll bars from the frame for the Home.htm file?

6 What HTML code would you enter to set the size of the margin above and below the Home.htm frame to 3 pixels?

7 What is the size of the margin to the right and left of the frame in Quick Check 6?

8 What HTML code would you enter to keep users from moving the frame borders for the Home.htm file?

You've completed your work with the frame layout and appearance for the Web presentation for The Colorado Experience. Debbie is pleased with the progress you've made. The page is not yet finished, however. You still must specify how the hyperlinks interact between one frame and another. You'll do this in the next session.

SESSION

5.2

In this session you will learn how hyperlinks work within frames. You will control which frame displays the source of an activated hyperlink. You'll also learn how to create a Web page that can be used both by browsers that support frames and browsers that do not. Finally, you'll examine some extensions to the <FRAME> and <FRAMESET> tags supported by the Netscape Navigator browser.

Working with Frames and Hypertext Links

Now that you've created the necessary frames for the Colorado Experience Web page, you're ready to work on the hypertext links on the page. The table of contents frame contains five hyperlinks: Home Page, Our Philosophy, Climbing Lessons, Tours, and Staff.

Figure 5-17 shows the files that each of these hyperlinks points to. The Home Page link points to the TCE.htm file; the Our Philosophy link points to Philsph.htm; Climbing Lessons points to Lessons.htm; Tours points to Tours.htm; and Staff points to the Staff.htm file.

Figure 5-17 ◄
Hyperlinks in
the Colorado
Experience
Web page

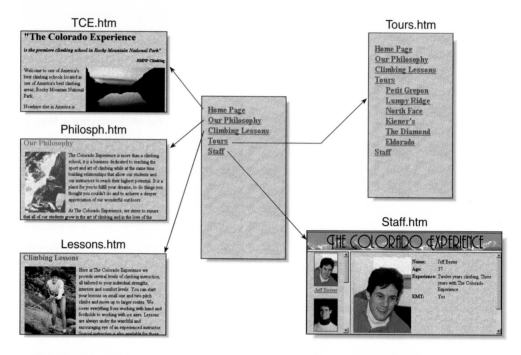

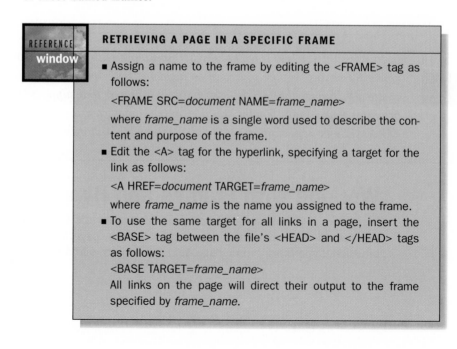

By default, clicking a hyperlink within a frame will open the linked file inside the same frame. However, this is not the way Debbie wants each of the hyperlinks to work. She wants the Home Page, Our Philosophy, and Climbing Lessons pages to open in the frame currently occupied by the home page. She wants the Tours page to replace the current table of contents, and finally she wants the Staff page to replace the entire frame structure.

When you want to control the behavior of hyperlinks in a framed page, you have to do two things: give each frame on the page a name and then point each hyperlink to one of those named frames.

REFERENCE
window

RETRIEVING A PAGE IN A SPECIFIC FRAME

- Assign a name to the frame by editing the <FRAME> tag as follows:

  <FRAME SRC=*document* NAME=*frame_name*>

  where *frame_name* is a single word used to describe the content and purpose of the frame.

- Edit the <A> tag for the hyperlink, specifying a target for the link as follows:

  <A HREF=*document* TARGET=*frame_name*>

  where *frame_name* is the name you assigned to the frame.

- To use the same target for all links in a page, insert the <BASE> tag between the file's <HEAD> and </HEAD> tags as follows:

  <BASE TARGET=*frame_name*>

  All links on the page will direct their output to the frame specified by *frame_name*.

Assigning a Name to a Frame

To assign a name to a frame, you use the NAME property. The syntax for this property is:

```
<FRAME SRC=document NAME=frame_name>
```

where *frame_name* is any single word you want to assign to the frame. Case is important in assigning names. A frame named "information" is different from one named "INFORMATION."

You'll name the three frames in the Colorado Experience page "Logo," "Links," and "Documents."

To assign names to the frames:

1. If you took a break after the previous session, start your text editor and open the Colorado.htm file.

2. Within the tag for the logo frame, enter the property **NAME=Logo**.

3. Within the tag for the links frame, enter the property **NAME=Links**.

4. Within the tag for the home page frame, enter the property **NAME=Documents**. Figure 5-18 shows the revised code for the Colorado.htm file.

Figure 5-18 ◀
Assigning
a name to
each frame

```
<FRAMESET ROWS="60,*">
    <!--- Company Logo --->
    <FRAME SRC="Head.htm" SCROLLING=NO MARGINHEIGHT=0 NORESIZE NAME=Logo>
    <!--- Nested frames --->
    <FRAMESET COLS="140,*">
        <!--- List of Colorado Experience hyperlinks --->
        <FRAME SRC="Links.htm" NORESIZE NAME=Links>
        <!--- Colorado Experience Web pages --->
        <FRAME SRC="TCE.htm" MARGINHEIGHT=0 MARGINWIDTH=10 NORESIZE NAME=Documents>
    </FRAMESET>
</FRAMESET>
```

5. Save your changes to the Colorado.htm file.

Now that you've named the frames, your next task is to specify the Documents frame as the target for the Home Page, Our Philosophy, and Climbing Lessons pages, so that each of these will open in the home page frame.

Specifying a Link Target

To display a page within a specific frame, you add the TARGET property to the <A> tag of the hyperlink. The syntax for this property is:

```
<A HREF=document TARGET=frame_name>
```

where *name* is the name you've assigned to a frame on your page. In this case the target name for the frame you need to specify is "Documents." To change the targets for the links, you have to edit the <A> tags in the Links.htm file. You'll start by editing only the <A> tags pointing to the Home Page, Our Philosophy, and Climbing Lessons pages. You'll work with the other hyperlinks later.

To specify the targets for the hypertext links:

1. In your text editor, open the **Linktext.htm** file from the Tutorial.05 folder on your Student Disk.

2. Within the <A> tag for the Home Page, Our Philosophy, and Climbing Lessons hyperlinks, enter the property **TARGET=Documents**. The revised code is shown in Figure 5-19.

Figure 5-19 ◀
Assigning a
target to
hyperlinks

the target is the
Documents frame on
the Web page

```
<A HREF="TCE.htm" TARGET=Documents>Home Page</A><BR>
<A HREF="Philosph.htm" TARGET=Documents>Our Philosophy</A><BR>
<A HREF="Lessons.htm" TARGET=Documents>Climbing Lessons</A><BR>
<A HREF="Tours.htm">Tours</A><BR>
<A HREF="Staff.htm">Staff</A>
```

3. Save the modified file as **Links.htm**. If you are prompted to overwrite the current version of Links.htm, click the **Yes** button.

   TROUBLE? If you need to return to the original version of the file, you can use the Linktext.htm file.

   Now test the first three hyperlinks in the list.

4. Open the **Colorado.htm** file in your Web browser.

5. Click the **Our Philosophy** link in the Links frame. The Our Philosophy Web page appears in the Documents frame. See Figure 5-20.

   TROUBLE? If the Our Philosophy page appears in the left frame, you either have to reload or reopen the Colorado.htm file.

Figure 5-20 ◀
Our Philosophy
page in the
Documents
frame

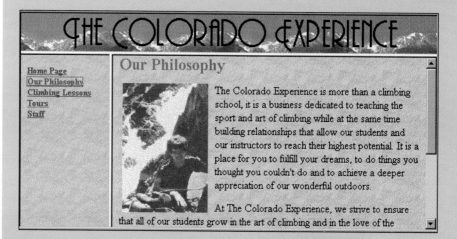

6. Click the **Home Page** and **Climbing Lessons** links to verify that the links are working properly.

Sometimes a table of contents frame will contain several such hyperlinks. It would be tedious to create TARGET properties for each link. Fortunately, HTML gives you a way to specify a target for all the hyperlinks in your file.

Using the <BASE> Tag

The <BASE> tag appears within the <HEAD> tags of your HTML file and is used to specify global options for the page. One of the properties of the <BASE> tag is the TARGET property, which identifies a default target for all of the page's hyperlinks. The syntax for this property is:

```
<BASE TARGET=name>
```

where *name* is the name of the target. The <BASE> tag is useful when your page contains a lot of hypertext links that all point to the same target. Rather than adding the TARGET property to each <A> tag, you can enter the information only once with the <BASE> tag.

If your file contains a few links that you do not want pointing to the target in the <BASE> tag, you can specify a different target for them. When the <BASE> tag points to one target, and an individual <A> tag points to a different target, the target in the <A> tag takes precedence.

To see how the <BASE> tag works, you'll use it to specify the Documents frame as the default target for all hyperlinks in the Links.htm file. In the process you'll remove the TARGET properties you've just entered.

To specify a default target with the <BASE> tag:

1. Return to the Links.htm file in your text editor.

2. Delete from the three <A> tags the TARGET=Documents properties you entered previously.

3. Insert the line **<BASE TARGET=Documents>** directly above the </HEAD> tag, as shown in Figure 5-21.

Figure 5-21 ◀
Specifying a
default target
for all
hyperlinks

default target ──────

```
<HTML>
<HEAD>
<TITLE>The Colorado Experience Hypertext Links</TITLE>
<BASE TARGET=Documents>
</HEAD>
<BODY BACKGROUND="Wall2.gif">
<FONT SIZE=2><B>
<A HREF="TCE.htm">Home Page</A><BR>
<A HREF="Philosph.htm">Our Philosophy</A><BR>
<A HREF="Lessons.htm">Climbing Lessons</A><BR>
<A HREF="Tours.htm">Tours</A><BR>
<A HREF="Staff.htm">Staff</A>
</B></FONT>
</BODY>
</HTML>
```

4. Save your changes, and then reload the Colorado.htm file in your Web browser. You might have to reopen the file to see the changes.

5. Test the hypertext links for the Home Page, Our Philosophy, and Climbing Lessons pages to verify that the pages appear within the Documents frame. Do not test the other hyperlinks yet.

   TROUBLE? If any hyperlinks do not work correctly, check the frame name and target name to verify that they match exactly, both in spelling and use of upper-case and lowercase letters.

You've so far worked with only the first three hyperlinks in the list. The remaining two links require different methods to display.

Using Magic Target Names

The last two tags in the list of hypertext links point to the tours offered by The Colorado Experience and to a staff information page, respectively. In both cases, the target of the hypertext link is not the Documents frame. The Tours hypertext link points to the Tours.htm file. The Tours.htm file does not contain any information about individual tours; instead, it is an expanded table of contents of Colorado Experience Web pages, some of which are devoted to individual tours. Each tour has its own Web page, as shown in Figure 5-22.

Figure 5-22 ◀
Tours page with
hyperlinks to
each tour

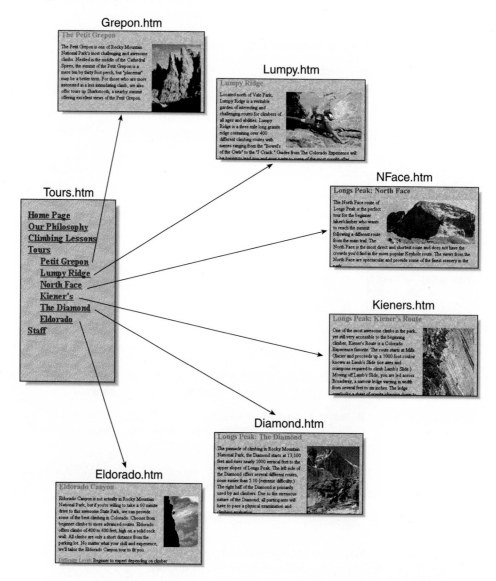

Debbie wants the Tours.htm file to appear in the Links frame. This will give the effect of expanding the table of contents whenever a user clicks the Tours hypertext link. Because the Tours.htm page will appear in the Links frame, you could specify Links (the name of the frame) as its target. However, there is another way to do this with magic target names.

Magic target names are special names reserved by HTML that can be used in place of a frame name as a target for a hypertext link. Magic target names are useful in situations where you want the page to appear in a new window or to replace the current frame layout. Figure 5-23 lists and describes the magic target names.

Figure 5-23 ◀
Magic target
names

Magic Target Name	Description
_blank	Loads the document into a new browser window
_self	Loads the document into the same frame or window that contains the hyperlink tag
_parent	In a layout of nested frames, loads the document into the frame that contains the frame with the hyperlink tag
_top	Loads the document into the full display area, replacing the current frame layout

All magic target names begin with the underscore character (_) to distinguish them from other target names. Note that magic target names are case-sensitive, so you must enter them in lowercase; otherwise, clicking the link could lead to unpredictable results.

Because Debbie wants the contents of the Tours.htm file to appear in the Links frame, you can use the _self magic target name, which will take precedence over the <BASE> tag and direct the browser to open the page in the same frame that contains the hypertext link.

To use the magic target name to specify the target for the Tours link:

1. Return to the Links.htm file in your text editor.

2. Within the <A> tag for the Tours hypertext link, enter the property **TARGET=_self**. See Figure 5-24.

Figure 5-24 ◀
Using the _self
magic target
name in the
Links.htm file

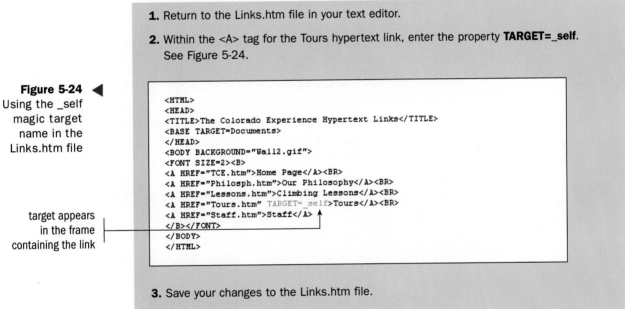

target appears
in the frame
containing the link

```
<HTML>
<HEAD>
<TITLE>The Colorado Experience Hypertext Links</TITLE>
<BASE TARGET=Documents>
</HEAD>
<BODY BACKGROUND="Wall2.gif">
<FONT SIZE=2><B>
<A HREF="TCE.htm">Home Page</A><BR>
<A HREF="Philosph.htm">Our Philosophy</A><BR>
<A HREF="Lessons.htm">Climbing Lessons</A><BR>
<A HREF="Tours.htm" TARGET=_self>Tours</A><BR>
<A HREF="Staff.htm">Staff</A>
</B></FONT>
</BODY>
</HTML>
```

3. Save your changes to the Links.htm file.

Because the Tours.htm file also acts as a table of contents for other Web pages, each page containing information about a specific tour, you need to specify the Documents frame as the default hyperlink target. This will cause the different tour pages to open in the home page frame. Also, the Tours.htm file contains a hyperlink that takes the user back to the Links.htm file. You should specify _self as the target for this hyperlink.

To modify the Tours.htm file as you did the Links.htm file:

1. In your text editor, open the **Tours.htm** file from the Tutorial.05 folder on your Student Disk.

2. Insert the tag **<BASE TARGET=Documents>** directly above the </HEAD> tag. This will allow the individual tour pages to be displayed properly in the Documents frame.

3. Within the <A> tag that points to the Links.htm file, enter the property **TARGET=_self**. This will redisplay the Links.htm file, containing the original table of contents. See Figure 5-25.

Figure 5-25 ◀
Revised
Tours.htm file

the default target
for hyperlinks on
this page

clicking this link
displays the
Links.htm file

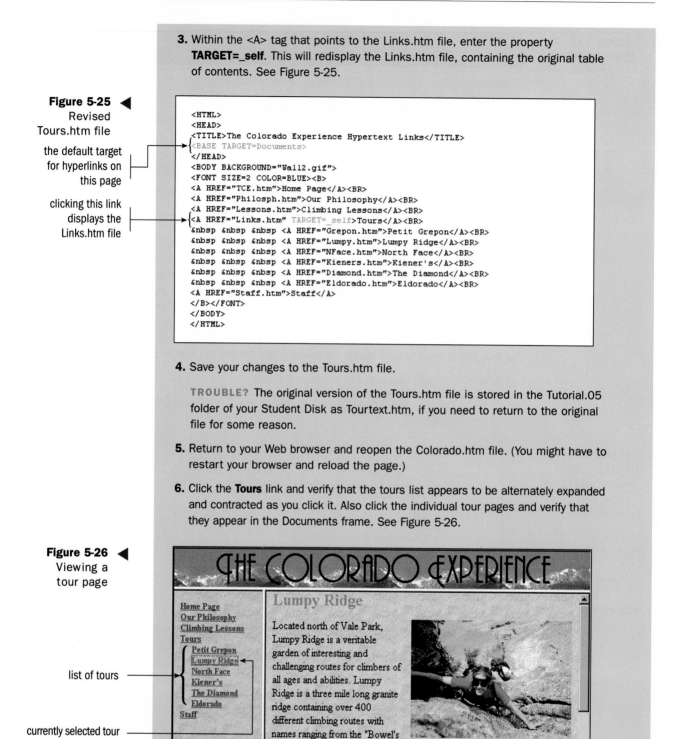

```
<HTML>
<HEAD>
<TITLE>The Colorado Experience Hypertext Links</TITLE>
<BASE TARGET=Documents>
</HEAD>
<BODY BACKGROUND="Wall2.gif">
<FONT SIZE=2 COLOR=BLUE><B>
<A HREF="TCE.htm">Home Page</A><BR>
<A HREF="Philosph.htm">Our Philosophy</A><BR>
<A HREF="Lessons.htm">Climbing Lessons</A><BR>
<A HREF="Links.htm" TARGET=_self>Tours</A><BR>
      <A HREF="Grepon.htm">Petit Grepon</A><BR>
      <A HREF="Lumpy.htm">Lumpy Ridge</A><BR>
      <A HREF="NFace.htm">North Face</A><BR>
      <A HREF="Kieners.htm">Kiener's</A><BR>
      <A HREF="Diamond.htm">The Diamond</A><BR>
      <A HREF="Eldorado.htm">Eldorado</A><BR>
<A HREF="Staff.htm">Staff</A>
</B></FONT>
</BODY>
</HTML>
```

4. Save your changes to the Tours.htm file.

TROUBLE? The original version of the Tours.htm file is stored in the Tutorial.05 folder of your Student Disk as Tourtext.htm, if you need to return to the original file for some reason.

5. Return to your Web browser and reopen the Colorado.htm file. (You might have to restart your browser and reload the page.)

6. Click the **Tours** link and verify that the tours list appears to be alternately expanded and contracted as you click it. Also click the individual tour pages and verify that they appear in the Documents frame. See Figure 5-26.

Figure 5-26 ◀
Viewing a
tour page

list of tours

currently selected tour

The technique employed here is a common one for tables of contents that double as hypertext links. Clicking the Tours hyperlink gives the effect that the list is expanding and contracting, but what is actually happening is that one table of contents is being replaced by another. You'll see this technique used on other pages on the Web.

The last link in the list points to a page of staff biographies, stored in the Staff.htm file. Debbie asked another employee to produce the contents of the page. The results are shown in Figure 5-27.

Figure 5-27 ◀
Staff Web page

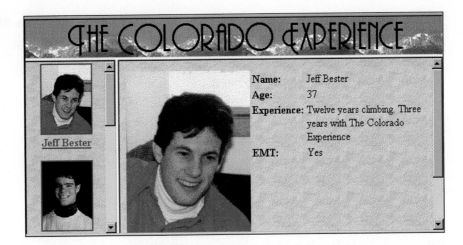

As you can see, this page also uses frames. How should this page be displayed within your frame layout? If you use the Documents frame as the target, you'll end up with the series of nested frame images shown in Figure 5-28.

Figure 5-28 ◀
One frame
image
appearing
inside another

This is not what Debbie wants. She wants the Staff page to load into the full display area, replacing the frame layout with its own layout. To target a link to the full display area, you use the _top magic target name. The _top target is often used when one framed page is accessing another. It's also used when you are linking to pages that lie outside your Web presentation, such as pages on the World Wide Web. For example, a link to the Colorado Tourism Board Web site should not appear within a frame on the Colorado Experience page for two reasons. First, once you go outside your Web presentation, you lose control of content, and you could easily end up with a nested frame layout problem. The second reason is that such a setup could confuse users, making it appear as if the Colorado Tourism Board is another component of the Colorado Experience climbing school, which would create an inaccurate impression.

Next, you'll add the _top magic target name for the Staff link to the link's <A> tag.

To use the _top magic target name to specify the target for the Staff link:

1. Open the **Links.htm** file in your text editor.

2. Within the <A> tag for the Staff link, enter the property **TARGET=_top**. See Figure 5-29.

Figure 5-29 ◄
Revised
Links.htm file
using the _top
magic target
name

```
<HTML>
<HEAD>
<TITLE>The Colorado Experience Hypertext Links</TITLE>
<BASE TARGET=Documents>
</HEAD>
<BODY BACKGROUND="Wall2.gif">
<FONT SIZE=2><B>
<A HREF="TCE.htm">Home Page</A><BR>
<A HREF="Philosph.htm">Our Philosophy</A><BR>
<A HREF="Lessons.htm">Climbing Lessons</A><BR>
<A HREF="Tours.htm" TARGET=_self>Tours</A><BR>
<A HREF="Staff.htm" TARGET=_top>Staff</A>
</B></FONT>
</BODY>
</HTML>
```

target is the top of
the document
window, replacing the
current frame layout

3. Save your changes to the Links.htm file.

Because the Tours.htm file also acts as a table of contents (with the added references to the tour pages), you should also edit the hyperlink to the Staff page in that file. In this way, a user can click the Staff hyperlink from both the table of contents with the expanded list of tours and from the original table of contents.

To edit the Tours.htm file:

1. Open the **Tours.htm** file in your text editor.

2. Within the <A> tag for the Staff link, enter the property **TARGET=_top**.

3. Save your changes to the Tours.htm file.

4. Reopen the Colorado Experience page in your Web browser and verify that the Staff link now opens the Staff page and replaces the existing frame layout with its own. Be sure to test the Staff link from both the original table of contents and the table of contents with the expanded list of tours.

   TROUBLE? If the Staff link does not work properly, verify that you used lower-case letters for the magic target name.

Debbie has viewed all the hypertext links on the Colorado Experience page and is satisfied with the results. However, she wonders what would happen if a user with an older browser encountered the page. Is there some way to accommodate browsers that don't support frames? Yes, using the <NOFRAMES> tag.

Using the <NOFRAMES> Tag

In most cases you do not need to include the <BODY> tags for pages containing frames. However, if you want your page to be viewable by browsers that do not support frames, as well as by those that do, you need to use the <BODY> tags. The difference is that the <BODY> tags must be placed within a pair of <NOFRAMES> tags. The <NOFRAMES> tag identifies a section of your HTML file that contains code to be read by frame-blind browsers. The general syntax for the <NOFRAMES> tag is:

```
<HTML>
<HEAD>
<TITLE>Page Title</TITLE>
</HEAD>
<FRAMESET>
    Frame Definitions
</FRAMESET>
<NOFRAMES>
<BODY>
    Page Layout
</BODY>
</NOFRAMES>
</HTML>
```

By examining this syntax, you can determine how the <NOFRAMES> tag works. If a browser that supports frames retrieves this code, it knows that it should ignore everything within the <NOFRAMES> tags and concentrate solely on the code within the <FRAME-SET> tags. If a browser that doesn't support frames retrieves this code, it doesn't know what to do with the <FRAMESET> and <NOFRAMES> tags, so it just ignores them. However it does know that it's supposed to render whatever appears within the <BODY> tags on the page. In this way, both types of browsers are supported within a single HTML file.

REFERENCE
window

SUPPORTING FRAME-BLIND BROWSERS

- Create a version of your page that does not use frames.
- In the framed version of the page, insert the following tags:
<NOFRAMES>
</NOFRAMES>
- Copy the HTML code between the <BODY> tags, including both the <BODY> and </BODY> tags, from the nonframed version of the page.
- Paste the copied code between the <NOFRAMES> and </NOFRAMES> tags in the framed version of the page.

The Colorado Experience has been using a nonframed version of its home page for some time now. This page is shown in Figure 5-30.

Figure 5-30 ◀
Nonframed
version of the
Colorado
Experience
Web page

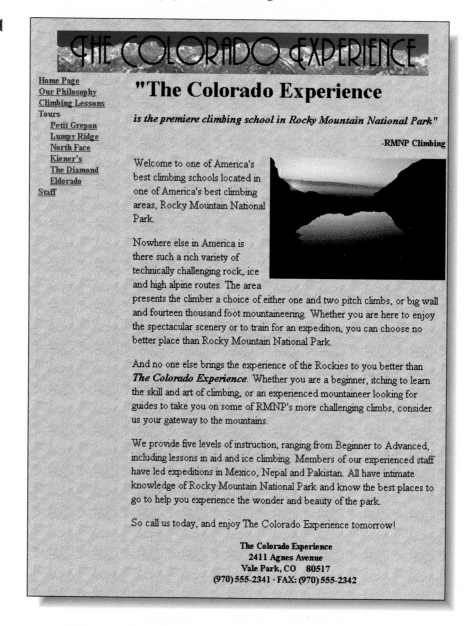

To display this page for frame-blind browsers, you need to copy the HTML code, including the <BODY> tags, and place it within a pair of <NOFRAMES> tags in the Colorado.htm file.

To insert support for frame-blind browsers:

1. Open the **Colorado.htm** file in your text editor.

2. Insert a blank line above the </HTML> tag.

3. Enter the following HTML code:

```
<!- - - Frameless version of this page - - ->
<NOFRAMES>
</NOFRAMES>
```

4. Save your changes to the Colorado.htm file.

Next you'll copy the code from the nonframed page into the Colorado.htm file.

5. In your text editor, open the **Noframes.htm** file from the Tutorial.05 folder on your Student Disk.

6. Copy the HTML code beginning with the <BODY> tag and down to the </BODY> tag. Be sure to include *both* the opening and closing <BODY> tags in your selection.

7. Open the **Colorado.htm** file in the text editor.

8. Insert a blank line below the <NOFRAMES> tag.

9. Paste the text you copied from the Noframes.htm file in the blank line below the <NOFRAMES> tag. Figure 5-31 shows a portion of the revised code.

Figure 5-31 ◀
Inserting the
NOFRAMES
code into the
Colorado.htm
file

```
<NOFRAMES>
<BODY BACKGROUND="Wall.gif">
<TABLE WIDTH=610>
<TR>
    <!--- Company Logo --->
    <TD ALIGN=CENTER COLSPAN=2>
        <IMG SRC="Logo.jpg" WIDTH=550 HEIGHT=60 ALT="The Colorado Experience">
    </TD>
</TR>
<TR>
```

```
        2411 Agnes Avenue<BR>
        Vale Park, CO     80517<BR>
        (970) 555-2341 &#183 FAX: (970) 555-2342
        </B></FONT></CENTER>
    </TD>
</TR>
</TABLE>

</BODY>
</NOFRAMES>
```

10. Save the file in your text editor.

To test your page, you should try to locate a browser that does not support frames (you can retrieve early versions of Netscape Navigator and Internet Explorer at their Web sites). Note that the table structure of the frameless page closely matches the frame layout you created. In this case, the first row is a single cell that spans two columns and displays the company logo, and the second row contains the list of links in the first cell and the home page text in the second cell.

Not all HTML editors support frames. If you try to use an HTML editor to edit a Web page, rather than working with the HTML code directly, you might find that the editor will only load the code between the <NOFRAMES> tags. The HTML editors that do not support frames, such as Netscape Gold, for example, will go directly to the first <BODY> tag they find. In these situations, you'll have to edit any code related to frames directly with a text editor.

TIPS FOR USING FRAMES

- Create framed and nonframed versions of your Web page to accommodate all browsers.
- Do not turn off vertical or horizontal scrolling unless you are certain that all the content will appear within the frame borders.
- Assign names to all of your frames to make your HTML code easier to interpret.
- Simplify your HTML code by using the <BASE> tag when most of the hyperlinks in your framed page point to the same target.
- Never display pages that lie outside your Web presentation (such as pages created by other authors on the World Wide Web) within a frame.

You're finished working with the Colorado Experience page. There are some additional features you can add to this page, which are not supported by all browsers. You'll investigate them next.

Using Frame Extensions

Netscape Navigator and Internet Explorer both support extensions to the <FRAME> tag that allow you to change border size and appearance. For example, you can remove borders from your frames to free up more space for text and images, or you can change the color of the frame border so that it matches your color scheme more closely. As with other extensions, you should use care when implementing these extensions, because they might not be supported by all browsers.

REFERENCE window

USING ENHANCEMENTS TO THE <FRAME> AND <FRAMESET> TAGS

(Netscape Navigator users only)
- To define a color for your frame borders, use the following tags:
  <FRAMESET BORDERCOLOR=*color*>
  or
  <FRAME BORDERCOLOR=*color*>
  where *color* is either the color name or color value. Enter the BORDERCOLOR property in the <FRAMESET> tag to change all of the frame border colors in a set of frames. Enter the property in the <FRAME> tag to change the color of a single frame border.
- To change the width of your frame borders, use the tag:
  <FRAMESET BORDER=*value*>
  where *value* is the width of the border in pixels. You cannot change the width of individual frame borders.

Setting the Border Color

One of the extensions supported by Netscape Navigator is the ability to change the color of a frame's border. The BORDERCOLOR property can be applied either to an entire set of frames (within the <FRAMESET> tag) or to individual frames (within the <FRAME> tag). The syntax for this property is:

```
<FRAMESET BORDERCOLOR=color>
or
<FRAME BORDERCOLOR=color>
```

where *color* is either a color name or a color value. Applying the BORDERCOLOR property to a set of frames colors all of the frames and nested frames within the set.

Debbie asks you to test the BORDERCOLOR property on the Colorado Experience page by changing the color of the Logo frame border to blue. You'll leave the colors of the rest of the frame borders as they are.

To change the Logo frame border color:

1. Return to the Colorado.htm file in your text editor.

2. Within the <FRAME> tag for the Logo frame, enter the property **BORDERCOLOR=BLUE**.

3. Save your changes to the file, and then reopen the file in the Netscape Navigator browser. Figure 5-32 shows the Logo frame with a blue border.

Figure 5-32
Logo frame with a blue border

blue frame border

TROUBLE? If you don't have the Netscape Navigator browser, or if your browser does not support the BORDERCOLOR property for frames, you will not be able to view the results of this set of steps. Continue reviewing the steps, however.

Another way of modifying frame borders is to change their widths.

Setting the Border Width

Netscape Navigator also supports the BORDER property, an extension that allows you to specify the width of the frame borders. Unlike the BORDERCOLOR property, this property can be used only in the <FRAMESET> tag, and not in individual <FRAME> tags. The syntax for the BORDER property is:

```
<FRAMESET BORDER=value>
```

where *value* is the width of the frame borders in pixels.

To see how this property affects the appearance of your page, Debbie asks you to use it to remove the frame borders by setting the width to 0 pixels. Once again, you can view the results of this property in the Netscape Navigator browser, version 3.0 or above.

To change the size of the frame borders:

1. Return to the Colorado.htm file in your text editor.

2. Locate the Logo <FRAME> tag and delete the BORDERCOLOR property that you entered in the previous set of steps. You don't need this property because you're going to remove the frame borders entirely.

3. Within the first <FRAMESET> tag, enter the property **BORDER=0**. See Figure 5-33.

Figure 5-33 ◀
Removing the
frame borders

width of each frame
border is 0 pixels

```
<HTML>
<HEAD>
<TITLE>The Colorado Experience</TITLE>
</HEAD>
<FRAMESET ROWS="60,*"  BORDER=0>
    <!--- Company Logo --->
```

4. Save your changes, and then reopen the Colorado.htm file in the Netscape Navigator browser. As shown in Figure 5-34, the frame borders have been removed from the page.

Figure 5-34 ◀
The Colorado
Experience
Web page
without frame
borders

By removing the borders, you created more space for the text and images in each of the pages. You've also created the impression of a "seamless" Web page. Some Web authors prefer to eliminate frame borders, in order to give the illusion of having a single Web page rather than three separate ones.

You can create a similar effect by using the FRAMEBORDER property. This is another property that is supported by both Netscape Navigator and Internet Explorer. Specifying FRAMEBORDER=NO in a <FRAMESET> tag removes the borders from the frames in your page.

Quick Check

1. When you click a hyperlink inside of a frame, what frame will the page appear in by default?
2. What HTML code would you enter to assign the name "Address" to a frame whose document source is Address.htm?
3. What HTML code would you enter to direct a hyperlink to a frame named "News"?
4. What HTML code would you enter to point a hyperlink to the document "Sales.htm" with the result that the Sales.htm file is retrieved into the entire display area, overwriting any frames in the process?
5. What tag would you enter to direct all hyperlinks in a document to the "News" target?
6. Describe what you would do to make your page readable by both browsers that support frames and those that do not.
7. What tag would you enter to set the frame border color of every frame on the page to red?
8. What tag would you enter to set the frame border width to 5 pixels?
9. What is the limitation of the tags you created in Quick Checks 7 and 8?

You've completed your work with the Web page for The Colorado Experience. Using frames, you created an interesting presentation that is easy to navigate and attractive to the eye. Debbie looks over your work and will get back to you with any changes.

Tutorial Assignments

Debbie has some suggestions for modifications to the Web presentation for The Colorado Experience. Recall that the Staff page already uses frames. Debbie would like you to make a few changes to the design of this page. Specifically, she wants you to:

- create a new frame containing a hyperlink pointing back to the Colorado.htm file
- remove any scroll bars from the frame and keep it from being resized by the user
- remove the frame borders for users of Netscape Navigator
- insert HTML code to support users with frame-blind browsers

To implement Debbie's suggestions:

1. Start your text editor and open the Stafftxt.htm file in the TAssign folder of the Tutorial.05 folder on your Student Disk, and then save the file as Staff.htm in the same folder.
2. Replace the <FRAME> tag and the corresponding comment tag in the first column of the second row with a <FRAMESET> tag to create two rows of nested frames. The height of the first row should be 25 pixels. The height of the second row should be whatever space is left.
3. Specify the file Return.htm as the source for the frame in the first row. Do not allow users to resize this frame, and remove any scroll bars. Set the width of the frame margins to 1 pixel. Name the frame "Return."
4. Specify the file Photos.htm as the source for the frame in the second row. Turn off frame resizing, but allow the browser to display scroll bars when needed. Set the margin height of this frame to 1 pixel, and set the margin width to 10 pixels. Name the frame "Photos."
5. Close off the two <FRAME> tags with a </FRAMESET> tag.
6. Insert an opening and closing <NOFRAME> tag below the last </FRAMESET> tag.
7. Copy the HTML code from the StaffNF.htm file (in the TAssign folder), including the <BODY> tags, and paste the code between the <NOFRAMES> tags in the Staff.htm file.
8. Change the border width of the frames in the Staff.htm file to 0 pixels.
9. Insert comment tags that document the different frames you created in the file.
10. Save your changes to the Staff.htm file.
11. Open the Retrntxt.htm file in the TAssign folder of the Tutorial.05 folder on your Student Disk, and then save the file as Return.htm in the same folder.

EXPLORE

12. Change the text "Go to home page" to a hyperlink pointing to the Colorado.htm file. Set up the hyperlink so that it loads Colorado.htm into the full display window when clicked.

13. Save your changes to the Return.htm file.

14. Open the Staff.htm file from the TAssign folder in your Web browser and verify that the frames appear correctly and all hyperlinks are working properly. Figure 5-35 shows the finished appearance of the page.

Figure 5-35 ◀

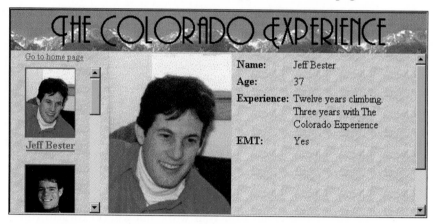

15. Print your Web page and the corresponding HTML code for the Staff.htm and Return.htm files.

16. Close your Web browser and your text editor.

Case Problems

1. Creating a Sales Report for Doc-Centric Copiers Doc-Centric Copiers, located in Salt Lake City, is one of the nation's leading manufacturers of personal and business copiers. The annual shareholders' convention in Chicago is approaching, and the general manager, David Edgars, wants you to create an online report for the convention participants. The report will run off a computer located in the convention hall and will be accessible to everyone. David feels that creating a Web presentation to run locally on the computer is the best way of presenting the sales data. Using hyperlinks between various reports will enable Doc-Centric Copiers to make a wealth of information available to shareholders in an easy-to-use format. Most of the Web pages have already been created for you. Your job is to combine the information into a single page using frames. A preview of the page you'll create is shown in Figure 5-36.

Figure 5-36 ◀

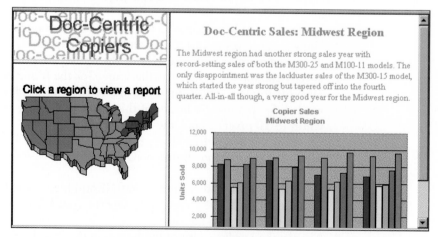

To create the Doc-Centric Copiers sales report page:

1. Open the file DCCtxt.htm in the Cases folder of the Tutorial.05 folder on your Student Disk, and then save the file as DCC.htm in the same folder.

2. Create a frame layout. The layout should consist initially of two columns. The left column should be 240 pixels wide, and the right column should fill up the rest of the display area.

3. Within the first frame column, insert two rows of nested frames. The frame in the first row should be 75 pixels high, and the second row should fill up the remaining space. The source for the first frame row is the Head.htm file, which contains the company logo. The source for the second frame row is the Map.htm file, which contains a map showing the different sales regions for the company. Name the first frame "Logo" and the second frame "USMap."

4. The source for the frame in the second column is the file Report.htm. This frame will contain the various sales reports that David wants displayed. Name the frame "Reports."

5. Complete the tags required for the frame layout and add comment tags describing each frame. Save your changes.

6. Open the file Maptxt.htm in the Cases folder of the Tutorial.05 folder on your Student Disk, and then save the file as Map.htm in the same folder.

EXPLORE

7. The Map.htm file contains an image map of the different sales regions. For each hyperlink in the Map.htm file, direct the link to the Reports target, so that the pages appear in the Reports frame. Save your changes.

8. View the DCC.htm file in your Web browser. What improvements could be made to the page? What things should be removed?

9. Return to the DCC.htm file in your text editor and reduce the margin for the Logo frame to 1 pixel. Reduce the margin width for the USMap frame to 1 pixel, and change the margin height to 30 pixels.

10. Remove scroll bars from both the Logo and USMap frames.

11. View the page again to verify that the problems you identified in Step 8 have been resolved.

12. Return to the DCC.htm file and lock the size of the frames to prevent users from inadvertently changing the frame sizes.

13. Reopen the Doc-Centric Copiers sales report page and test the image map in the USMap frame. Verify that each of the four sales reports is correctly displayed in the Reports frame.

14. Print a page displaying one of the sales reports. Print a copy of both the DCC.htm and Map.htm files.

15. Close your Web browser and your text editor.

2. Creating a Tour Page for Travel Scotland! You've been asked to create a Web presentation for a touring agency called Travel Scotland!, which organizes tours to Scotland and the British Isles. The page will display an itinerary and photo for four popular tours: the Lake District tour, the Castles of Scotland tour, a tour of the Scottish Highlands, and, finally, a tour of the Hebrides. A page with a frame layout has been created for each tour. Your task is to create a page that ties the four separate Web pages into a single presentation. A preview of the completed Web page is shown in Figure 5-37.

Figure 5-37 ◀

To create the Travel Scotland! page:

1. Open the file Scottxt.htm in the Cases folder of the Tutorial.05 folder on your Student Disk, and then save the file as Scotland.htm in the same folder.

2. Create a frame layout for the Scotland.htm page that consists of three rows of frames. The size of the first row should be 45 pixels, the third row should be 70 pixels, and the middle row should occupy whatever space is left.

3. Specify the file TSLogo.htm—a file containing the company logo—as the source for the first frame. The source for the second frame is Laketour.htm, a file describing the Lake District tour. Finally, the source for the third frame is TSList.htm, a page containing a graphic with the four tour names.

4. Assign the following names to the frames: Logo, Tours, and TourList, respectively.

5. Save your changes to the Scotland.htm file.

6. The TourList frame refers to a file that contains an inline image with titles for the four main tours offered by Travel Scotland! Change this graphic to an image map:

   a. Open the file TSLtxt.htm in the Cases folder of the Tutorial.05 folder on your Student Disk, and then save the file as TSList.htm in the same folder.

   b. Assign an image map named "TourList" to the inline image with the following hotspots:
      - a rectangular hotspot at (17,0) (158,59) that points to Laketour.htm
      - a rectangular hotspot at (159,0) (306,59) that points to Casttour.htm
      - a rectangular hotspot at (307,0) (454,59) that points to Hightour.htm
      - a rectangular hotspot at (455,0) (593,59) that points to Hebdtour.htm

   c. For each hotspot in the graphic, specify the Tours frame as the target.

   d. Save your changes to TSList.htm.

7. Open the Scotland.htm file in your Web browser. What problems do you see? Reopen Scotland.htm in your text editor and fix the problems.

8. Reopen Scotland.htm in your browser. Is the problem fixed? If so, return to the file in your text editor and lock the size and position of the frame borders by preventing users from resizing the frames. Reopen the page in the browser.

9. Test the hyperlinks in the image map. Note that when you click a hyperlink, two frames are updated in the page. This is because the source for the frame in the middle row is itself a framed page. This is one way you can have two frames updated with a single click of a hyperlink.

10. Print the Travel Scotland! Web page and the source code in the Scotland.htm and TSList.htm files.

11. Trace the code for the series of hyperlinks and framed pages in this Case Problem and create a diagram showing how all of the files are connected.

12. Close your Web browser and your text editor.

3. Creating a Sonnets Page for English 220 Professor Sherry Lake is teaching a course on 16th and 17th century poetry. She's asked you to help her create a Web presentation of a section of her course dealing with sonnets. She has collected ten sonnets written by John Donne, William Shakespeare, and Edmund Spenser, that she wants the students to learn and has placed them in HTML files. She has also created a page that shows the title of the course and a list of the ten sonnets. She wants you to organize this material using frames. A preview of the page you'll create is shown in Figure 5-38.

Figure 5-38 ◀

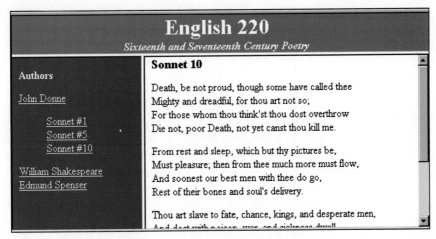

The table of contents for this page appears in the leftmost frame. Sherry wants the links in the table of contents frame to work as follows:

- If a user clicks the name of an author, a list of sonnets by that author alternately expands and contracts in the table of contents frame.
- If a user clicks the name of a sonnet, the sonnet appears in the rightmost frame.

Sherry doesn't want the layout of the page to be locked in; that is, she wants to give students the ability to resize the frames when they're viewing the page.

To create the sonnets page:

1. Open the file Sontxt.htm in the Cases folder of the Tutorial.05 folder on your Student Disk, and then save the file as Sonnet.htm in the same folder.
2. Create a frame layout in which the first frame row is 65 pixels high, and the height of the second frame row is whatever space remains on the page.
3. Within the second frame row, create a nested frame layout of two columns. The first column should be 220 pixels wide, and the second column should cover the rest of the page.
4. The source for the first frame is Eng220.htm. The source for the second frame is SonTOC.htm, and the source for the third frame is Blank.htm.
5. Name the first frame "Head," the second frame "List," and the third frame "Sonnet."
6. Set the margin height for the Head and Sonnet frames to 1 pixel. Set the margin width for the Sonnet frame to 10 pixels.
7. Save your changes to Sonnet.htm, and then close the file.
8. Open the SnTOCtxt.htm file in the Cases folder of the Tutorial.05 folder on your Student Disk, and then save the file as SonTOC.htm in the same folder.
9. Set the base target for all hyperlinks in this file to the magic target name that loads the document into the same frame that contains the hyperlink tag.
10. Convert the names of the three authors to hypertext links: "John Donne" should point to the SonnetJD.htm file, "William Shakespeare" to SonnetWS.htm, and "Edmund Spenser" to SonnetES.htm. Save your changes to SonTOC.htm, and then close the file.
11. Open the John Donne file, JDtxt.htm, in the Cases folder of the Tutorial.05 folder on your Student Disk, and then save the file as SonnetJD.htm in the same folder.
12. Convert the author names and sonnet names to hypertext links. The sonnets should point to the files SonJD1.htm, SonJD5.htm, and SonJD10.htm, respectively. The author name "John Donne" should point back to the SonTOC.htm file, and the author names "William Shakespeare" and "Edmund Spenser" should point to the files SonnetWS.htm and SonnetES.htm, respectively.
13. Set the Sonnet frame as the base target for hyperlinks in this document. Set the target for each author name to the magic target name that loads the document into the same frame that contains the hyperlink tag. Save your changes.

14. Repeat Steps 11 through 13 for the William Shakespeare file, WStxt.htm. Save the file as SonnetWS.htm. Create hyperlinks to the sonnet files SonWS12.htm, SonWS18.htm, SonWS116.htm, and SonWS130.htm. The author name "William Shakespeare" should point back to the SonTOC.htm file, and the author names "John Donne" and "Edmund Spenser" should point back to SonnetJD.htm and SonnetES.htm, respectively. Save your changes.

15. Repeat Steps 11 through 13 for the Edmund Spenser file, EStxt.htm. Save the file as SonnetES.htm. Create hyperlinks to the sonnet files SonES54.htm, SonES64.htm, and SonES79.htm. The author name "Edmund Spenser" should point back to the SonTOC.htm file, and the author names "John Donne" and "William Shakespeare" should point back to SonnetJD.htm and SonnetWS.htm, respectively. Save your changes.

16. Open Sonnet.htm in your Web browser. Verify that by clicking the names of the authors, the list of sonnets is alternately expanded and contracted, and that by clicking the names of the sonnets, the text of the sonnet appears in the rightmost frame.

17. Print a copy of the Web page and the code for the following files: Sonnet.htm, SonTOC.htm, SonnetJD.htm, SonnetWS.htm, and SonnetES.htm.

18. Close your Web browser and your text editor.

4. Creating a Web Presentation for Warner Peripherals Warner Peripherals, a company located in Tucson, makes high-quality peripherals for computers. The company leads the industry in disk drives and tape drives. Its most popular products include the SureSave line of tape drives and the SureRite line of disk drives. You've been asked to consolidate several Web pages describing these products into a single Web presentation that uses frames. The files shown in Figure 5-39 are available for your use.

Figure 5-39 ◀

File	Contents
Drive15L.htm	Description of the 15L SureRite hard drive
Drive20M.htm	Description of the 20M SureRite hard drive
Drive30M.htm	Description of the 33M SureRite hard drive
Drive60M.htm	Description of the 60M SureRite hard drive
Tape800.htm	Description of the 800 SureSave tape backup drive
Tape3200.htm	Description of the 3200 SureSave tape backup drive
Tape9600.htm	Description of the 9600 SureSave tape backup drive
WLogo.htm	Web page containing the Warner Peripherals logo

To create the Warner Peripherals Web presentation:

1. Create a table of contents page that includes hyperlinks to the files listed in Figure 5-39. The layout and appearance of this page are up to you. Save this page as WTOC.htm in the Cases folder of the Tutorial.05 folder on your Student Disk.

2. Create a file named Warner.htm that consolidates the logo page, table of contents page, and product description pages into a single page using frames. The layout of the frames is up to you. Include comment tags in the file describing each element of the page. Save the Warner.htm file in the Cases folder of the Tutorial.05 folder on your Student Disk.

3. Test your page and verify that each link works properly and appears in the correct frame.

4. Print a copy of the page and the HTML code.

5. Close your Web browser and your text editor.

Answers to Quick Check Questions

SESSION 3.1

1 Color names and color values. Color names are easier to work with but the color name may not exist for exactly the color you want to use. Also your color name may not be supported by all browsers. Color values allow you to exactly describe a color, but they can be difficult to work with.

2 <BODY BGCOLOR=GRAY TEXT=RED LINK=BLUE VLINK=YELLOW>

3 Spot color is color that affects only a few sections of a page such as a single character, word or phrase.

4 <FONT COLOR=red SIZE=+5>Major Sale</FONT>

5 <FONT FACE="Times New Roman, MS Serif">Major Sale</FONT>

6 <BODY BACKGROUND="Stars.gif">

7 overwhelming the page's text, using a large image file that will make the page take longer to load, and using an image that displays visible seams

SESSION 3.2

1 when you want to use transparent colors, when you want to use an animated image, and when your image has only 256 colors or less

2 for photographic images, for images that contain more than 256 colors, and to reduce file size through compression

3 <IMG SRC="mwu.jpg" ALT="MidWest University">

4 <IMG SRC="mwu.jpg" ALIGN=TOP>

5 <IMG SRC="mwu.jpg" ALIGN=RIGHT> This tag will not work for browsers that don't support the LEFT align property such as versions of Netscape Navigator and Internet Explorer prior to 3.0.

6 <IMG SRC="mwu.jpg" HSPACE=10 VSPACE=10>

7 <IMG SRC="mwu.jpg" HEIGHT=85 WIDTH=120>

8 When an image with many colors is displayed on a monitor that does not support all those colors, the monitor will attempt to approximate the appearance of those colors. The Safety Palette is a palette of 211 colors that is guaranteed to be displayed on all browsers without resorting to dithering.

SESSION 3.3

1 A hotspot is a defined area of the image that acts as a hypertext link. An image map lists the coordinates on the image that define the boundaries of the hotspots.

2 Server-side and client-side. The server-side is the older, more accepted method of creating image maps and relies on the Web server to interpret the image map and create the hypertext jump. The client-side image map is newer and is not supported by all browsers (though this is rapidly changing). Because the user's machine interprets the image map, the image map is interpreted more quickly, it can be tested on the local machine, and information about the various hotspots appears in the status bar of the Web browser.

3 <AREA SHAPE=RECT COORDS="5,20,85,100" HREF="Oregon.htm">

4 <AREA SHAPE=CIRCLE COORDS="44,81,23" HREF="LA.htm">

5 <AREA SHAPE=POLY COORDS="5,10,5,35,25,35,30,20,15,10" HREF="Hawaii.htm">

6 <IMG SRC="WestCoast.gif" USEMAP="#States">

7 <IMG SRC="WestCoast.gif" BORDER=5>

SESSION 4.1

1 Text tables and graphical tables. The text table is supported by all browsers and is easier to create. The graphical table is more difficult to create but provides the user with a wealth of formatting options. Graphical tables are also more flexible and attractive since the text tables have to be created in a fixed width font.

2 A proportional font assigns different widths to each character based on the character's shape. A fixed-width font assigns the same width to each character regardless of shape.

3 the <PRE> tag

4 The <TABLE> tag identifies the beginning of a table. The <TR> tag identifies the beginning of a table row. The <TD> tag identifies individual table cells, and the <TH> tag identifies table cells that will act as table headers.

5 The number of rows in a table is determined by the number of <TR> tags. The number of columns is equal to the largest number of <TD> or <TH> tags within a single table row.

6 Text within the <TH> tag is automatically bolded and centered within the table cell.

7 <CAPTION ALIGN=BOTTOM>Product Catalog</CAPTION> Place this tag anywhere between the <TABLE> and </TABLE> tags.

SESSION 4.2

1 <TABLE BORDER=5 CELLSPACING=3 CELLPADDING=4>

2 <TD VALIGN=TOP> or <TH VALIGN=TOP>

3 <TR ALIGN=CENTER>

4 In pixels or as a percentage of the display area. Use pixels if you want to exactly control the size of the table. Use percentages if you want your table to adapt itself to the user's monitor resolution.

5 <TABLE WIDTH="50%">

6 <TD WIDTH=60> or <TH WIDTH=60>. This will not keep the cell from exceeding 60 pixels in width. The only way to do that is to set the width of *all* cells in that table column to 60 pixels.

7 <TABLE BGCOLOR=YELLOW> This property is not supported by earlier browsers.

8 <TD ROWSPAN=3 COLSPAN=2> or <TH ROWSPAN=3 COLSPAN=2>

SESSION 4.3

1 <TABLE>
<TR><TD>
<TABLE><TR><TD></TD><TD></TD></TR><TR><TD></TD><TD></TD></TR></TABLE>
</TD>
<TD></TD>
</TR>
<TR>
<TD></TD>
<TD></TD>
</TR>
</TABLE>

2 <! Nested table starts here>

3 <TABLE BORDERCOLOR=YELLOW>

4 <TABLE BORDERCOLORDARK=BLUE BORDERCOLORLIGHT=RED>

5 <TABLE FRAME=ABOVE>

6 <TABLE RULES=COLS>

7 It works for browsers that support HTML 4.0. It may not work for older browsers that support the earlier HTML specifications.

SESSION 5.1

1 Frames are windows appearing within the browser's display area, each capable of displaying the contents of a different HTML file.

2 Because there is no page body. Instead the browser displays the <BODY> tags from other pages.

3 <FRAMESET ROWS="200,50%,*">

4 <FRAME SRC="Home.htm">

5 <FRAME SRC="Home.htm" SCROLLING=NO>

6 <FRAME SRC="Home.htm" MARGINHEIGHT=3>

7 3 pixels

8 <FRAME SRC="Home.htm" NORESIZE>

SESSION 5.2

1 the frame containing the hyperlink

2 <FRAME SRC="Address.htm" NAME=Address>

3 <A HREF=*URL* TARGET=News>

4 <A HREF="Sales.htm" TARGET=_top>

5 Place the tag, <BASE TARGET=News>, in the <HEAD> section of the HTML file.

6 Create a section starting with the <NOFRAMES> tag. After the <NOFRAMES> tag enter a <BODY> tag to identify the text and images you want frame-blind browsers to display. Complete this section with a </BODY> tag followed by a </NOFRAMES> tag.

7 <FRAMESET BORDERCOLOR=RED>

8 <FRAMESET BORDERWIDTH=5>

9 They cannot be used by all browsers.

Creating Web Pages with HTML **Index**

If you are using this text as part of our Custom Edition Program, you will find entries in the Index and Task Reference that do not apply to your custom tutorials.

COLOR NAME	HEXADECIMAL VALUE	PREVIEW

Extended Color Names

The following is a list of extended color names and their corresponding hexadecimal triplets supported by most Web browsers. To view these colors, you must have a video card and monitor capable of displaying up to 256 colors. As with other aspects of Web page design, you should test these color names on a variety of browsers before committing to their use. Different browsers may render these colors differently, or not at all.

COLOR NAME	HEXADECIMAL VALUE	PREVIEW
ALICEBLUE	#F0F8FE	
ANTIQUEWHITE	#FAEBD7	
AQUA	#00FFFF	
AQUAMARINE	#70DB93	
AZURE	#F0FFFF	
BEIGE	#F5F5DC	
BLACK	#000000	
BLUE	#0000FF	
BLUEVIOLET	#9F5F9F	
BRASS	#B5A642	
BRIGHTGOLD	#D9D919	
BRONZE	#8C7853	
BROWN	#A52A2A	
CADETBLUE	#5F9F9F	
CHOCOLATE	#D2691E	
COOLCOPPER	#D98719	
COPPER	#B87333	

Appendix A **HTML Extended Color Names**

COLOR NAME	HEXADECIMAL VALUE	PREVIEW
CORAL	#FF7F00	
CORAL	#FF7F50	
CRIMSON	#DC143C	
CYAN	#00FFFF	
DARKBLUE	#00008B	
DARKBROWN	#5C4033	
DARKCYAN	#008B8B	
DARKGOLDENROD	#B8860B	
DARKGRAY	#A9A9A9	
DARKGREEN	#006400	
DARKKHAKI	#BDB76B	
DARKMAGENTA	#8B008B	
DARKOLIVEGREEN	#4F4F2F	
DARKORANGE	#FF8C00	
DARKORCHID	#9932CD	
DARKPURPLE	#871F78	
DARKSALMON	#E9967A	
DARKSLATEBLUE	#6B238E	
DARKSLATEGRAY	#2F4F4F	
DARKTAN	#97694F	

Appendix A **HTML Extended Color Names**

COLOR NAME	HEXADECIMAL VALUE	PREVIEW
DARKTURQUOISE	#7093DB	
DARKVIOLET	#9400D3	
DARKWOOD	#855E42	
DIMGRAY	#545454	
DUSTYROSE	#856363	
FELDSPAR	#D19275	
FIREBRICK	#8E2323	
FORESTGREEN	#238E23	
GOLD	#CD7F32	
GOLDENROD	#DBDB70	
GRAY	#C0C0C0	
GREEN	#00FF00	
GREENCOPPER	#527F76	
GREENYELLOW	#93DB70	
HOTPINK	#FF69B4	
HUNTERGREEN	#215E21	
INDIANRED	#4E2F2F	
INDIGO	#4B0082	
IVORY	#FFFFF0	
KHAKI	#9F9F5F	

Appendix A **HTML Extended Color Names**

COLOR NAME	HEXADECIMAL VALUE	PREVIEW
LAVENDER	#E6E6FA	
LIGHTBLUE	#C0D9D9	
LIGHTCORAL	#F08080	
LIGHTCYAN	#E0FFFF	
LIGHTGRAY	#A8A8A8	
LIGHTGREEN	#90EE90	
LIGHTPINK	#FFB6C1	
LIGHTSTEELBLUE	#8F8FBD	
LIGHTWOOD	#E9C2A6	
LIME	#00FF00	
LIMEGREEN	#32CD32	
MAGENTA	#FF00FF	
MANDARINORANGE	#E47833	
MAROON	#8E236B	
MEDIUMAQUAMARINE	#32CD99	
MEDIUMBLUE	#3232CD	
MEDIUMFORESTGREEN	#6B8E23	
MEDIUMGOLDENROD	#EAEAAE	
MEDIUMORCHID	#9370DB	
MEDIUMSEAGREEN	#426F42	

Appendix A **HTML Extended Color Names**

COLOR NAME	HEXADECIMAL VALUE	PREVIEW
MEDIUMSLATEBLUE	#7F00FF	
MEDIUMSPRINGGREEN	#7FFF00	
MEDIUMTURQUOISE	#70DBDB	
MEDIUMVIOLETRED	#DB7093	
MEDIUMWOOD	#A68064	
MIDNIGHTBLUE	#2F2F4F	
MINTCREAM	#F5FFFA	
MISTYROSE	#FFE4E1	
NAVYBLUE	#23238E	
NEONBLUE	#4D4DFF	
NEONPINK	#FF6EC7	
NEWMIDNIGHTBLUE	#00009C	
NEWTAN	#EBC79E	
OLDGOLD	#CFB53B	
OLIVE	#808000	
ORANGE	#FF7F00	
ORANGERED	#FF2400	
ORCHID	#DB70DB	
PALEGOLDENROD	#EEE8AA	
PALEGREEN	#8FBC8F	

Appendix A **HTML Extended Color Names**

COLOR NAME	HEXADECIMAL VALUE	PREVIEW
PALETURQUOISE	#AFEEEE	
PINK	#BC8F8F	
PLUM	#EAADEA	
POWDERBLUE	#B0E0E6	
PURPLE	#800080	
QUARTZ	#D9D9F3	
RED	#FF0000	
RICHBLUE	#5959AB	
ROYALBLUE	#4169E1	
SADDLEBROWN	#8B4513	
SALMON	#6F4242	
SANDYBROWN	#F4A460	
SCARLET	#8C1717	
SEAGREEN	#238E68	
SIENNA	#8E6B23	
SILVER	#E6E8FA	
SKYBLUE	#3299CC	
SLATEBLUE	#007FFF	
SNOW	#FFFAFA	
SPICYPINK	#FF1CAE	

Appendix A **HTML Extended Color Names**

COLOR NAME	HEXADECIMAL VALUE	PREVIEW
SPRINGGREEN	#00FF7F	
STEELBLUE	#236B8E	
SUMMERSKY	#38B0DE	
TAN	#DB9370	
TEAL	#008080	
THISTLE	#D8BFD8	
TOMATO	#FF6347	
TURQUOISE	#ADEAEA	
VERYDARKBROWN	#5C4033	
VERYDARKGRAY	#CDCDCD	
VIOLET	#4F2F4F	
VIOLETRED	#CC3299	
WHEAT	#D8D8BF	
WHITE	#FFFFFF	
YELLOW	#FFFF00	
YELLOWGREEN	#99CC32	

Appendix B HTML Special Characters

CHARACTER	CODE	CODE NAME	DESCRIPTION

The following table lists the extended character set for HTML, also known as the ISO Latin-1 Character set. Characters in this table can be entered either by code number or code name. For example, to insert the registered trademark symbol, ®, you would use either &reg or &#174.

Not all code names are recognized by all browsers. Some older browsers that support only the HTML 2.0 standard will not recognize the code name &times, for instance. Code names that may not be recognized by older browsers are marked with an asterisk. If you are planning to use these symbols in your document, you may want to use the code number instead of the code name.

CHARACTER	CODE	CODE NAME	DESCRIPTION
	&#00 - &#08		Unused
	&#09		Tab
	&#10		Line feed
	&#11 - &#31		Unused
	&#32		Space
!	&#33		Exclamation mark
"	&#34	&quot	Double quotation mark
#	&#35		Pound sign
$	&#36		Dollar sign
%	&#37		Percent sign
&	&#38	&amp	Ampersand
'	&#39		Apostrophe
(	&#40		Left parenthesis
)	&#41		Right parenthesis
*	&#42		Asterisk
+	&#43		Plus sign
,	&#44		Comma
-	&#45		Hyphen
.	&#46		Period
/	&#47		Forward slash
0 - 9	&#48 - &#57		Numbers 0 - 9
:	&#58		Colon
;	&#59		Semicolon
<	&#60	&lt	Less than sign

Appendix B HTML Special Characters

CHARACTER	CODE	CODE NAME	DESCRIPTION
=	&#61		Equals sign
>	&#62	&gt	Greater than sign
?	&#63		Question mark
@	&#64		Commercial at
A - Z	&#65 - &#90		Letters A - Z
[	&#91		Left square bracket
\	&#92		Back slash
]	&#93		Right square bracket
^	&#94		Caret
_	&#95		Horizontal bar
`	&#96		Grave accent
a - z	&#97 - &#122		Letters a - z
{	&#123		Left curly brace
|	&#124		Vertical bar
}	&#125		Right curly brace
~	&#126		Tilde
	&#127 - &#129		Unused
,	&#130		Low single comma quotation mark
ƒ	&#131		Function sign
„	&#132		Low double comma quotation mark
…	&#133		Ellipses
†	&#134		Dagger
‡	&#135		Double dagger
ˆ	&#136		Caret
‰	&#137		Per mile sign
Š	&#138		Capital S with hacek
<	&#139		Less than sign
Œ	&#140		Capital OE ligature

CHARACTER	CODE	CODE NAME	DESCRIPTION
	&#141 - &#144		Unused
'	&#145		Single beginning quotation mark
'	&#146		Single ending quotation mark
"	&#147		Double beginning quotation mark
"	&#148		Double ending quotation mark
•	&#149		Middle dot
–	&#150		En dash
—	&#151		Em dash
~	&#152		Tilde
™	&#153	&trade*	Trademark symbol
š	&#154		Small s with hacek
›	&#155		Greater than sign
œ	&#156		Small oe ligature
	&#157 - &#158		Unused
Ÿ	&#159		Capital Y with umlaut
		*	Non-breaking space
¡	&#161	&iexcl*	Inverted exclamation point
¢	&#162	&cent*	Cent symbol
£	&#163	&pound*	Pound sterling
¤	&#164	&curren*	General currency symbol
¥	&#165	&yen*	Yen sign
¦	&#166	&brvbar*	Broken vertical bar
§	&#167	&sect*	Section sign
¨	&#168	&uml*	Umlaut
©	&#169	&copy*	Copyright symbol
ª	&#170	&ordf*	Feminine ordinal
«	&#171	&laquo*	Left angle quotation mark
¬	&#172	&not*	Not sign

Appendix B HTML Special Characters

CHARACTER	CODE	CODE NAME	DESCRIPTION
–	&#173	&shy*	Soft hyphen
®	&#174	&reg*	Registered trademark
¯	&#175	&macr*	Macron
°	&#176	&deg*	Degree sign
±	&#177	&plusmn*	Plus/minus symbol
²	&#178	&sup2*	Superscript 2
³	&#179	&sup3*	Superscript 3
´	&#180	&acute*	Acute accent
µ	&#181	&micro*	Micro symbol
¶	&#182	&para*	Paragraph sign
·	&#183	&middot*	Middle dot
¸	&#184	&cedil*	Cedilla
¹	&#185	&sup1*	Superscript 1
º	&#186	&ordm*	Masculine ordinal
»	&#187	&raquo*	Right angle quotation mark
¼	&#188	&frac14*	Fraction one-quarter
½	&#189	&frac12*	Fraction one-half
¾	&#190	&frac34*	Fraction three-quarters
¿	&#191	&iquest*	Inverted question mark
À	&#192	&Agrave	Capital A, grave accent
Á	&#193	&Aacute	Capital A, acute accent
Â	&#194	&Acirc	Capital A, circumflex accent
Ã	&#195	&Atilde	Capital A, tilde
Ä	&#196	&Auml	Capital A, umlaut
Å	&#197	&Aring	Capital A, ring
Æ	&#198	&Aelig	Capital AE ligature
Ç	&#199	&Ccedil	Capital C, cedilla
È	&#200	&Egrave	Capital E, grave accent

Appendix B **HTML Special Characters**

CHARACTER	CODE	CODE NAME	DESCRIPTION
É	&#201	&Eacute	Capital E, acute accent
Ê	&#202	&Ecirc	Capital E, circumflex accent
Ë	&#203	&Euml	Capital E, umlaut
Ì	&#204	&Igrave	Capital I, grave accent
Í	&#205	&Iacute	Capital I, acute accent
Î	&#206	&Icirc	Capital I, circumflex accent
Ï	&#207	&Iuml	Capital I, umlaut
Ð	&#208	&ETH*	Capital ETH, Icelandic
Ñ	&#209	&Ntilde	Capital N, tilde
Ò	&#210	&Ograve	Capital O, grave accent
Ó	&#211	&Oacute	Capital O, acute accent
Ô	&#212	&Ocirc	Capital O, circumflex accent
Õ	&#213	&Otilde	Capital O, tilde
Ö	&#214	&Ouml	Capital O, umlaut
×	&#215	&times*	Multiplication sign
Ø	&#216	&Oslash	Capital O slash
Ù	&#217	&Ugrave	Capital U, grave accent
Ú	&#218	&Uacute	Capital U, acute accent
Û	&#219	&Ucirc	Capital U, circumflex accent
Ü	&#220	&Uuml	Capital U, umlaut
Ý	&#221	&Yacute	Capital Y, acute accent
Þ	&#222	&THORN	Capital THORN, Icelandic
ß	&#223	&szlig	Small sz ligature
à	&#224	&agrave	Small a, grave accent
á	&#225	&aacute	Small a, acute accent
â	&#226	&acirc	Small a, circumflex accent
ã	&#227	&atilde	Small a, tilde
ä	&#228	&auml	Small a, umlaut

Appendix B HTML Special Characters

CHARACTER	CODE	CODE NAME	DESCRIPTION
å	&#229	&aring	Small a, ring
æ	&#230	&aelig	Small AE ligature
ç	&#231	&ccedil	Small C, cedilla
è	&#232	&egrave	Small e, grave accent
é	&#233	&eacute	Small e, acute accent
ê	&#234	&ecirc	Small e, circumflex accent
ë	&#235	&euml	Small e, umlaut
ì	&#236	&igrave	Small i, grave accent
í	&#237	&iacute	Small i, acute accent
î	&#238	&icirc	Small i, circumflex accent
ï	&#239	&iuml	Small i, umlaut
ð	&#240	&eth	Small ETH, Icelandic
ñ	&#241	&ntilde	Small N, tilde
ò	&#242	&ograve	Small o, grave accent
ó	&#243	&oacute	Small o, acute accent
ô	&#244	&ocirc	Small o, circumflex accent
õ	&#245	&otilde	Small o, tilde
ö	&#246	&ouml	Small o, umlaut
÷	&#247	&divide*	Division sign
ø	&#248	&oslash	Small o slash
ù	&#249	&ugrave	Small u, grave accent
ú	&#250	&uacute	Small u, acute accent
û	&#251	&ucirc	Small u, circumflex accent
ü	&#252	&uuml	Small u, umlaut
ý	&#253	&yacute	Small y, acute accent
þ	&#254	&thorn	Small thorn, Icelandic
ÿ	&#255	&yuml	Small y, umlaut

Appendix C
Putting a Document on the World Wide Web

Once you've completed your work on your HTML file, you're probably ready to place it on the World Wide Web for others to see. To make a file available to the World Wide Web, you have to transfer it to a computer connected to the Web called a **Web server**.

Your **Internet Service Provider** (**ISP**)—the company or institution through which you have Internet access—usually has a Web server available for your use. Because each Internet Service Provider has a different procedure for storing Web pages, you should contact your ISP to learn its policies and procedures. Generally you should be prepared to do the following:

- Extensively test your files under a variety of browsers and under different display conditions. Weed out any errors and design problems before you place the page on the Web.
- If your HTML documents have a three-letter "HTM" extension, rename those files with the four-letter extension "HTML." Some Web servers will require the four-letter extension for all Web pages.
- Check the hyperlinks and inline objects in each of your documents to verify that they point to the correct filenames. Verify the filenames with respect to upper and lower cases. Some Web servers will distinguish between a file named "Image.gif" and one named "image.gif." To be safe, match the uppercase and lowercase letters.
- If your hyperlinks use absolute pathnames, change them to relative pathnames.
- Find out from your ISP the name of the folder into which you'll be placing your HTML documents. You may also need a special user name and password to access this folder.
- Use **FTP**, a program used on the Internet that transfers files, or e-mail to place your pages in the appropriate folder on your Internet Service Provider's Web server. Some Web browsers, like Internet Explorer and Netscape Navigator, have this capability built in, allowing you to transfer your files with a click of a toolbar button.
- Decide on a name for your site on the World Wide Web (such as "http://www.jackson_electronics.com"). Choose a name that will be easy for customers and interested parties to remember and return to.
- If you select a special name for your Web site, you may have to register it. Registration information can be found at http://www.internic.net. This is a service your ISP may also provide for a fee. Registration is necessary to ensure that any name you give to your site is unique and not already in use by another party. Usually you will have to pay a yearly fee to keep control of a special name for your Web site.
- Add your site to the indexes of search pages on the World Wide Web. This is not required, but it will make it easier for people to find your site. Each search facility has different policies regarding adding information about Web sites to its index. Be aware that some will charge a fee to include your Web site in their list.

Once you've completed these steps, your work will be available on the World Wide Web in a form that is easy for users to find and access.

HTML Tag Reference

TAGS AND PROPERTIES	DESCRIPTION	HTML	NETSCAPE	IE

The following is a list of the major HTML tags and properties. The three columns at the right indicate the earliest HTML, Netscape and Internet Explorer versions which started supporting these tags. For example a version number of "3.0" for Internet Explorer indicates that versions of Internet Explorer 3.0 *and above* will support the tag or attribute. Both opening and closing tags are displayed where they are required (e.g. <TABLE> ... </TABLE>). A single tag means that no closing tag is needed.

You can view more detailed information about the latest HTML specifications at http://www.w3.org. Additional information about browser support for different HTML tags is available at http://www.htmlcompendium.org/.

Since the World Wide Web is always in a constant state of change, you should check this information against the current browser versions.

Properties are of the following types.
- *Color*   A recognized color name or color value.
- *CGI Script*   The name of a CGI script on the Web server.
- *Document*   The file name or URL of file.
- *List*   List of items separated by commas. Usually enclosed in double quotes.
- *Options*   Limited to a specific set of values (values are shown below the property).
- *Text*   Any text string.
- *URL*   The URL for a Web page or file.
- *Value*   A number, usually an integer.

Block-Formatting Tags

Block-Formatting tags are tags that are used to format the appearance of large blocks of text.

TAGS AND PROPERTIES	DESCRIPTION	HTML	NETSCAPE	IE
<ADDRESS> ... </ADDRESS>	The <ADDRESS> tag is used for information such as addresses, authorship and so forth. The text is usually italicized and in some browsers it is indented.	2.0	1.0	1.0
<BASEFONT>	The <BASEFONT> tag specifies the default font size, in points, for text in the document. The default value is 3.	3.2	1.0	2.0
SIZE=*Value*	*Value* is the size (in points) of the text font.	3.2	*1.1*	2.0
<BLOCKQUOTE> ... </BLOCKQUOTE>	The <BLOCKQUOTE> tag is used to set off long quotes or citations by usually indenting the enclosed text on both sides. Some browsers italicize the text as well.	2.0	1.0	2.0
 	The tag forces a line break in the text.	2.0	1.0	2.0
CLEAR=*Option* (LEFT | RIGHT | ALL | NONE)	Causes the next line to start at the spot in which the specified margin is clear.	3.0	1.0	2.0
<CENTER> ... </CENTER>	The <CENTER> tag centers the enclosed text or image horizontally.	3.2	1.1	2.0
<DFN> ... </DFN>	The <DFN> tag is used for the defining instance of a term, i.e. the first time the term is used. The enclosed text is usually italicized.	2.0		2.0
<DIV> ... </DIV>	The <DIV> tag is to set the text alignment of blocks of text or images. Supported by older browsers, it has been made obsolete by newer tags.	3.0	2.0	3.0

HTML Tag Reference

TAGS AND PROPERTIES	DESCRIPTION	HTML	NETSCAPE	IE
`<HR>`	The `<HR>` tag creates a horizontal line.	1.0	1.0	2.0
ALIGN=*Option* (LEFT | CENTER | RIGHT)	Alignment of the horizontal line. The default in CENTER.	3.2	1.1	2.0
COLOR=*Color*	Specifies a color for the line.			3.0
NOSHADE	Removes 3D shading from the line.	3.0	1.1	3.0
SIZE=*Value*	The size (height) of the line in pixels.	3.2	1.1	2.0
WIDTH=*Value*	The width (length) of the line either in pixels or as a percentage of the display area.	3.2	1.1	2.0

`<H1> ... </H1>`
`<H2> ... </H2>`
`<H3> ... </H3>`
`<H4> ... </H4>`
`<H5> ... </H5>`
`<H6> ... </H6>`
	The six levels of text headings ranging from the largest (`<H1>`) to the smallest (`<H6>`). Text headings appear in a bold face font.	1.0	1.0	1.0

ALIGN=*Option* (LEFT | RIGHT | CENTER)	The alignment of the heading.	3.0	4.0	2.0
`<LISTING> ... </LISTING>`	The `<LISTING>` tag displays text in a fixed width font resembling a typewriter or computer printout. This tag has been rendered obsolete by some newer tags.	2.0		3.0
`<NOBR> ... </NOBR>`	The `<NOBR>` tag prevents line breaks for the enclosed text. This tag is not often used.		1.1	2.0
`<P> ... </P>`	The `<P>` tag defines the beginning and ending of a paragraph of text.	1.0	1.0	1.0
ALIGN=*Option* (LEFT | CENTER | RIGHT)	The alignment of the text in the paragraph.	1.0	1.1	3.0
`<PLAINTEXT> ... </PLAINTEXT>`	The `<PLAINTEXT>` tag displays text in a fixed width font. An obsolete tag which authors should avoid using. It is supported by some earlier versions of Netscape, but in an erratic way.	2.0	4.0	2.0
`<PRE> ... </PRE>`	The `<PRE>` tag retains the preformatted appearance of the text in the HTML file, including any line breaks or spaces. Text is usually displayed in a fixed width font.	1.0	1.0	1.0
`<WBR> ... </WBR>`	The `<WBR>` tag overrides other tags that may preclude the creation of line breaks and directs the browser to insert a line break if necessary. Used in conjunction with the `<NOBR>` tag. This tag is not often used.		1.1	2.0
`<XMP> ... </XMP>`	The `<XMP>` tag displays blocks of text in a fixed width font. The tag is obsolete and should not be used.	3.2		5.0

HTML Tag Reference

TAGS AND PROPERTIES	DESCRIPTION	HTML	NETSCAPE	IE
Character Tags	Character tags modify the appearance of individual characters, words or sentences from that of the surrounding text. Character tags usually appear nested within Block-Formatting tags.			
<ABBR> ... </ABBR>	The <ABBR>tag indicates text in an abbreviated form (e.g. WWW, HTTP, URL, etc.).	4.0		
<ACRONYM> ... </ACRONYM>	The <ACRONYM> tag indicates a text acronym (e.g. WAC, radar, etc.).	4.0		4.0
<B> ... </B>	The <B> tag displays the enclosed text in bold type.	1.0	1.0	1.0
<BIG> ... </BIG>	The <BIG> tag increases the size of the enclosed text. The exact appearance of the text depends on the browser and the default font size.	3.0	2.0	3.0
<BLINK> ... </BLINK>	The <BLINK> tag causes the enclosed text to blink on and off.		1.0	
<CITE> ... </CITE>	The <CITE> tag is used for citations and is usually displayed in italics.	1.0	1.0	2.0
<CODE> ... </CODE>	The <CODE> tag is used for text taken from the code for a computer program. It is usually displayed in a fixed width font.	1.0	1.0	1.0
<EM> ... </EM>	The <EM> tag is used to emphasize text. The enclosed text is usually displayed in italics.	1.0	1.0	2.0
<FONT> ... </FONT>	The <FONT> tag is used to control the appearance of the text it encloses.	3.0	1.1	2.0
COLOR=*Color*	The color of the enclosed text.	3.0	2.0	2.0
FACE=*List*	The font face of the text. Multiple font faces can be specified, separated by commas. The browser will try to render the text in the order specified by the list.	3.0	3.0	2.0
SIZE=*Value*	Size of the font in points, it can be absolute or relative. Specifying SIZE=5 sets the font size to 5 points. Specifying SIZE=+5 sets the font size 5 points larger than that specified in the <BASEFONT> tag.	3.0	4.0	2.0
<I> ... </I>	The <I> tag italicizes the enclosed text.	1.0	1.0	1.0
<KBD> ... </KBD>	The <KBD> tag is used for text made to appear as if it came from a typewriter or keyboard. Text is displayed with a fixed width font.	1.0	1.0	2.0
<SAMP> ... </SAMP>	The <SAMP> tag displays text in a fixed width font.	1.0	1.0	2.0

HTML Tag Reference

TAGS AND PROPERTIES	DESCRIPTION	HTML	NETSCAPE	IE
\<SMALL> ... \</SMALL>	The \<SMALL> tag decreases the size of the enclosed text. The exact appearance of the text depends on the browser and the default font size.	3.0	2.0	3.0
\<STRIKE> ... \</STRIKE>	The \<STRIKE> tag displays the enclosed text with a horizontal line striking through it. Note: future revisions to HTML may be phase out STRIKE in favor of the more concise S tag from HTML 3.0	3.2	3.0	2.0
\<STRONG> ... \</STRONG>	The \<STRONG> tag is used to strongly emphasize the enclosed text, usually in a bold font.	1.0	1.0	1.0
_{... \}	The \<SUB> tag displays the enclosed text as a subscript.	1.0	2.0	3.0
\^{... \}	The \<SUP> tag displays the enclosed text as a superscript.	1.0	2.0	3.0
\<TT> ... \</TT>	The \<TT> tag displays text in a fixed width, teletype style font.	1.0	1.0	1.0
\<U> ... \</U>	The \<U> tag underlines the enclosed text. The \<U> tag should be avoided because it will confuse users with hypertext, which is typically underlined.	1.0	3.0	2.0
\<VAR> ... \</VAR>	The \<VAR> tag is used for text that represents a variable is usually displayed in italics.	1.0	1.1	1.0

Document Tags

Document tags are tags that specify the structure of the HTML file or control its operations and interactions with the Web server.

TAGS AND PROPERTIES	DESCRIPTION	HTML	NETSCAPE	IE
\<!>	The \<!> tag is used for comments in documenting the features of your HTML file.	1.0	1.0	1.0
\<BASE>	The \<BASE> tag allows you to specify the URL for the HTML document. It is used by some browsers to interpret relative hyperlinks.	1.0	1.0	2.0
HREF=*URL*	Specifies the URL from which all relative hyperlinks should be based.	1.0	4.0	2.0
TARGET=*Text*	Specifies the default target window or frame for every hyperlink in the document.	4.0	2.0	3.0
\<BODY> ... \</BODY>	The \<BODY> tag encloses all text, images and other elements that will be visible to the user on the Web page.	1.0	1.0	1.0
ALINK=*Color*	Color of activated hypertext links, which are links the user has pressed with the mouse button but have not yet released.	1.0	1.1	2.0
BACKGROUND=*Document*	The graphic image file used for the Web page background.	1.0	1.1	2.0
BGCOLOR=*Color*	The color of the Web page background.	3.2	1.1	2.0

HTML Tag Reference

TAGS AND PROPERTIES	DESCRIPTION	HTML	NETSCAPE	IE
BGPROPERTIES=FIXED	Keeps the background image fixed so that it does not scroll with the Web page.			2.0
LEFTMARGIN=*Value*	Indents the left margin of the page the number of pixels specified in *value*.			2.0
LINK=*Color*	Color of all unvisited links.	1.0	1.1	2.0
TEXT=*Color*	Color of all text in the document.	1.0	1.1	2.0
TOPMARGIN=*Value*	Indents the top margin of the page the number of pixels specified in *value*.			2.0
VLINK=*Color*	Color of previously visited links.	1.0	1.1	2.0
<HEAD> ... </HEAD>	The <HEAD> tag encloses code that provides information about the document.	1.0	1.0	1.0
<HTML> ... </HTML>	The <HTML> tag indicates the beginning and end of the HTML document.	1.0	1.0	1.0
<ISINDEX>	The <ISINDEX> tag identifies the file as a searchable document.	1.0	1.0	2.0
ACTION=*CGI Program*	Sends the submitted text to the program identified by *CGI Program*.			2.0
PROMPT=*Text*	The text that should be placed before the index's text-input field.	3.0	1.1	2.0
<LINK>	The <LINK> tag specifies the relationship between the document and other objects.	1.0	3.0	2.0
HREF=*URL*	The URL of the LINK tag, hotlinks the user to the specified document.	1.0		2.0
ID=*Text*	The file, URL or text that acts as a hypertext lik to another document.	1.0	3.0	3.0
REL=*URL*	Directs the browser to link forward to the next page in the document.	1.0		2.0
REV=*URL*	Directs the browser to go back to the previous link in the document.	2.0		2.0
TITLE=*Text*	The title of the document named in the link.	1.0		2.0
<META>	The <META> tag is used to insert information about the document not defined by other HTML tags and properties. It can include special instructions for the Web server to perform.	1.0	1.0	1.0
CONTENT=*Text*	Contains information associated with the NAME or HTTP-EQUIV properties.	1.0	1.1	2.0
HTTP-EQUIV=*Text*	Directs the browser to request the server to perform different HTTP operations.	2.0	1.1	2.0
NAME=*Text*	The type of information specified in the CONTENT property.	2.0	1.1	2.0
<TITLE> ... </TITLE>	The <TITLE> tag is used to specify the text that appears in the Web browser's title bar.	2.0	1.1	2.0
Form Tags	Form tags are used to create user-entry forms.			
<BUTTON> ... </BUTTON>	Buttons created with the <BUTTON> tag, function just like buttons created with the <INPUT> tag, but they offer richer rendering possibilities. For example, the BUTTON element may have content.	4.0	4.0	4.0

HTML Tag Reference

TAGS AND PROPERTIES	DESCRIPTION	HTML	NETSCAPE	IE
NAME=*Text*	Specifies the button name.	4.0		5.0
VALUE=*Text*	Specifies the initial value of the button.	4.0		5.0
TABINDEX=*Value*	Specifies the tab order in the form.	4.0		5.0
TYPE=*Option* (SUBMIT | RESET | BUTTON)	Specifies the type of button. Setting the type to "BUTTON" creates a push button for use with client-side scripts.	4.0		4.0
<FIELDSET> ... </FIELDSET>	<The FIELDSET> tag allows authors to group form controls and labels. Grouping controls makes it easier for users to understand their purpose while simultaneously facilitating moving between fields.	4.0		4.0
ALIGN=*Option* (TOP | BOTTOM | MIDDLE | LEFT | RIGHT)	Specifies the alignment of the legend with respect to the field set (see the <LEGEND> tag for more information.)	4.0		4.0
<FORM> ... </FORM>	The <FORM> tag marks the beginning and end of a Web page form.	1.0	1.0	1.0
ACTION=*URL*	Specifies the URL to which the contents of the form are to be sent.	1.0	2.0	2.0
ENCTYPE=*Text*	Specifies the encoding type used to submit the data to the server.	2.0	2.0	2.0
METHOD=*Option* (POST | GET)	Specifies the method of accessing the URL indicated in the ACTION property.	2.0	2.0	2.0
TARGET=*Text*	The frame or window that displays the form's results.	4.0	2.0	3.0
<INPUT> ... </INPUT>	The <INPUT> tag creates an input object for use in a Web page form.	1.0	1.0	2.0
ALIGN=*Option* (LEFT | RIGHT | TOP | TEXTTOP | MIDDLE | ABSMIDDLE | BASELINE | BOTTOM | ABSBOTTOM)	Specifies the alignment of an input image. Similar to the ALIGN option with the <IMG> tag.	1.0	1.1	2.0
CHECKED	Specifies that an input checkbox or input radio button is selected.	1.0	2.0	2.0
MAXLENGTH=*Value*	Specifies the maximum number of characters inserted into an input text box.	1.0	2.0	2.0
NAME=*Text*	The label given to the input object.	1.0	2.0	2.0
SIZE=*Value*	The visible size, in characters, of an input text box.	1.0	2.0	2.0
SRC=*Document*	The source file of the graphic used for an input image object.	1.0	2.0	2.0
TABINDEX=*Value*	Specifies the tab order in the form.	4.0		4.0
TYPE=*Option* (CHECKBOX | HIDDEN | IMAGE | PASSWORD | RADIO | RESET | SUBMIT | TEXT | TEXTAREA)	Specifies the type of input object. CHECKBOX creates a checkbox. HIDDEN creates a hidden object. IMAGE creates an image object. PASSWORD creates a text box which hides the text as the user enters it. RADIO creates a radio button. RESET creates a button that resets the form's fields when pressed. SUBMIT creates a button that submits the form when pressed. TEXT creates a text box. TEXTAREA creates a text box with multiple line entry fields.	1.0	2.0	2.0

TAGS AND PROPERTIES	DESCRIPTION	HTML	NETSCAPE	IE
USEMAP=#*Map_Name*	Identifies the input image as an image map. Similar to the USEMAP property used with the <IMG> tag.	1.0	2.0	2.0
VALUE=*Value*	Specifies the information that is initially displayed in the input object.	2.0	2.0	2.0
VSPACE=*Value*	The amount of space above and below the image, in pixels.	1.0	2.0	2.0
WIDTH=*Value*	The width of the input image in pixels.	1.0	2.0	2.0
<LEGEND> ... </LEGEND>	The <LEGEND> tag allows authors to assign a caption to a FIELDSET (see the <FIELDSET> tag above.)	4.0		4.0
ALIGN=*Option* (TOP | BOTTOM | LEFT | RIGHT)	Specifies the position of the legend with respect to the field set.	4.0		4.0
<OPTION> ... </OPTION>	The <OPTION> tag is used for each item in a selection list. This tag must be placed within <SELECT> tags.	1.0	1.0	1.0
SELECTED	The default or selected option in the selection list.	1.0	2.0	2.0
VALUE=*Value*	The value returned to the server when the user selects this option.	2.0	2.0	2.0
<SELECT> ... </SELECT>	The <SELECT> tag encloses a set of <OPTION> tags for use in creating selection lists.	1.0	2.0	2.0
MULTIPLE	Allows the user to select multiple options from the selection list.	2.0	2.0	2.0
NAME=*Text*	The name assigned to the selection list.	1.0	2.0	2.0
SIZE=*Value*	The number of visible items in the selection list.	2.0	2.0	2.0
TABINDEX=*Value*	Specifies the tab order in the form.	4.0		4.0
<TEXTAREA> ... </TEXTAREA>	The <TEXTAREA> tag creates a text box.	1.0	1.0	2.0
COLS=*Value*	Specifies the height of the text box in characters.	1.0	2.0	2.0
NAME=*Text*	Specifies the name assigned to the text box.	1.0	1.0	2.0
ROWS=*Value*	Specifies the width of the text box in characters.	1.0	2.0	2.0
TABINDEX=*Value*	Specifies the tab order in the form.	4.0		4.0
WRAP=*Option* (OFF | VIRTUAL | PHYSICAL)	Specifies how text should be wrapped within the text box. OFF turns off text wrapping. VIRTUAL wraps the text, but sends the text to the server as a single line. PHYSICAL wraps the text and sends the text the server as it appears in the text box.		2.0	2.0

Frame Tags

TAGS AND PROPERTIES	DESCRIPTION	HTML	NETSCAPE	IE
Frame Tags	Frame tags are used for creating and formatting frames.			
<IFRAME> ... </IFRAME>	The <IFRAME> tag allows authors to insert a frame within a block of text. Inserting an inline frame within a section of text allow you to insert an HTML document in the middle of another, and they may both be aligned with surrounding text.	4.0		3.0

HTML Tag Reference

TAGS AND PROPERTIES	DESCRIPTION	HTML	NETSCAPE	IE
ALIGN=*Option* (LEFT | RIGHT | MIDDLE | JUSTIFY)	Specifies the alignment of the floating frame.	4.0		3.0
HEIGHT=*Value*	Specifies the height of the floating frame, in pixels.	4.0		4.0
MARGINHEIGHT=*Value*	Specifies the amount of space above and below the frame object and the frame borders.	4.0		3.0
MARGINWIDTH=*Value*	Specifies the amount of space to the left and right of the frame object, in pixels.	4.0		3.0
NAME=*Text*	Label assigned to the frame.	4.0		3.0
SCROLLING=*Option* (YES | NO | AUTO)	Specifies whether scroll bars are visible. AUTO (the default) displays scroll bars only as needed.	4.0		3.0
SRC=*Document*	Specifies the document or URL of the object to be displayed in the frame.	4.0		3.0
WIDTH=*Value*	Specifies the width of the floating frame, in pixels.	4.0		3.0
<FRAME>	The <FRAME> tag defines a single frame within a set of frames.	4.0	2.0	3.0
BORDERCOLOR=*Color*	Specifies the color of the frame border.		3.0	4.0
FRAMEBORDER=*Option* (YES | NO)	Specifies whether the frame border is visible.	4.0	3.0	3.0
FRAMESPACING=*Value*	Specifies the amount of space between frames, in pixels.			3.0
MARGINHEIGHT=*Value*	Specifies the amount of space above and below the frame object and the frame borders.	4.0	2.0	3.0
MARGINWIDTH=*Value*	Specifies the amount of space to the left and right of the frame object, in pixels.	4.0	2.0	3.0
NAME=*Text*	Label assigned to the frame.	4.0	2.0	3.0
NORESIZE	Prevents users from resizing the frame.	4.0	2.0	3.0
SCROLLING=*Option* (YES | NO | AUTO)	Specifies whether scroll bars are visible. AUTO (the default) displays scroll bars only as needed.	4.0	2.0	3.0
SRC=*Document*	Specifies the document or URL of the object to be displayed in the frame.	4.0	2.0	3.0
<FRAMESET> ... </FRAMESET>	The <FRAMESET> tag marks the beginning and the end of a set of frames.	4.0	2.0	3.0
BORDER=*Value*	The size of the borders, in pixels.		3.0	3.0
BORDERCOLOR	The color of the frame borders.		3.0	3.0
COLS=*List*	The size of each column in set of frames. Columns can be specified either in pixels, as a percentage of the display area or with an asterisks (*) indicating that any remaining space be allotted to that column. e.g.COLS="40,25%,*"	4.0	2.0	3.0
ROWS=*List*	The size of each row in set of frames. Rows can be specified either in pixels, as a percentage of the display area or with an asterisks (*) indicating that any remaining space be allotted to that column. e.g.ROWS="40,25%,*"	4.0	2.0	3.0
<NOFRAMES> ... </NOFRAMES>	Enclosing body tags to be used by browsers which do not support frames.	4.0	2.0	3.0

HTML Tag Reference

TAGS AND PROPERTIES	DESCRIPTION	HTML	NETSCAPE	IE
Graphic and Link Tags	Graphic and Link tags are used for hypertext links and inline images.			
<A> ... </A>	The <A> tag marks and the beginning an end of a hypertext link.	1.0	1.0	1.0
HREF=*URL*	Indicates the target, file name or URL that the hypertext points to.	1.0	1.0	1.0
NAME=*Text*	Specifies a name for the enclosed text, allowing it to be a target of a hyperlink.	1.0	1.0	2.0
REL=*Text*	Specifies the relationship between the current page and the link specified by the HREF property.	1.0		2.0
REV=*Text*	Specifies a reverse relationship between the current page and the link specified by the HREF property.	1.0		2.0
TABINDEX=*Value*	Specifies the tab order in the form.	4.0		4.0
TARGET=*Text*	Specifies the default target window or frame for the hyperlink.	4.0	1.0	3.0
TITLE=*Text*	Provides a title for the document whose address is given by the HREF property.	1.0		2.0
<AREA>	The <AREA> tag defines the type and coordinates of a hotspot within an image map.	3.2	1.0	2.0
COORDS=*Value 1, value 2...* Rectangle: COORDS=*x_left, y_upper, x_right, y_lower* CIRCLE: COORDS= *x_center, y_center, radius* POLYGON: COORDS= $x_1, y_1, x_2, y_2, x_3, y_3, ...$	The coordinates of the hotspot. The coordinates depend upon the shape of the hotspot:	3.2	1.0	2.0
HREF=*URL*	Indicates the target, file name or URL that the hotspot points to.	3.2	1.0	2.0
SHAPE=*Option* (RECT | CIRCLE | POLY)	The shape of the hotspot.	3.2	1.0	2.0
TABINDEX=*Value*	Specifies the tab order in the form.	4.0		4.0
TARGET=*Text*	Specifies the default target window or frame for the hotspot.	4.0	2.0	3.0
<IMG>	The <IMG> tag is used to insert an inline image into the document.	1.0	1.0	2.0
ALIGN=*Option* (LEFT | RIGHT | TOP | TEXTTOP | MIDDLE | ABSMIDDLE | BASELINE | BOTTOM | ABSBOTTOM)	Specifies the alignment of the image. Specifying an alignment of LEFT or RIGHT aligns the image with the left or right page margin. The other alignment options align the image with surrounding text.	1.0	1.1	2.0
ALT=*Text*	Text to display if the image cannot be displayed by the browser.	2.0	1.1	2.0
BORDER=*Value*	The size of the border around the image in pixels.	3.2	1.1	2.0
CONTROLS	Display VCR-like controls under moving images. Used in conjunction with the DYNSRC property.			2.0
DYNSRC=*Document*	Specifies the file of a video, AVI clip or VRML worlds displayed inside the page.			2.0

HTML Tag Reference

HTML Tag Reference

TAGS AND PROPERTIES	DESCRIPTION	HTML	NETSCAPE	IE
HEIGHT=*Value*	The height of the image in pixels.	3.0	1.1	2.0
HSPACE=*Value*	The amount of space to the left and right of the image, in pixels.	3.0	1.1	2.0
ISMAP	Identifies the graphic as an image map. For use with server-side image maps.	3.0	2.0	2.0
LOOP=*Value*	Specifies the number of times a moving image should be played. The value must be either a digit or INFINITE.			2.0
LOWSRC=*Document*	A low-resolution version of the graphic that the browser should initially display before loading the high resolution version.		1.0	4.0
SRC=*Document*	The source file of the inline image.	1.0	1.0	2.0
START=*Item* (FILEOPEN | MOUSEOVER)	Tells the browser when to start displaying a moving image file. FILEOPEN directs the browser to start when the file is open. MOUSEOVER directs the browser to start when the mouse moves over the image.			2.0
USEMAP=#*Map_Namet*	Identifies the graphic as an image map and specifies the name of image map definition to use with the graphic. For use with client-side image maps.	3.2	2.0	2.0
VSPACE=*Value*	The amount of space above and below the image, in pixels.	3.2	1.1	2.0
WIDTH=*Value*	The width of the image in pixels.	3.0	1.1	2.0
<MAP> ... </MAP>	The <MAP> specifies information about a client-side image map. (Note that it must enclose <AREA> tags.)	3.2	1.0	2.0
NAME=*Text*	The name of the image map.	3.2	2.0	2.0

List Tags

TAGS AND PROPERTIES	DESCRIPTION	HTML	NETSCAPE	IE
	List tags are used to create a variety of different kinds of lists.			
<DD>	The <DD> tag formats text to be used as relative definitions in a<DL> list.	1.0	1.0	2.0
<DIR> ... </DIR>	The <DIR> tag encloses an unordered list of <LI> items, formatted in narrow columns.	1.0	1.0	2.0
TYPE=*Option* (CIRCLE | DISC | SQUARE)	Specifies the type of bullet used for displaying each <LI> item in the <DIR> list.		2.0	
<DL> ... </DL>	The <DL> tag encloses a definition list in which the <DD> definition term, is left aligned and the <DT> relative definition, is indented.	1.0	1.0	2.0
<DT>	The <DT> tag is used to format the definition term in a <DL> list.	1.0	1.0	2.0
<LI>	The <LI> tag identifies list items in a <DIR>, <MENU>, <OL> or <UL> list.	1.0	1.0	2.0
<MENU> ... </MENU>	The <MENU> tag encloses an unordered list of items, similar to a <UL> or <DIR> list.	1.0	1.0	2.0

HTML Tag Reference

TAGS AND PROPERTIES	DESCRIPTION	HTML	NETSCAPE	IE
<OL> ... </OL>	The <OL> tag encloses an ordered list of <LI> items. Typically ordered lists are rendered as numbered lists.	1.0	1.0	1.0
START=*Value*	The *value* of the starting number in the ordered list.	3.2	2.0	2.0
TYPE=*Option* (A | a | I | i | 1)	Specifies how ordered items are to be marked. A = uppercase letters. a = lowercase letters. I = uppercase Roman numerals. i = lowercase Roman numerals. 1 = Digits. The default is 1.	3.2	2.0	2.0
<UL>	The <UL> tag encloses an unordered list of <LI> items. Typically unordered lists are rendered as bulleted lists.	1.0	1.0	1.0
Type=*Option* (CIRCLE | DISK | SQUARE)	Specifies the type of bullet used for displaying each <LI> item in the <UL> list.	3.2	2.0	

Miscellaneous Tags

TAGS AND PROPERTIES	DESCRIPTION	HTML	NETSCAPE	IE
	Miscellaneous tags do not fit into any specific category. These tags are currently only supported by Internet Explorer 3.0 and above.			
<BGSOUND>	The <BGSOUND> is used to play a background sound clip when the page is first opened.			2.0
LOOP=*Value*	Specifies the number of times the sound clip should be played. LOOP can either be a digit or INFINITE.			3.0
SRC=*Document*	The sound file used for the sound clip.			2.0
<MARQUEE> ... </MARQUEE>	The <MARQUEE> tag is used to create an area containing scrolling text.			2.0
ALIGN=*Option* (TOP | MIDDLE | BOTTOM)	The alignment of the scrolling text within the marquee.			2.0
BEHAVIOR=*Option* (SCROLL | SLIDE | ALTERNATE)	Controls the behavior of the text in the marquee. SCROLL causes the text to repeatedly scroll across the page. SLIDE causes the text to slide onto the page and stop at the margin. ALTERNATE causes the text to bounce from margin to margin.			2.0
BGCOLOR=*Color*	The background color of the marquee.			2.0
DIRECTION=*Option* (LEFT | RIGHT)	The direction that the text scrolls on the page.			2.0
HEIGHT=*Value*	The height of the marquee in either pixels or as a percentage of the display area.			2.0
HSPACE=*Value*	The amount of space to the left and right of the marquee, in pixels.			2.0
LOOP=*Value*	The number of times the marquee will be scrolled, can be either a digit or INFINITE			2.0
SCROLLAMOUNT=*Value*	The amount of space between successive draws of the text in the marquee.			2.0
SCROLLDELAY=*Value*	The amount of time between scrolling actions, in milliseconds.			2.0
VSPACE=*Value*	The amount of space above and below the marquee, in pixels.			2.0

HTML Tag Reference

TAGS AND PROPERTIES	DESCRIPTION	HTML	NETSCAPE	IE
WIDTH=*Value*	The width of the marquee in either pixels or as a percentage of the display area.			2.0

Script and Applet Tags

TAGS AND PROPERTIES	DESCRIPTION	HTML	NETSCAPE	IE
	Script tags are used for client-side scripts, including JavaScript and VBScript. Applet tags are used for Java applets.			
<APPLET> ... </APPLET>	The <APPLET> tag, supported by all Java-enabled browsers, allows designers to embed a Java applet in an HTML document. It has been deprecated in favor of the <OBJECT> tag in HTML 4.0.	3.2	2.0	3.0
ALIGN=*Option* (TOP | BOTTOM | MIDDLE | LEFT | RIGHT)	Specifies the alignment of the applet with the surrounding text.	3.2	2.0	3.0
ALT=*Text*	Specifies alternate text to be displayed in place of the Java applet.	3.2	3.0	3.0
ARCHIVE=*List*	List of archives containing classes and other resources that will be "preloaded" for use with the Java applet.	4.0	3.0	
CODEBASE=*URL*	Specifies the base URL for the applet. If not specified, the browser assumes the same location as the current document.	3.2	2.0	3.0
CODE=*Text*	Specifies the name of the CLASS file that contains the Java applet.	3.2	2.0	3.0
HEIGHT=*Value*	Specifies the height of the applet, in pixels.	3.2	2.0	3.0
HSPACE=*Value*	Specifies the horizontal space around the applet, in pixels.	3.2	2.0	3.0
NAME=*Text*	The name assigned to the Java applet.	3.2	2.0	3.0
OBJECT=*Text*	Specifies a resource containing a serialized representation of an applet's state. It is interpreted relative to the applet's codebase. The serialized data contains the applet's class name but not the implementation. The class name is used to retrieve the implementation from a class file or archive.	4.0		
VSPACE=*Value*	Specifies the vertical space around the applet, in pixels.	3.2	2.0	3.0
WIDTH=*Value*	The width of the applet, in pixels.	3.2	2.0	3.0
<NOSCRIPT> ... </NOSCRIPT>	The <NOSCRIPT> tag is used to enclose HTML tags for browsers that do not support client-side scripts.	4.0	3.0	3.0
<OBJECT> ... </OBJECT>	Most user browsers have built-in mechanisms for rendering common data types such as text, GIF images, colors, fonts, and a handful of graphic elements. To render data types they don't support natively, user agents generally run external applications. The <OBJECT> tag allows authors to control whether data should be rendered externally or by some program, specified by the author, that renders the data within the user agent.	2.0	1.1	1.0

HTML Tag Reference

TAGS AND PROPERTIES	DESCRIPTION	HTML	NETSCAPE	IE
ALIGN=Option (TOP | BOTTOM | MIDDLE | LEFT | RIGHT)	Specifies the alignment of the embedded object relative to the surrounding text.	4.0	2.0	3.0
BORDER=Value	Specifies the width of the embedded object's border, in pixels.	4.0		3.0
CLASSID=URL	Specifies the URL of the embedded object.	4.0		3.0
CODEBASE=URL	Specifies the base path used to resolve relative references within the embedded object.	4.0	2.0	3.0
CODETYPE=Text	Specifies the type of data object.	4.0		3.0
DATA=URL	Specifies the location of data for the embedded object.	4.0	2.0	3.0
HEIGHT=Value	Specifies the height of the embedded object, in pixels.	4.0	2.0	3.0
HSPACE=Value	Specifies the horizontal space around the embedded object, in pixels.	4.0		3.0
NAME=Text	Specifies the name of the embedded object.	4.0		3.0
STANDBY=Text	Specifies a message the browser should display while rendering the embedded object.	4.0		3.0
TABINDEX=Value	Specifies the tab order of the object when it is placed within a form.	4.0		4.0
TYPE=Text	Specifies the type of data object.	4.0	2.0	3.0
VSPACE=Value	Specifies the vertical space around the embedded object, in pixels.	4.0		3.0
WIDTH=Value	Specifies the width of the embedded object, in pixels.	4.0	2.0	3.0
<PARAM> ... </PARAM>	<PARAM> tags specify a set of values that may be required by an object at run-time. Any number of PARAM elements may appear in the content of an <OBJECT> or <APPLET> tag, in any order, but must be placed at the start of the content of the enclosing <OBJECT> or <APPLET> tag.	3.2	1.0	3.0
NAME=Text	Specifies the name of the parameter.	3.2	2.0	3.0
VALUE=Text	Specifies the value of the parameter.	3.2	2.0	3.0
VALUETYPE=Option (DATA | REF | OBJECT)	Specifies the type of the value attribute.	4.0		3.0
<SCRIPT> ... </SCRIPT>	The <SCRIPT> tag places a client-side script within a document. This element may appear any number of times in the HEAD or BODY of an HTML document.	3.2	3.0	3.0
LANGUAGE=Text	Specifies the language of the client-side script.	4.0	3.0	3.0
SRC=URL	Specifies the source of the external script file.	4.0	3.0	3.0
TYPE=Text	Specifies the type of scripting language.	4.0	3.0	3.0

Table tags

Table tags are used to define the structure and appears of graphical tables.

TAGS AND PROPERTIES	DESCRIPTION	HTML	NETSCAPE	IE
<CAPTION> ... </CAPTION>	The <CAPTION> tag encloses the table caption.	3.0	1.1	2.0
ALIGN=Option (LEFT | RIGHT | CENTER | TOP | BOTTOM)	Specifies the alignment of the caption with respect to the table. The LEFT, RIGHT and CENTER options are only supported by Internet Explorer 3.0	3.0	2.0	2.0

HTML Tag Reference

TAGS AND PROPERTIES	DESCRIPTION	HTML	NETSCAPE	IE
VALIGN=*Option* (TOP | BOTTOM)	Specifies the vertical alignment of the caption with respect to the table.			2.0
<COL> ... </COL>	The <COL> tag specifies the default settings for a column or group of columns.	3.0		4.0
ALIGN=*Option* (CENTER | JUSTIFY | LEFT | RIGHT)	Specifies the horizontal alignment of text within a column.	4.0		4.0
SPAN=*Value*	Specifies the columns modified by the <COL> tag.	4.0		4.0
VALIGN=*Option* (TOP | MIDDLE | BOTTOM)	Specifies the vertical alignment of text within a column.	4.0		4.0
<COLGROUP> ... <COLGROUP>	The <COLGROUP> tag encloses a group of <COL> tags, grouping columns together to set their alignment properties.	3.0		4.0
ALIGN=*Option* (CENTER | JUSTIFY | LEFT | RIGHT)	Specifies the horizontal alignment of text within a column group.	4.0		4.0
SPAN=*Value*	Specifies the columns within the column group.	4.0		4.0
VALIGN=*Option* (TOP | MIDDLE | BOTTOM)	Specifies the vertical alignment of text within a column group.	4.0		4.0
<TABLE> ... </TABLE>	The <TABLE> tag is used to specify the beginning and ending of the table.	1.0	1.1	1.0
ALIGN=*Option* (LEFT | CENTER | RIGHT)	Specifies the horizontal alignment of the table on the page. Only LEFT and RIGHT are supported by Netscape 3.0 and Internet Explorer 3.0.	3.0	2.0	3.0
BACKGROUND=*Document*	Specifies a background image for the table.			4.0
BGCOLOR=*Color*	Specifies a background color for the table.	4.0	3.0	2.0
BORDER=*Value*	Specifies the width of the table border in pixels.	3.0	2.0	2.0
BORDERCOLOR=*Color*	Specifies the color of the table border.			2.0
BORDERCOLORDARK=*Color*	Specifies the color of the shaded edge of the table border.			2.0
BORDERCOLORLIGHT=*Color*	Specifies the color of the unshaded edge of the table border.			2.0
CELLPADDING=*Value*	Specifies the space between table cells in pixels.	3.2	2.0	2.0
CELLSPACING=*Value*	Specifies the space between cell text and the cell border in pixels.	3.2	2.0	2.0
FRAME=*Option* (ABOVE | BELOW | BOX | HSIDES | LHS | RHS | VOID | VSIDES)	Specifies the display of table borders. ABOVE = Top border only. BELOW = Bottom border only. BOX = Borders on all four sides. HSIDES = Top and bottom borders. LHS = Left side border. RHS = Right side border. VOID = No borders. VSIDES = Left and right side borders.	3.0		3.0
HEIGHT=*Value*	The height of the table in pixels or as a percentage of the display area.		4.0	4.0

HTML Tag Reference

HTML Tag Reference

TAGS AND PROPERTIES	DESCRIPTION	HTML	NETSCAPE	IE
RULES=*Option* (ALL | COLS | NONE | ROWS)	Specifies the display of internal table borders. ALL = Borders between every row and column. COLS = Border between every column. NONE = No internal table borders. ROWS = Borders between every row.	3.0		3.0
WIDTH=*Value*	The width of the table in pixels or as a percentage of the display area.	3.0	2.0	2.0
<TBODY> ... </TBODY>	The <TBODY> tag identifies text that appears in the table body as opposed to text in the table header (<THEAD> tag) or the table footer (TBODY tag).	3.0		4.0
HALIGN=*Option* (LEFT | CENTER |RIGHT)	The horizontal alignment of text in the cells of the table body.	4.0		4.0
VALIGN=*Option* (TOP | MIDDLE | BOTTOM)	The vertical alignment of text in the cells in the table body.	4.0		4.0
<TD> ... </TD>	The <TD> tag encloses the text that will appear in an individual table cell.	1.0	1.1	2.0
ALIGN=*Option* (LEFT | CENTER | RIGHT)	Specifies the horizontal alignment of cell text.	1.0	2.0	2.0
BACKGROUND=*Document*	Specifies a background image for the cell.			4.0
BGCOLOR=*Color*	Specifies a background color for the cell.	4.0	3.0	2.0
BORDERCOLOR=*Color*	Specifies the color of the cell border.			2.0
BORDERCOLORDARK=*Color*	Specifies the color of the shaded edge of the cell border.			2.0
BORDERCOLORLIGHT=*Color*	Specifies the color of the unshaded edge of the cell border.			2.0
COLSPAN=*Value*	Specifies the number of columns the cell should span.	3.2	2.0	2.0
HEIGHT=*Value*	The height of the cell in pixels or as a percentage of the display area.	3.2	2.0	2.0
NOWRAP	Prohibits the browser from wrapping text in the cell.	3.0	2.0	2.0
ROWSPAN=*Value*	Specifies the number of rows the cell should span.	3.2	2.0	2.0
VALIGN=*Option* (TOP | MIDDLE | BOTTOM)	Specifies the vertical alignment of cell text.	3.0	2.0	2.0
WIDTH= *Value*	The width of the cell in pixels or as a percentage of the width of the table.	3.2	2.0	2.0
<TFOOT> ... </TFOOT>	The <TFOOT> tag encloses footer information that will be displayed in the table footer when the table is printed on multiple pages.	4.0		4.0
ALIGN=*Option* (LEFT | CENTER |RIGHT)	The horizontal alignment of the table footer.	4.0		4.0
VALIGN=*Option* (TOP | MIDDLE | BOTTOM)	The vertical alignment of the table footer.	4.0		4.0
<TH> ... </TH>	The <TH> tag encloses the text that will appear in an individual table header cell.	1.0	1.1	2.0
ALIGN=*Option* (LEFT | CENTER | RIGHT)	Specifies the horizontal alignment of header cell text.	1.0	2.0	2.0
BACKGROUND=*Document*	Specifies a background image for the header cell.			4.0

HTML Tag Reference

TAGS AND PROPERTIES	DESCRIPTION	HTML	NETSCAPE	IE
BGCOLOR=*Color*	Specifies a background color for the header cell.	4.0	3.0	2.0
BORDERCOLOR=*Color*	Specifies the color of the header cell border.			2.0
BORDERCOLORDARK=*Color*	Specifies the color of the shaded edge of the header cell border.			3.0
BORDERCOLORLIGHT=*Color*	Specifies the color of the unshaded edge of the header cell border.			3.0
COLSPAN=*Value*	Specifies the number of columns the header cell should span.	1.0	2.0	2.0
HEIGHT=*Value*	The height of the header cell in pixels or as a percentage of the display area.	3.2	2.0	2.0
NOWRAP	Prohibits the browser from wrapping text in the header cell.	3.0	2.0	2.0
ROWSPAN=*Value*	Specifies the number of rows the header cell should span.	3.0	2.0	2.0
VALIGN=*Option* (TOP | MIDDLE | BOTTOM)	Specifies the vertical alignment of header cell text.	3.0	2.0	2.0
WIDTH= *Value*	The width of the header cell in pixels or as a percentage of the width of the table.	3.2	2.0	2.0
<THEAD> ... </THEAD>	The <THEAD> tag encloses header information that will be displayed in the table header when the table is printed on multiple pages.	3.0		3.0
ALIGN=*Option* (LEFT | CENTER |RIGHT)	The horizontal alignment of the table header.	3.0		3.0
VALIGN=*Option* (TOP | MIDDLE | BOTTOM)	The vertical alignment of the table header.	3.0		3.0
<TR> ... </TR>	The <TR> tag is encloses table cells within a single row.	3.0	1.1	2.0
ALIGN=*Option* (LEFT | CENTER | RIGHT)	Specifies the horizontal alignment of text in the row.	3.0	2.0	2.0
BGCOLOR=*Color*	Specifies a background color for the header cell.	4.0	3.0	2.0
BORDERCOLOR=*Color*	Specifies the color of the header cell border.			2.0
BORDERCOLORDARK=*Color*	Specifies the color of the shaded edge of the header cell border.			2.0
BORDERCOLORLIGHT=*Color*	Specifies the color of the unshaded edge of the header cell border.			2.0
VALIGN=*Option* (TOP | MIDDLE | BOTTOM)	The vertical alignment of the text in the table row.	3.0	2.0	2.0